# FROM

# MANAGEMENT

## TO

# *Leadership*

Interpersonal Skills
for Success in Health Care

# JO MANION

press

American Hospital Publishers, Inc.
*An American Hospital Association Company*
CHICAGO

*This book is sincerely dedicated to all of the leaders who have been part of my life:*

*To my clients for trusting me enough to share their challenges, difficulties, and experiences, for generously providing countless opportunities that lifted me to new levels of learning, and for so enriching my professional life.*

*To my colleagues for inspiring me with their sense of commitment, for their courage and perseverance in the face of great obstacles, and for sharing their wisdom and challenging me to grow.*

*To my family and friends for providing unwavering support for my ideas and ventures, for encouraging me to always seek out and give my best, and for believing in me when I was uncertain.*

**Library of Congress Cataloging-in-Publication Data**

Manion, Jo.
    From management to leadership : interpersonal skills for success in health care / by Jo Manion..
        p.      cm.
    Includes bibliographical references and index.
    ISBN 1-55648-233-7
    1. Health services administration—Psychological aspects.
2. Leadership—Psychological aspects. 3. Interpersonal relations—
Psychological aspects. I. Title.
    [DNLM: 1. Health Services Administration. 2. Leadership.
3. Interpersonal Relations. 4. Health Facility Administrators.
5. Efficiency, Organizational.      WX 155 M278f 1998]
RA440.6.M26    1998
362.1'068—dc21
DNLM/DLC
for Library of Congress                                                      98-9873
                                                                                    CIP

Item Number: 108101

# Contents

# About the Author

**Jo Manion, BSN, MA, CNAA,** is the president of her own organizational development consulting practice, Manion & Associates, located in Altamonte Springs, Florida. A nationally recognized professional speaker, seminar leader, consultant, and author, she specializes in offering practical strategies for personal and organizational leadership development. Her more than 32 years of health care experience in a variety of organizations and positions has created expertise in the areas of leadership development, change management, and development of effective teams. She is coauthor of *Team-Based Health Care Organizations* (1996) and author of *Change from Within: Nurse Intrapreneurs as Health Care Innovators* (1990) as well as many journal articles.

# *Preface*

The development of leaders is a critical challenge facing health care organizations today. Tumultuous change is occurring at breakneck speed, creating the need for individuals who can effectively lead others during these demanding times. Required are leaders who effect a new direction, win the commitment of employees and other key stakeholders, and influence others to do what needs to be done to achieve a future vision. Unprecedented changes are occurring in health care's executive and managerial roles and in the manner in which health care organizations function. Health care leaders must assume nontraditional roles for which they may feel inadequately equipped; new roles demand mastery of new skills. Present leaders face a tremendous challenge in balancing the demands of day-to-day organizational life while continually learning for the future.

Some organizations meet the challenge of leadership development by recruiting strong leaders. However, vibrant, dynamic, and flourishing organizations are also committed to developing leaders from within the existing ranks of their managers and other employees. Working in partnership with employees to develop their leadership skills is in the organization's best interests. By providing opportunities, coaching, and guidance, the organization creates an ever-expanding source of new leaders. Without strong leaders, it will be difficult, if not impossible, to navigate successfully amid the turmoil of the new millennium.

Leadership development is more than an organizational issue—it is an intensely personal issue for all health care workers, who are being asked to assume more responsibility, to be involved in making decisions about issues that were previously the manager's domain, and to serve in leadership roles. Loren Ankario (1993) notes that "by the next decade, anyone who is not a leader in his or her own way probably won't have a job." More significantly, many employees are seeking—in some

**ix**

instances, demanding—opportunities to serve in roles that influence their work environment more broadly. When organizations transform their traditional structure into a team-based design, leaders are consciously developed at every level in the organization.

The concept of "leaders at all levels" corresponds to current societal trends. Overall, the health care workforce is more mature and experienced than ever. Today's successful health care management understands that the old "command-and-control" methodology is no longer appropriate for today's workers. Instead, the work relationship has evolved into a partnership model in which leadership roles are fluid and dynamic and individuals move in and out of these roles on a seemingly constant basis. Facilitating the development of employee leadership skills makes sense because the entire organization benefits. The foundation of the organization is stronger, the structure more solid, and future viability more likely in an organization filled with individuals who are leaders or are capable of moving into leadership roles when needed.

This book is written for all health care leaders and aspiring leaders. Seasoned leaders will find that the concepts and skills presented here are essential as they reshape and redefine their roles. The book may also serve as a reference or reminder to which the "master" leader may turn when faced with a particular challenge. For new or aspiring leaders, this book can serve as a road map for the development of interpersonal skills that enhance leadership success.

In his book *On Becoming a Leader*, Warren Bennis (1989) notes that leadership courses can only teach *skills* and cannot teach character or vision. He believes character and vision develop in an individual over time, as they are most often based on life experiences—learning that occurs beyond reading and course work. However, Peter Drucker believes that all aspects of leadership can and must be learned (Hesselbein, Goldsmith, and Beckhard 1996). The purpose of this book is to explore the essential interpersonal skills needed by an effective leader that *can* be taught and learned: skills that, with study and practice, can increase a leader's effectiveness. It is only through using these skills that they are developed.

The American Hospital Association Press and the Center for Health Care Leadership of the American Hospital Association conducted market research on the nature of the leadership gap in health care. Focus groups were held comprising more than 60 well-known chief executive officers, board members, physician leaders, consultants, academics, and community activists. These groups revealed five administrative pitfalls driving the emerging new paradigm of health care leadership. These five weaknesses include:

1. Little or no sense of shared vision and mission within the health care organization

2. Ineffective communication skills, particularly at the executive level
3. Unwillingness to abandon hierarchical control structures, particularly at the executive and board levels
4. Refusal to let go of the "hospital mentality" and traditional modes of service
5. Denial of the inevitability of rapid evolution toward capitated reimbursement and managed care

Consequences of these pitfalls are significant, impacting organizational health and future viability. To offset these weaknesses, leaders need to take on some nontraditional roles for which they may feel unprepared. Mastery of new skills is critical to the successful transition into these roles; and the research shows that these nontraditional skills are clustered into two domains:

1. Systems thinking, including skills in collaborative envisioning, strategic planning, broad-based decision making, innovative problem solving, and stewardship.
2. Interpersonal abilities, including communication skills—both verbal and nonverbal—coaching, giving constructive feedback, conflict management, consensus building, delegation of responsibility, team building, and change management

This book addresses these skills, although in a somewhat unusual format. It is based on the premise that leadership exists only within a relationship: If there are no followers, there is no need for a leader. Interpersonal skills in leadership are critical success factors, yet little is written about developing these skills within the leadership context. This book identifies the fundamental interpersonal competencies every leader needs, and it maps out suggestions for improving these skills. Examples from health care leaders at all levels are shared to emphasize key points. The concepts in this book are immediately applicable in leadership practice at any level and in any setting where leadership exists.

The first chapter explores the difference between management and leadership, a concept even experienced managers and leaders have trouble grasping concretely. A working definition of leadership is offered and key interpersonal requirements are identified. Why leadership is more crucial today is examined, as are the challenges faced by today's leaders. Each of the remaining chapters fully examines a key leadership competency.

Chapter 2 focuses on establishing the leader-follower relationship. The three key elements of this relationship—trust, respect, and communication—are addressed, and the nature of collaboration and aspects of forming a partnership are included. Tomorrow's leaders will be successful only if they are willing and able to work in partnership with others.

Building commitment among followers is the theme of chapter 3. Compliance, or conformance, is achieved by managers and executives who inform employees of decisions made. Most changes being made require full commitment from followers to be successful. Commitment may be described as a *buy-in*, or a feeling of ownership that goes well beyond mere compliance. What can a leader do to increase the likelihood that key stakeholders—employees, physicians, community members— will commit to the direction taken by the organization? When there is a sense of connection and shared values, a leader with the ability to col- laboratively develop inspiring, energizing visions is more likely to develop commitment on the part of followers.

Chapter 4 deals with the leader's role in communicating with clar- ity. Although seemingly the simplest of the interpersonal competencies, it is central to establishing the leader-follower relationship. Verbal and nonverbal communication are thoroughly explored within the context of contemporary leadership practice. Long-known principles and con- cepts are reexamined in light of today's workplace and challenges. Spe- cial communication issues—such as communicating during times of change, communicating long distance, and with teams—are addressed. Barriers to effective communication are identified, such as gender and style differences and tribal language.

Many leaders and managers have learned their skills in work envi- ronments that emphasized outcomes rather than processes. The deci- sive get-it-done individual was often rewarded and promoted, while the individual spending the time needed to ensure that an appropriate process was followed may have been seen as slow and plodding. Today's leaders must be able to integrate these two approaches and achieve effective outcomes through constructive processes. Key princi- ples of managing process are identified in chapter 5. In addition, the critical processes—such as empowering others, resolving conflict, problem solving, decision making, creating teams, and managing change—are scrutinized.

The major interpersonal competency, developing others, is the sub- ject of chapter 6. Everyone agrees that leaders today must be coaches, but there is little practical, concrete advice available on filling this role. Principles of coaching, teaching, encouraging others are the subject of this chapter. Effective leaders are continual learners, and they expect others around them to continually develop, learn, and stretch. Good leaders are serious about tapping the potential within each person to expand their reach, to grow, and to establish their own leadership skills. Systems thinking and collaborative learning are key characteristics of a leader-coach-teacher.

Although mastery of these key competencies does not guarantee immediately successful leadership, it can help the individual who has character and vision to become more effective. Developing and refining leadership is a lifelong journey. Circumstances continually alter, creating the need for new skills sets. This book is offered to stimulate thought and to provoke creative action for those on the path of leadership development.

# *Acknowledgments*

The author gratefully acknowledges the following people who were instrumental in helping make this book a reality:

Rosemary Jacobson, CEO and president of Altru Health Care in Grand Forks, North Dakota, who was generous with her time and spirit. As a leader, she is a source of inspiration to many.

Rick Hill, senior editor at AHA Press, who "saw" the book long before I did and convinced me there was a manuscript here waiting to be written. His gentle prodding and persistence was as helpful as his insightful challenges and questions.

Winnie Schmeling, friend and colleague who "started the ball rolling."

The many unnamed leaders who over the years have contributed themselves to my learning and understanding of leadership.

And, finally, my husband, Craig, who gave the support and encouragement I needed, who listened and thoughtfully questioned, and who, once again, patiently "gave me up" to my writing.

# 1

## Leadership: An Elusive Concept

"Leadership has to take place every day. It cannot be the responsibility of the few, a rare event, or a once-in-a-lifetime opportunity."

—*R. A. Heifetz and D. L. Laurie*

N o issue is as important in health care today as the development and continual evolution of leaders. "Leadership is the pivotal force behind successful organizations. . . . To create vital and viable organizations, leadership is necessary to help organizations develop a new vision of what they can be, then mobilize the organization to change toward the new vision" (Bennis and Nanus 1985, 12). An organization's success is directly correlated to the strength of its leaders. The failure of an organization to develop leaders at all levels, relying instead on a few strong leaders at the top, results in dismal outcomes. In the foreword of Gifford and Elizabeth Pinchot's book *The Intelligent Organization*, Warren Bennis notes that "traditional bureaucratic organizations have failed and continue to fail, in large part, because they tend to rely exclusively on the intelligence of those at the very top of the pyramid" (1996, x).

In the same way, relying only on formal managers for leadership limits the tremendous possibilities that exist when leaders are differentiated from managers. "Solutions . . . reside not in the executive suite but in the collective intelligence of employees at all levels, who need to use one another as resources, often across boundaries, and learn their way to those solutions" (Heifetz and Laurie 1997, 124).

Unfortunately, few people understand clearly the distinction between leadership and management, and as a result, the field from which organizational leaders might emerge is narrowed. In some instances, leaders who do emerge from the ranks go unrecognized and are even resisted and labeled as troublemakers or dissatisfied employees. This chapter explores the concept of leadership, differentiates it

1

from management, identifies reasons leadership is so critical in today's health care organizations, and illuminates the major challenges facing current health care leaders.

## LEADERSHIP DEFINED

Defining leadership is the first step. Most authorities on the topic generally define leadership as influencing others to do what needs to be done, especially those things the leader believes need to be accomplished. Max DePree believes the art of leadership is "liberating people to do what is required of them in the most effective and humane way possible" (1989, xx). This definition implies that leadership is not something *done to* or *for* the follower but is instead releasing the potential already present within an individual. The leader sets the stage and then steps out of the way to let others perform. True leadership enables the follower to realize their full potential—potential that perhaps was unsuspected by the follower. Also implied in any definition is that leadership is work. It is about performance, achieving outcomes, getting needed results. Peter Drucker says that "it has little to do with 'leadership qualities' and even less to do with 'charisma.' It is mundane, unromantic, and boring. Its essence is performance" (1992, 199).

Leadership is mobilizing the interest, energy, and commitment of all people at all levels of the organization. It is a means to an end. "An effective leader knows that the ultimate task of leadership is to create human energies and human vision" (Drucker 1992, 122). Bardwick clearly states that leadership is not intellectual or cognitive but, rather, emotional. She points out that at the emotional level, leaders create followers because they generate "confidence in people who are frightened, certainty in people who were vacillating, action where there was hesitation, strength where there was weakness, expertise where there was floundering, courage where there were cowards, optimism where there was cynicism, and a conviction that the future will be better" (Bardwick 1996, 14).

Noted author Warren Bennis (1989) has spent almost two decades studying leaders, and he offers three key ingredients for successful leadership:

1.  A clear vision of what needs to be accomplished
2.  Passion or an intense level of personal commitment
3.  Integrity or character

None of these are teachable by the methods often used for leadership development, such as reading or attending seminars and formal educational courses. However, all can be learned or perfected through life's experiences. For most people, the development of leadership ability is lifelong work—a trial-and-error method of perfecting techniques and approaches, the evolution of personality and spirituality. Often the leader is not even aware of exactly *how* they influenced a follower. An opportunity or need to lead appeared and the leader stepped forward to meet the challenge.

## DIFFERENTIATING MANAGEMENT AND LEADERSHIP

How does leadership differ from management? Most would agree that not all managers are good leaders and not all leaders are good managers. However, differentiating between these two concepts concisely and concretely is a difficult task. A common misconception is that the legitimate authority of a position, such as holding a management job or an elected position, automatically confers leadership skills upon the holder of that position. Nothing is further from the truth. Leadership and management are two separate and distinct concepts although they may exist simultaneously in the same person. In an interview by Joe Flower (1990), Bennis compares management and leadership on several key points. As discussed below, his viewpoint greatly increases clarity about these two concepts.

### *Efficiency versus Effectiveness*

The first differentiating point is related to the essential focus of the individual. A manager is concerned with efficiency, or getting things done right, better, and faster. Increasing productivity and streamlining current operations are important, and employees are often exhorted by managers to "work smarter, not harder." In contrast, a leader is more concerned with effectiveness, asking: "Are we doing the right thing?" The initial question is not "How can we do this faster?" but "Should we be doing this at all?" In answer to the latter question, a key deciding factor is if the activity in question directly supports the overall purpose and mission of the organization.

A classic example of this difference occurred some years ago in a 480-bed midwestern medical center. As the hospital's volume increased over the years, traffic flow on the elevators became a major problem. Several quality teams, at various times, attacked the problem but came up with no lasting or truly effective solution. After years of frustration, a quality team assigned to this issue finally came up with a solution that involved building a new set of elevators designated FOR PATIENTS ONLY.

The intent was to move patients faster and more efficiently—which was accomplished for several hundred thousand dollars.

A couple of years later the organization went through a major reengineering and work-redesign effort where the first questions asked were: "Why are we transporting patients all over the organization? Aren't there any services that can be deployed to the patient-care unit to reduce the amount of travel that patients experience?" These are leadership questions—instead of asking how patients can be moved faster, they asked: "Should they be moved at all? How can movement of patients be reduced?"

## How *versus* What *and* Why

A second differentiating characteristic is that management is about *how* while leadership is about *what* and *why*. A good manager is usually one who understands the work processes and can demonstrate and explain how to accomplish the work assigned to an employee. These phenomena are clearly valued in health care, where there is a history of promoting people with job expertise to management and supervisory roles. The highly skilled practitioner becomes a manager, and overall this is the typical pattern regardless of the department in question. Health care workers tend to highly value job expertise in their managers and, in fact, often show disdain for the manager who cannot perform at a highly competent level the work of the staff they manage. This is understandable when health care's history is examined. Early hospitals were led and managed by individuals with a high level of technical clinical expertise (physicians and nurses). Only in recent decades have a significant number of executives and managers with nonclinical backgrounds entered health care institutions. There still exists today some skepticism and doubt by clinical health care workers that these individuals with nonclinical backgrounds can possibly understand enough to be effective leaders in health care organizations.

Knowing and controlling work processes are essential components of the managerial role, and rightly so. The origins of management sprang from the factories of the last century. The workforce of the late 1800s was very different from today's workforce. Most early factory workers were newly arrived immigrants, women, and children—poorly informed, uneducated, non–English speaking, and uninvolved employees working for survival wages. The work was compartmentalized, broken down into small manageable pieces that could be taught easily to these early workers. The manager was responsible for ensuring that work was done correctly.

In contrast, a leader focuses on what needs to be done and why. More time is spent explaining the general direction and purpose of the work, and then the leader gets out of the way so the follower can do it. Someone once characterized a leader as an individual who describes what needs to be done followed by "It's up to you to impress me with how you do it."

This implies several different points. First, the leader knows what needs to be done and can clearly articulate this to others in a way that convinces the follower it is an appropriate direction. Second, the leader has the patience to share the reasons this course has been chosen and ensure those reasons are acceptable and valid to the follower. Finally, the leader accepts that the follower may find a new and different way to accomplish the goals. The leader is not wedded to his or her way of performing a task or carrying out a responsibility.

Multiple examples of this leadership approach abound in the last few years in organizations undergoing major work-redesign or restructuring initiatives. In one medical center, the CEO addressed employees before redesigning work was begun, explaining the organization's current status, the external environment, and why the board of trustees and executive team believed work redesign was necessary for future viability of the organization. The reasons were clear and, in most instances, were viewed as important and valued by the employees. A team of employees was then formed that was instrumental in determining how results were to be achieved and how the project would be carried out. In other organizations, work redesign has failed because it was undertaken with only a "hospital mentality"—a controlling leader who believed there was one right way to achieve needed outcomes—rather than a systems approach. Employees may have participated, but they did not believe in or value the reasons behind the project.

### Structure versus People

Bennis points out that management is about systems, controls, procedures, and policies—all of which create structure—while leadership is about people (Flower 1990). Managers spend much of their time dealing with organizational structure. Anyone who has successfully participated in an accreditation visit by an outside agency has a sense of the number of policies and procedures generated by the average health care institution. There is usually a policy or procedure for every aspect of organizational and professional life. Infection control monitoring, risk management reporting, and patient-complaint resolution are only a few among the multitude of control systems designed to oversee organizational processes. These systems ensure that work is progressing as expected; they are designed to alert the manager to any deviation so that it can be investigated and corrected.

Leadership is about people and relationships. Leadership only exists within the context of a relationship. If there are no followers, there is no need for leadership, just independent action. Leadership occurs when there is leader behavior that influences someone else to act in a certain manner, and at the core of this people connection is trust. These concepts are explored in depth in chapter 2. Leadership as a relationship may be disturbing news for managers who have limited "people skills," for it is virtually impossible to become a fully effective leader if an individual has difficulty in working with others. A book on policies and procedures cannot replace this key relationship.

### Status Quo versus Innovation

Whereas maintaining and managing the status quo are appropriate managerial behaviors (Bennis 1989), leaders are more concerned with innovation and creating new procedures for the future. This is a difficult area for many health care leaders because most health care organizations have not customarily encouraged or highly valued either creativity or innovation. The terms are found in many mission statements, but only rarely are health care organizations flexible and fluid enough to encourage true innovation. Most are bureaucratic structures where deviations from standard practice are often responded to as something that needs to be stamped out, controlled, or limited in some manner.

Punitive responses to mistakes are common and many managers have learned to not rock the boat. The incident-reporting mechanism is a common example. If a mistake is reported, a familiar response by the manager is to determine what went wrong and how the employee needs to change so that the mistake never occurs again—a return to the status quo. Less frequent is a response that investigates the mistake in partnership with the employee to determine why the mistake occurred and what needs to change in the system so that the problem will not occur again. Recent emphasis on the quality process has stimulated a move toward more creative problem solving and resolution.

Leaders are always looking for ways to improve the current situation; they are never satisfied with the status quo. A leader's automatic response to a problem or mistake is to consider ways to capitalize on the opportunity that has been created. For this reason "bureaucracies tend to suppress real leadership because real leaders disequilibrate systems; they create disorder and instability, even chaos" (Flower 1990, 62).

Because of their trust in people, a leader knows that the follower can always find a way to improve on the current situation. DePree (1989) describes highly effective leaders as those who are comfortable abandoning themselves to the strengths of others and admitting that they themselves cannot know or do everything. This can be frightening to those who are not up to the challenge of continually questioning their own performance or established practices. Fearful individuals may react to this drive for continual improvement as implied criticism: "It was not good enough and now we have to change it."

## Bottom Line versus Horizon

Managers keep their eyes on the bottom line while leaders focus on the horizon. Managers ask: "Are we within budget?" "Are we meeting our goals?" "What's the deadline?" There is an emphasis on counting, recording, and measuring to ensure that everything is on target. It is easy to forget, expressed by Linda Ellerbee so eloquently: "Not everything that counts can be counted."

By its very nature, leadership and its results are difficult to measure. How do you measure a relationship? What are the concrete, observable outcomes? Good leaders see beyond the bottom line to the horizon, where a vision of a different future for themselves and their followers guides their day-to-day decision making. This vision inspires them to make very difficult decisions on behalf of the organization and the people within it.

A leader with a vision of empowered employees who feel ownership of their jobs, who make decisions impacting work in their span of control, and who work in partnership with the organization's managers knows that to attain this vision the employees will need continual learning and educational opportunities. In many organizations today, employees are being asked to contribute more, learn additional skills, and take on more responsibility at the same time that education departments and learning resources have been severely reduced. Leadership decisions to invest in employee education may not look good on the bottom line, but they are at the core of the vision of the future. Exemplary leaders recognize that without investment in the development of internal staff resources, there will be a much higher price to pay in the future.

## Management versus Leadership: A Final Word

That there is a difference between management and leadership is clear. None of this is to imply, however, that there is not a need for good, capable managers in today's health care organizations. Managers will always be needed, and the role is in fact so crucial that everyone in the organization must share managerial responsibilities. Highly efficient employees who understand their work, who are able to organize and structure it, and who can measure outcomes and take corrective action will always be in high demand. With a great number of experienced and mature workers in health care today, there are higher expectations of employees than ever before. As more employees become self-managing, the number of formal managers may be reduced. At the same time, however, there is an increasing need for leaders. According to many recognized students of American leadership, organizations in this country have been overmanaged and underled (Bennis and Nanus 1985; Kouzes and Posner 1987; Peters 1987).

## WHY LEADERSHIP IS IN DEMAND TODAY

During the 1970s health care organizations had a burgeoning interest in management development programs. Recognition that promoting technically competent employees into management positions produced a responsibility on the part of the organization to provide management and supervisory training and education. In the last ten years there has been a shift in all sectors of our society to emphasize the importance of leadership skills. Simply reviewing in a popular bookstore the number of titles about leadership reflects this emphasis. Why the sudden interest in leadership? Why the need to differentiate it from management? There are at least three major reasons:

1. The unrelenting crush of change
2. Rapidly shifting paradigms
3. Survival

### Change

*Change* is the byword for the 1990s. Never has the pace of change been so fast nor have the changes altered so deeply the way people live and work. "The change and upheaval of the past years have left us with no place to hide. We need anchors in our lives, something like a trim-tab factor, a guiding purpose. Leaders fill that need" (Bennis 1989, 15). Fundamental changes in health care are occurring so rapidly it is hard to keep pace. What were believed to be significant organizational changes in 1982—revised job descriptions, new management positions, novel performance appraisals—pale by comparison to today's changes, which include moving services off site, transforming department-based structures to team-based, replacing employees by automation, outsourcing, cross training of skills, forming partnerships within the community, simultaneously collaborating and competing with the same entity, and merging with another organization or developing an entirely new system. Annison states the case clearly: "During periods of stability we can be successful by doing more of what we already do; the focus is on management and maintaining the present. During periods of change, the emphasis is on changing what we do and the focus is on leadership" (1994, 1).

## Shifting Paradigms

*Paradigms*, or the models through which the world is viewed, are rapidly shifting. As described by Barker, "A paradigm shift, then, is a change to a new game, a new set of rules" (1992, 37). This shift creates confusion and unease as well as new possibilities. In some instances the paradigm is changed by a player in the health care sector, while in other situations the impetus comes from without. The rules and game plan may suddenly change, leaving those in the game to figure out the new rules.

Competition in health care is a good example of a paradigm that continues to shift. Not so long ago the major competitor for a hospital was the other hospital in town, "just down the road." Today competition comes from everywhere: stand-alone health care facilities, such as ambulatory-care centers and diagnostic centers in physician offices; hospitals from other communities that set up satellite or full-service facilities outside their communities; and even previous customers who decide to become providers on a limited basis.

The lines and boundaries are no longer clear. As demonstrated elsewhere in the business world, there are times when one must collaborate with close competitors (Annison 1997). Consumers buying an Apple computer today are purchasing a machine manufactured by Toshiba. MasterCard and Visa collaborate on automatic teller machines and choose to compete on marketing and customer service. Similarly, in health care, two hospitals from competing systems have jointly built a wellness facility in their community, and a major medical center has partnered with a large clinic-based physician practice on several joint projects while competing with it on several others.

During times of great change and rapidly shifting paradigms, leaders are needed. As Barker points out: "You manage within a paradigm. You lead between paradigms." When times are stable and game rules remain consistent and known, there are structures, standards, and protocols that enhance the manager's ability to optimize the paradigm. In fact, this describes the manager's job exactly. However, during a shift to new paradigms, leadership is required, as Barker explains: "Leaving one paradigm while it is still successful and going to a new paradigm that is as yet unproved looks very risky. But leaders, with their intuitive judgment, assess the seeming risk, determine that shifting paradigms is the correct thing to do, and, because they are leaders, instill the courage in others to follow them" (1992, 164).

When paradigms shift and the rules change, everyone involved "goes back to zero." Put simply in the words of a colleague: "What got you to the party won't keep you there!" It is time to let go of past successes and look for new ways of doing things. There is no guarantee that because the organization, group, or individual was very good with the old game rules that they will be as good with the new ones. In fact, the more successful the individual or organization was with the old model, the more difficult to engage in a new way of thinking.

One of the major leadership gaps identified through market research for this book was a refusal to let go of the "hospital mentality" and traditional modes of service. Potential consequences of this pitfall include:

- Belief that past or current success automatically leads to future success
- Reluctance to make changes rapidly enough to successfully adapt to the changing external environment
- Overreliance on internal expertise and past experience
- Aversion to risk sharing with physicians and key stakeholders and risk taking by executives and board members
- Attempts to control and dictate community health initiatives rather than collaborating with community stakeholders

This issue is easy to talk about but difficult to deal with when faced with a shifted paradigm. During one surgical services leadership team retreat, initial discussion revolved around changes the team and service were experiencing. The anesthesiologists were especially upset because, with increasing managed-care penetration in their community, surgery was for the first time being considered a *cost* center rather than a revenue source for the organization. In their words, "We used to be able to get whatever we wanted; now we're being seen as a drain on the resources of the organization." This leadership team needed to figure out how to be successful with the new game rules in order to continue to thrive.

## Survival

The final and perhaps most important reason that leadership is needed today is viewed simply as survival. Bennis (1989) notes that a few years ago a scientist at the University of Michigan listed what he considered to be the ten basic dangers to our society. The top three are:

1. A nuclear war or accident, capable of destroying the human race
2. A worldwide epidemic, disease, famine, or financial depression
3. The quality of management and leadership in our institutions

Leaders are responsible for the effectiveness of an organization. As an industry, health care is vulnerable as a result of technological pressures, globalization, changing demographics, and environmental challenges. Strong leadership is needed to take us into a very uncertain future. Gifford and Elizabeth Pinchot eloquently describe the need for leaders:

> The more machines take over routine work and the higher the percentage of knowledge workers, the more leaders are needed. The work left for humans involves innovation, seeing things in new ways, and responding to customers by changing the way things are done. We are reaching a time when every employee will take turns leading. Each will find circumstances when they see what must be done and must influence others to make their vision of a better way a reality. (1996, 18)

Finally, the role of leaders as it influences the integrity of organizations is crucial. "There is a pervasive, national concern about the integrity of our institutions. Wall Street was, not long ago, a place where a man's word was his bond. The recent investigations, revelations, and indictments have forced the industry to change the way it conducted business for 150 years. Jim Bakker and Jimmy Swaggart have given a new meaning to the phrase 'children of a lesser God'" (Bennis 1989, 15–16). Health care is not immune to the issue of integrity. Hospital executives indicted for Medicare fraud, home health agencies led by criminals previously convicted of fraud, or a community hospital's senior executives convicted of embezzlement—all are headlines seen in recent years. Never has the need for ethical, exemplary leaders been more crucial as the challenges of the next century are faced.

## CHALLENGES FACING TODAY'S LEADERS

Today the opportunities and possibilities for leaders are endless, as are the challenges. Demands are different for today's leaders and have ramifications for anyone aspiring to lead others. The more these issues are understood, the more likely a leader can find the necessary strength and courage to meet the test presented by these five challenges:

1. The rapidity of change
2. People in transition
3. The dejobbing of America
4. The "new employment contract"
5. New organizational structures

## The Rapidity of Change

As discussed previously, change is occurring at an accelerated pace today with change experts assuring the public that the rate of change will continue to increase through the end of the century and into the early years of the next millennium. According to Connor, change encountered in previous eras is different in magnitude and pace, the approach required, the increasing seriousness of its implication, and the short shelf life of solutions: "In tumultuous environments, every solution brings more complex problems, not worse necessarily, but ones requiring more creative approaches. For example, the world is not worse off because of the invention of the computer. But even with all the good that these machines have provided, information systems have complicated our lives in unforeseen ways" (Connor 1993, 39). It can be discouraging when a leader realizes that today's solution may become tomorrow's problem. Leaders know that the current change simply brings you closer to the next one.

Change takes energy, and as more change is experienced, it can feel like an endless energy drain. Because it is difficult to influence others in a positive way when exhausted, leaders must take good care of themselves during changing times. Not all changes are for the better, and a leader is challenged to remain optimistic and enthusiastic, yet truthful. This can be arduous in the face of personal discouragement. As described by Connor (1993), effective leaders have a high degree of resilience in their ability to demonstrate courage, strength, and flexibility in the face of change and frightening disorder.

Sometimes the challenge for a leader lies in determining what changes are to be made and which to forgo. It is easy to become swept up in the tide of change and go overboard. Many leaders find change exhilarating and forget that the organization's ability to sustain a certain pace of change may not match the leader's personal capacity for change. Winston Churchill said, "When it is not necessary to change, it is necessary *not* to change." This sage advice is easy to forget when all the changes look positive. The knack of looking beyond the initial excitement and potential promise to determine whether the change is a necessary and beneficial one is a leadership skill worth developing.

This tendency to get caught up in unnecessary change happened inadvertently in a community hospital undergoing a major restructuring and work-redesign effort. As departments were restructured, some employees were asked to reapply for their positions. There was concern that the secretaries and executive assistants in the organization would not have the same opportunity (yes, it was considered an opportunity). As a result, all employees in secretarial positions were allowed to apply for a transfer into any position for which they were suited. The outcome was an extreme version of "fruit basket upset." The secretary for the behavioral health department transferred to education; the education secretary went to human resources; the human resource secretary transferred to purchasing; the infection control secretary went to administration; and so on. The result was mass confusion and significantly decreased effectiveness in the organization for a good six months while these people were being oriented: all for what was, in the end, unnecessary change.

Peter Drucker talks about this same issue in an interview by Joe Flower, but he refers to it as being effective. He says the leader has to sometimes say no. "The secret of effectiveness is concentration of the very meager resources you have where you can make a difference" (Flower 1991, 53). Thus, the leader's role is to carefully assess what changes are most important and likely to help achieve the goals and attain the vision of the organization while avoiding the energy drain of nonessential change.

Every major sector of society is undergoing massive change. The entire structure of health care is changing. Some of these changes were highlighted in a recent book edited by Chawla and Renesch (1995), which found such factors at work requiring critical shifts in thinking by health care leaders as:

- A shift from fee-for-service to discounts and capitation wherein providers are responsible for quality and cost
- A shift from inpatient acute care to outpatient services, requiring health care leaders to rethink traditional hospital boundaries, investments, and relationships with key stakeholders
- The rise of primary care physicians as gatekeepers and care managers in a capitated environment
- A shift from a discipline-centered production organization to a customer-focused service orientation
- A shift from an illness and disease model to a wellness paradigm with a focus on alternative or complementary medicine

## People in Transition

This second challenge goes hand in hand with the rapidity of change. Change means to alter or make something different. Transition is the psychological adaptation to change and is not over until the person can function and find meaning in the new situation (Bridges 1991). If a transition has occurred, something has been lost, even if it is as simple as loss of comfort with the old way. Thus, stages of transition include stages of grief, which engender some of the most difficult emotions humans face. Anger, depression, anxiety, fear, and just plain contrariness are often experienced and expressed. Trying to lead people who are grieving is fraught with difficulties and can tax even the most proficient leader.

These emotions are complex enough to face in an individual much less when multiplied by hundreds and even thousands in an organization. Understanding where people are in their cycle helps prevent inappropriate or unhelpful responses. The fact that they may all be in different places at the same time makes the challenge more intense. Complexity is further increased by the fact that the leader may be feeling some of these difficult emotions as well. Chapter 5 explores the transition process in more detail.

## The "Dejobbing" of America

A fundamental shift in work life is occurring across America and impacting people in unexpected ways. The shift is away from the job as a concept. William Bridges, author of several best-selling books, including *Transitions, Making Transitions* and *Surviving Corporate Transitions,* has recently written the book *JobShift* (1994). He notes that the concept of a job was only invented at the beginning of the industrial revolution, when people went to work in factories. Now, with the decline of manufacturing and the evolution of the information age, the very concept of *job* is disintegrating.

"As a way of organizing work, [the job] is a social artifact that has outlived its usefulness. Its demise confronts everyone with unfamiliar risks—and rich opportunities" (Bridges 1994b, 62). This trend is disturbing to many people who have held a job their entire work life. It is difficult to conceive of a "dejobbed" health care organization, and yet many examples are already apparent. There is an increase in outsourcing and using consultants and independent contractors. Part-timers outnumber full-time employees in some organizations; it's not uncommon to have employees with two to three jobs; and there is consistent use of per diem or registry staff. These are all examples that support this trend toward "dejobbing" health care.

Although it is unlikely that health care will ever be completely dejobbed (Flower 1997), this trend does have implications for leaders. "The main impact is . . . that tomorrow's leadership is going to have to be able to activate and focus the efforts of people who lack long-term connections with or loyalty to the organization. You don't lead a group of freelancers the way you lead long-term employees" (Bridges 1995, 5). Influencing these people and getting commitment from them is much tougher than when the employees' connections to the organization were stronger.

## The New Employment Contract

Closely related to the dejobbing challenge yet different is the altered "contract" that organizations have with their employees. Not so very long ago, when employees were initially hired by an institution, the implication—*and* reality—of the agreement was that as long as work was completed according to expected standards, the employee retained the job. Even in the face of economic downturns, health care workers enjoyed fairly high job security. Not so anymore. There are no longer any guarantees of any kind but, instead, what author David Noer describes as a new employment contract: "This psychological contract fits the new reality. It says that even the best performer or the most culturally adaptive person cannot count on long-term employment. It replaces loyalty to an organization with loyalty to one's work" (1993, 13).

Examples of this abound in health care. In one case, a director of staff development attended a professional seminar on a Friday—the topic was "Change in the Workplace." When she returned to work the following Monday, she was informed she needed to decide by noon which two employees she would cut from staff. At one o'clock she was informed she would be reporting directly to the vice president of human resources because the director of education (to whom she reported) had been eliminated. None of these employees were doing a bad job; the positions were simply restructured out of existence.

In another organization, several long-term, excellent employees were eliminated when their function in the human resource department was outsourced. In yet another organization, the vice president of human resources helped lead the "rightsizing" campaign only to discover that the last position to be eliminated was his own! Many organizations are combining management positions and eliminating people even though they are contributing and highly committed employees. Of two managers competing for the same position in one organization, the weaker manager was selected because there was a belief that the more capable and better-educated manager would have no trouble finding a new position! Entire categories of positions have been eliminated, such as supervisors, clinical nurse specialists, assistant managers, clinicians, and charge nurses, to cite a few examples.

Certainly not all of these changes are bad; perhaps they merely reflect a transition to a more fluid, flexible organization of the future. Noer believes that in the past there was an unhealthy, outdated organizational codependency. It was not unusual for employees to depend on the organization for far more than a job or a way to earn a living. It was the old "company store" mentality, and the organization was expected to provide everything from a network of friends, a social life, education support, to even health and recreational needs.

This battle is among the most important struggles that we and our organizations will ever face. Individuals must break the chains of their unhealthy, outdated organizational codependency and recapture their self-esteem; organizations must achieve their potential and thrive in the new world economy. For the organization, holding on to the familiar old is not the answer. For the individual, holding on to the job is not always the most healthy option. (Noer 1993, 4)

Noer's advice is striking: "The only way you provide security for yourself is by making sure that your work experience is as up-to-date as possible so that if tomorrow happens, you are able to go out and get another job because you have skills people want. That's the only way you have security. You aren't going to get it from the company. It will never be that way again" (1993, 15).

This new employment contract has significant ramifications for health care leaders. These chains of organizational codependency can be as difficult to break for those who have provided these benefits and implied job security as for those who have been the recipients of the supposed rewards. Many leaders still feel a benevolence toward employees and do not want to accept that a healthier relationship is a full partnership between the employee and the organization. The generosity of the "we will take care of you" attitude has inadvertently created employees who are overly dependent on the organization. And, as benefits are reduced and there is less talk of the "big, happy family," employees naturally respond as if what they are entitled to is being taken away.

## New Organization Structures

Another challenge for today's leader is the changing organizational structures that are emerging. Most of today's leaders have spent the majority of their organizational life in a bureaucratic structure, and it is the form with which they are comfortable. Whether this structure can survive into the future is debatable. New, more fluid and flexible structures are being tried with the belief that these newer structures enhance response to customers, increase the rate of innovation, and create work environments that stimulate commitment, curiosity, and ownership on the part of employees. In their book *The Intelligent Organization*, the Pinchots say: "The transformation from bureaucracy to organizational intelligence is a move from relationships of dominance and submission up and down the chain of command to horizontal relationships of peers across a network of voluntary cooperation and market-based exchanges" (1996, xiv).

Bureaucracies are not well equipped to meet changing times. "Bureaucracies are self-sustaining only in times of stability, when the environment is placid. They are very ineffective when times are changing. When the world is turbulent, the managerial environment is spastic, fluid, and volatile. Then the bureaucracy seems to be particularly inadequate because it keeps repeating yesterday's lessons and fighting the last war" (Flower 1990, 62). Organizations of the future are more likely to be based on a network or a flattened hierarchy model. In fact, Bennis is very clear on this point when he says, "Organizations that operate on the nineteenth-century model of the bureaucracy—a model based on the words *control*, *order*, and *predict*—are just not going to cut it. . . . They already aren't."

One new form of organizational model is described by Waterman as the "adhocracy," which is any organizational form that challenges the bureaucracy in order to embrace new ways of doing things. He notes that the concept of adhocracy is not new. In the mid-1960s, "Warren Bennis argued the need for adaptive, problem-solving, temporary systems of diverse specialists linked together . . . in an organic flux" (Waterman 1992, 18). This is much more difficult to do in a bureaucracy than it appears. People hold specific jobs and have responsibilities that must be accomplished regardless of "temporary assignments" or project team commitments. In health care during the past five to seven years, there has been more of a move toward "flexible assignments" than was in evidence prior to this time. When undergoing major reengineering or work-redesign initiatives, many organizations appointed employees or managers as project directors or project team members. This pulled employees and managers out of their jobs and moved them into these semipermanent yet temporary assignments. It allowed organizations to move some of their "best and brightest" to the critical initiative of the day.

This resulted in many other difficulties, however, the prime predicament being what to do with these people when the temporary work was completed and the individual's previous job had been filled or eliminated. It is the same problem in other businesses and industries, as Waterman notes: "Today's companies need, but seldom have, the ability to move seamlessly from bureaucracy to adhocracy and back again. Today's managers need, but seldom have, the skill and security to leave their posts for a while and become effective members of project teams. But without that ability, companies and people go on making the same old mistakes. They do not learn. This is the Achilles' heel of corporate America" (1996, 26).

Another promising new organizational form is the team-based organization. This new structure "replaces or supplements traditional hierarchical structures with semiautonomous teams in order to flatten management, revitalize employees, and enhance productivity" (Manion, Lorimer, and Leander 1996, xi). Employee work teams replace the department as the smallest unit of an organization's structure. The true essence of teams involves transfer of real responsibility and authority to the team and formation of a collaborative relationship between manager and team. "Teams are a remarkable way to forge a partnership between leaders and employees, producing an undreamed-of synergy as they build on the strengths of everyone in the organization. Teams thrive on the challenges of the future and give us the best chance for capitalizing on the scarcely tapped energy of human potential" (Manion, Lorimer, and Leander 1996, xii). Creating a true team-based organization challenges leadership tremendously. It simply cannot occur without strong leaders who have a clear vision of a different future.

## CONCLUSION

Developing leaders is one of the most important issues currently facing health care organizations. In defining leadership, it is important to distinguish between leadership and management. The growing need for strong leadership is directly related to the unrelenting crush of change being experienced today—which in the health care world is reflected in the rapid shifting of paradigms and concern for survival into the future. Thus, the challenges facing today's leaders include the rapidity of change, the number of people undergoing major transitions, the dejobbing of America and health care, the new employment contract, and changing organizational structures. These factors have resulted in a tremendous sense of urgency in health care organizations and have made clear the need for the identification and development of internal leaders as well as the mastery of new, nontraditional skills for these leaders.

# 2

## Cultivating the Leadership Relationship

"The only definition of a leader is someone who has followers. Some people are thinkers. Some are prophets. Both roles are important and badly needed. But without followers, there can be no leaders."

—*Peter Drucker*

L eadership exists only within the context of a relationship. It is an intensely personal experience, a process of relating to another person, who if influenced becomes a follower. All definitions of leadership include the ability to influence others to do what needs to be done. It is a dynamic interaction between both leader and follower, changing each irrevocably.

The quality of the leader and follower's relationship directly affects the abilities of the leader. Without the foundation for a healthy relationship, the aspiring leader cannot attain extraordinary outcomes. Although troubled leaders seldom return to the basic components of a healthy relationship when they are frustrated by followers who do not follow, the answer to their difficulties often lies within this basic concept. This chapter outlines the essential elements of a healthy leader-follower relationship and identifies several future-oriented forms of association that today's leaders must understand.

## ESSENTIAL ELEMENTS OF A HEALTHY RELATIONSHIP

Leaders who relate comfortably to others often take their talent for granted. There is a naturalness and a spontaneity in their relationships that result in mutually beneficial outcomes. When a particular leader-follower situation is not going well, the relationship-centered leader often reflects first on the connection with the supporter to determine the issues. And because this leader is already skillful in this area, the assessment process is not likely to produce undue anxiety. If, however, the leader is not naturally skilled at forming strong relationships, this impacts both the accuracy and ease of the assessment process.

Often, established, effective leaders intuitively understand the essential elements of a healthy relationship. And when something is wrong, the leader is alerted by intuitive signals. There are three essential elements to a successful leader-follower relationship:

1. Trust
2. Mutual respect
3. Communication

These three elements are described as essential because the absence of any one can damage the relationship.

### Trust

According to *Webster's Encyclopedic Unabridged Dictionary*, *trust* means you can rely on the "integrity, strength or ability of a person or thing. Confidence implies conscious trust because of good reasons, definite evidence or past experience." Without trust or confidence in the person attempting to influence them, people will not follow that person's direction or lead. In an organization, when the individual attempting to lead uses the authority of his or her position, the relative health of the relationship can be deceptive. People may do what that leader wants, not because they agree or believe in the direction set or the request made, but because they believe they must comply or there may be painful or uncomfortable personal consequences.

Understanding the concept of trust is imperative for anyone aspiring to lead others. Warren Bennis offers a concrete, applicable framework for understanding trust within the context of a leadership role (Flower 1990). He defines three essential ingredients for trust as competence, congruence, and constancy. Examination of these three components of trust provides a guide for any leader who is seeking to more fully understand their personal effectiveness.

**Competence**    *Webster's* defines *competence* as the "possession of required skill, knowledge, qualification or capacity." The application of this definition in a leadership context is clear. Supporters must believe that the leader has the skill and knowledge to do what is required. "Whenever we step in front of the crowd and say, 'Follow me,' the implication is that we know where we're going and what we want to achieve and that we're committed to giving our very best efforts" (Melrose 1996, 20). Confidence in a leader develops from working with that person, and from evidence of the leader's past performance demonstrating competence. Both skill *and* knowledge are included in this definition. Knowledge alone is insufficient. The leader may know that followers need accurate information and clear communication, but an unskilled leader is greatly hampered if unable to articulate clearly.

This is why changing key leaders in organizations can result in a troublesome situation. It takes time to establish trust and confidence in new leadership. Nevertheless many health care organizations embarking on major change choose to alter the managerial and executive structure, eliminating or combining positions. Entire departments find themselves in a new reporting relationship. Leaders in these new positions are then expected to lead their followers through the changes, yet are severely disadvantaged because they must first form a trusting relationship. Although this sequence of events may be appropriate, its impact on the time required to change should be carefully considered.

*Qualification:* Qualification is an interesting factor in competence. In health care there is a notable emphasis on expertise as a necessary qualification (discussed in chapter 1). Some people simply do not follow an individual unless the person has a particular qualification believed to be important, such as a clinical discipline background or a certain academic degree. Whether the qualification actually prepares or enables the leader to function competently is a moot point; from the perception of a potential follower, it can become a critical issue with significant repercussions. In a restructured medical center, a newly appointed patient-care department leader encountered significant obstacles because of his background as manager of environmental services. Right or wrong, it simply took longer for him to establish a trust relationship with his staff because of a need to prove competence in the face of what appears to be a significant qualification issue to clinical caregivers.

*Capacity:* Capacity issues influence the level of trust in the leader. If a leader is seen by others as simply having too much to do, too many responsibilities—"juggling too many balls"—a question of trust may arise. Can this leader handle the current situation? Will it be too much? What if it pushes the leader over the edge? Appearing frazzled and out of control creates uneasy followers. Personal endurance and a phenomenal capacity for work often go hand in hand with effective leadership. The motto "Never let them see you sweat" may be appropriate but should not imply that a good leader never lets followers see the reality of a difficult situation.

In one West Coast hospital where significant restructuring was occurring, a newly appointed care center leader had a personality style characterized by spontaneity, impulsiveness, and a high degree of self-disclosure. As the restructuring progressed, this leader was given more and more responsibility because she was very capable. She quickly reached the point of overload and began manifesting counterproductive behaviors such as volatility, extreme distractibility, and pure panic. Her communication patterns became dysfunctional as a result of her intense anxiety. Her erratic behavior with her followers clearly transmitted her anxiety, and she began to lose their trust. In this instance, skill, knowledge, and qualifications were not at issue. Instead, her followers feared she could not handle the heavy load.

**Congruence**   The second key element of trust in this context is *congruence*, meaning consistency or agreement between verbal messages and the leader's behavior (Lorimer and Manion 1996). A leader with a high degree of congruence between what is said and the behaviors observed by followers is perceived as more honest and trustworthy. If the leader says one thing but does another, the result is an enormous credibility gap with followers. Most would agree that leaders must "walk the talk." Integrity and character of the leader are important. Followers need to believe that leaders act in accordance with their personal beliefs and are honest not only with themselves but with followers. This is more important than agreeing with the leader's beliefs. "Effective leadership . . . is not based on being clever; it is based primarily on being consistent" (Drucker 1992, 122).

*Common discrepancies:* Examples of discrepancies are common in any work setting. One department leader in hospital maintenance established employee work teams and assured team members that they would have responsibility for input into or making decisions that impacted their work. After almost a year of working together as a team, they were joined one day by two new team members that no one on the team had expected. Their manager had hired these additional members without including the team in the decision. Consequently the team members felt betrayed by the manager, and the ensuing breach of trust was difficult to repair.

One of the most serious problems with congruency is that inconsistent messages are often inadvertent. The leader usually does not purposely engage in behavior that is contrary to previous messages sent but instead, without realizing it, acts in direct contradiction to the oral and written messages delivered. This happened in one organization where competence was a stated organization value. Yet when attempting to relocate people during a massive restructuring and reassignment process, tenure was the key selection criteria. Tenure and competence are not the same thing, and many employees were offended and angered by what appeared to be a decision-making criterion inconsistent with a stated, and often touted, organization value. When this was questioned, the senior executive leading the initiative became defensive and angry but eventually listened to the feedback and changed the decision-making criteria. Tenure was used as a final determining factor *only* if the employees in question first met the criterion of competency.

A similar situation in another hospital was handled differently. When confronted with the incongruity between the stated organization value of competence and using tenure as selection criterion, the administration of this community hospital retained tenure as the deciding criterion. They cited the reason that this was not the appropriate time to correct problems with employee competency issues that had not been dealt with previously by managers. Though it may sound reasonable, the choice remains a major credibility issue. They were basically admitting that they had never held true to the organization's stated value of competence when saying that managers had never dealt properly with unacceptable or poor employee performance.

*Avoiding discrepancies:* A leader must scrupulously examine and be aware of behavior that might be interpreted as incongruent, although it is virtually impossible to avoid *all* discrepancies. Thus it is especially important for a leader to promote openness and honest feedback from followers. An executive team in one northeastern medical center worked diligently to establish such an open environment, making certain that employees knew their leaders wanted feedback if behaviors appeared incongruent. These leaders knew that their initial reaction to feedback would determine the amount and usefulness of future feedback given and were very careful to listen fully when discordant messages were brought to their attention and to react nondefensively. In some instances, behavior deemed incongruent was changed to fit the message. In other cases, communication was unclear and through sharing additional information, the problem was resolved. This openness did not occur overnight. Many employees were—and some still are—hesitant to provide feedback because of fear of reprisal. This fear is a common obstacle when the leader also holds a hierarchical position.

Giving the leader feedback on incongruent behavior is much more difficult than it may appear. Bennis observes that "7 out of 10 staff won't say anything when they feel the leader is about to make a mistake. They may speak up once, but if what they say is discounted, either by words or body language, they won't speak up again, sometimes with costly consequences." Some of this reluctance to speak freely and honestly is related to early socialization messages. Chaleff explains that young people are taught from an early age to obey authority, to say "Yes, sir" and "Yes, ma'am," and that this conditioning runs very deep. It takes work to overcome these deep internal messages. "We are afraid that if we question authority we will be viewed as a nuisance, pushed out of the loop, overlooked for promotion, even fired. We fear the consequences of speaking up far more than we are afraid of the more serious consequences of not speaking up" (Chaleff 1996, 16).

Another way to view congruence involves congruity between what leaders do in their personal and public lives. People who do not live up to commitments to their family or who cheat their neighbors often hide behind the belief that what happens in their personal lives should not affect their leadership roles. Like it or not, if untrustworthy personal behavior is seen by followers, it impacts the level of trust given their leaders.

***Constancy***    Constancy is the third and final ingredient of trust as identified by Bennis (Flower 1990). It implies that the leader is reliable, dependable, and consistent. A good leader keeps commitments and follows through on promises made. If it becomes clear that a promise or commitment cannot be met, the leader communicates openly and honestly with followers to inform them of the changed circumstances— ideally *before* being confronted by followers.

*Availability and accessibility:* To many followers, availability and accessibility are part of constancy. For leaders to be most effective, they must be accessible to followers and not just at prescheduled, formal times. Some of the best dialogues occur in a completely spontaneous fashion. When the leader is also a manager or executive, formal trappings of the role may serve to distance the leader from followers. Common examples of this are isolated office locations or the presence of secretaries who see their role as "protecting" or buffering the leader from others. Although it is not possible to be completely available 24 hours a day, neither should the leader be inaccessible to followers. A balance must be found, for the perception that the leader is available is a potent one in creating a collegial relationship with followers.

Visibility of the leader has been promoted by many authors. Peters and Austin (1985) promote "management by walking around," or MBWA. It suggests that the closer a leader is physically to followers, the more a sense of connection and understanding is established. And it is true that the leader who sees a situation with his or her own eyes is certainly better informed than one hearing about it from a third, potentially biased party. As time pressures increase, visibility and availability are often sacrificed. Whatever constraints may exist, they are never as serious as the threat to a leader's effectiveness from followers who do not feel a sense of connection, and, as a result, do not follow.

These ideas seem like common sense or intuitive knowledge that is self-evident. However, availability and accessibility are difficult to achieve in these demanding times. The massive amount of change occurring creates an environment filled with uncertainty, and followers have many questions. Followers may not perceive all changes as positive and may be very unhappy, even angry, about the current direction of the organization. Every leader today knows how daunting it is to face a crowd of antagonistic followers, and it is a natural tendency to avoid these situations and withdraw from contact with followers. Herein lies one major difference between the excellent leader and the not-so-effective leader: the excellent leader stays *more* visible and involved, *more* accessible and available to followers during these times. Similar to a sporting event where a team finds inspiration from cheerleaders when it falls behind and is losing the game, the excellent leader knows the importance of being present when there is significant unrest.

Being able to count on the presence of the leader is important to followers, although some leaders feel uncomfortable if they do not have answers to complex or difficult questions raised by followers. Many of today's leaders are managers, or were managers in the past, who have been socialized to believe that the manager's job is to have answers. A good leader understands and accepts, however, that it is impossible to have all of the answers. It takes phenomenal courage to stay "present" with others when they are looking to the leader for answers that the leader does not have. Yet followers respect leaders who are not afraid to admit they do not have the answers. They are encouraged when a leader communicates belief that the answers will be found by working together. This presence during trying times is a tremendous gift the leader gives to others.

*Support:* Constancy of support offered by the leader is a vital issue affecting the quality of the leader-follower relationship. *Support* means to nurture or to provide sustenance, a two-way street within the context, going from followers to leaders and from leaders to followers. Consistency of support is critical; without it trust wavers. If support is offered only when everything is going smoothly and then withdrawn during vulnerable times, it is of virtually no value because it cannot be counted on. The net result in the relationship is one of uneasiness, of being uncertain whether this time the support will be there or not. It is ironic that support is most needed during the times when it is most frequently withdrawn—when mistakes occur and when poor decisions or errors in judgment are made. In a healthy relationship, support is consistent, offered freely, and visible to the receiver.

A leader's response to mistakes or errors is often the clue followers have as to the consistency of support that is extended. If punitive consequences are the norm, people do not feel supported. Punitive consequences to mistakes can occur in the form of shaming, blaming, humiliation, or reduction of future opportunities. Simply stepping in and taking over, relieving the follower of responsibility for correcting the consequences that resulted, can be seen as a lack of support. Interestingly, if the leader is observed engaging in negative, punitive behavior with any follower, it is enough to damage trust with followers not even directly involved. This is not to imply that appropriate consequences would not be taken for a person making the same mistakes repeatedly.

*Behavior:*  Constancy may also refer to stability of personal characteristics. The leader who experiences extreme fluctuations in mood, who is quick to anger, or who responds with knee-jerk reactions may have more trust problems with followers. Take the leader who is excessively positive about ideas, unrealistically optimistic about the chances for success of a project, and effusive with praise on one day—but the next day is exactly the opposite. Followers are left with an uncomfortable feeling of uncertainty, and trust is impaired. It is next to impossible for a leader to be completely balanced and thoroughly predictable. However, the degree to which the leader avoids these surprises for followers enhances trust in the relationship. Consistency of behavior is important.

**Repairing Broken Trust**    The three key ingredients of competence, congruence, and constancy must all be present for a healthy relationship. If mistrust is present, examining these three areas can help to sort out the probable causes. When mistrust is apparent in potential followers, one possible approach to the solution is to ask: "What has happened to damage trust?" Leaders with the courage to ask this question are often rewarded with insight. Unless the question is asked sincerely, however, followers may be reluctant to discuss situations in which they believe they were let down by a leader. Bennis (1989) points out that good leaders encourage respectful dissent so that they can know the truth about a situation, even if it is not what the leader would like to hear. In fact, good leaders need people around who have contrary views and serve as devil's advocates.

Rogers (1994) identifies three steps to repairing broken trust:

1.  Acknowledgment
2.  Apology
3.  Making amends

*Acknowledgment:*  The first step, acknowledging broken trust, is tough for many leaders. Few leaders purposefully set out to destroy trust, and it is difficult to admit that something has happened to damage it in this relationship. In fact, some leaders prefer to call it something else, anything else, rather than accept it as a lack of trust. Some people believe acknowledging a lack of trust implies a personal fault of some kind, and this belief makes it especially onerous to honestly examine these situations.

Susan is a senior vice president in a community hospital in Texas. In her organization the hierarchy is very rigid, and rules and policies are plentiful. One expectation is that all employees, including managers and executives, use a time card. For years employees were required to have their time cards signed by the individual to whom they reported, but this wasn't practiced for managers and executives. Problems developed with one manager, including questionable entries and not accurately recording sick or absent time. As a result, Susan began to require that all managers and executives have their time cards signed. The reaction was predictable—people felt they were no longer trusted. Susan was adamant that her requirement for the double check on the time cards was "just policy," but her assurances did nothing to assuage their feelings. When pushed she finally admitted it was because there were "performance problems" with one individual. Even when confronted directly, she continued to deny that there were any trust issues. It was clearly a lack of trust (albeit well deserved) in the one individual who had been found altering and falsifying time cards.

*Apology:* Apologizing for a breach of trust is difficult for many leaders. This does not mean accepting fault for something that is not the leader's responsibility. If it is the leader's responsibility, the apology may sound like this: "I made a mistake and I am sorry" or "I am sorry that this decision has caused these difficulties for you." If the leader is not culpable, the apology may sound different: "I am sorry to hear you feel this way; the decision was right for this situation" or "I am sorry that is what you heard. Let me try explaining this again."

Apologies are very difficult for some people because they believe it diminishes their stature or damages the respect held by the other person. Many managers and executives have been socialized in a hierarchical system where formal leaders just do not admit mistakes to employees, perhaps because they believe it may weaken their authority. The problem with this attitude is that what is most hoped to be avoided is exactly what occurs. People lose respect for individuals who cannot admit they were wrong or made a mistake.

In one community hospital undergoing a major work-redesign initiative, employees showed significant distrust of administration. Five years previously a layoff had occurred, and there were several very visible and devastating mistakes made in the way the process had been handled. While the executives talked about these mistakes behind closed doors, employees talked about them openly. The executives closed ranks and never talked with employees about these mistakes. The pervasive feeling was an antagonistic workforce who did not trust the executives to manage this new challenge because employees did not believe the executives had learned anything from the layoff. How different the environment would have been if there was open dialogue and a sharing of ideas about what had been learned during and since the layoff.

*Making amends:* The last step in repairing broken trust is to make amends. If something can be corrected or behavior not repeated, these are ways of making amends. Sometimes the easiest thing to do is to ask, "How can I make this right? How can I make amends?" In many instances, an apology is enough. However, if there is behavior to be changed and a commitment is made to do so, the leader must follow through on this commitment. It may take longer to reestablish trust than expected. People will be watching closely to determine whether they can believe the leader's promises.

Making amends also implies some reciprocal behavior from the follower. If the leader changes his or her behavior and maintains it, followers at some point need to let go of past wrongs. A leader in one organization found that his early behavior when first appointed to his position resulted in a reputation that still haunts him even though it has been ten years! This lack of trust from followers needs to be addressed, and he should perhaps ask for their trust.

## Mutual Respect

The second essential element in forming a healthy relationship is mutual respect between leader and follower, which means having esteem for or valuing the other person or their skill or characteristics. In a leadership relationship, respect is offered unconditionally to followers. It is not contingent upon superficial attributes such as position, education, or socioeconomic status but recognizes the contributions, both actual and potential, of the individual. Relating to followers as colleagues is a characteristic of a transformational leader (Burns 1978).

In health care, because patients and families are extended unconditional respect regardless of their situation, it is often assumed that this same respect exists among health care workers. All too often, however, respect is offered because of the status or authority inherent in a title. Just as a person leaving a position becomes a nonentity because they no longer have a title, certain employees are not recognized as leaders because they have no formal title. Individuals with particular educational qualifications are believed to be most capable or the only ones with the ability to solve certain problems. These are all examples of respect based on superficial attributes. A leader understands fully that in another situation positions may be reversed, placing the leader in a follower position.

Respect extended to followers is a result of a sincere belief that followers are partners, that they have ideas, abilities, solutions, and a keen interest in the situation. Max DePree says that the excellent leader begins with understanding the diversity and breadth of people's gifts, talents, and skills. "Understanding and accepting diversity enables us to see that each of us is needed. It also enables us to begin to think about being abandoned to the strengths of others, of admitting that we cannot know or do everything" (DePree 1989, 9). Extending respect to others includes seeking input, soliciting opinions and ideas, and then using these in making decisions. It also means providing freedom within the relationship, allowing a give-and-take to occur.

### Communication

The third essential element of healthy relationships is open and honest communication. No leader is effective without the ability to communicate with others. This involves excellent communication skills and a willingness to talk through issues. A leader may be highly skilled but unwilling to take the necessary time to do the time-consuming work of communicating. Because of the scope and importance of this element, chapter 4 is devoted entirely to the skills of communication.

## LEADERSHIP RELATIONSHIPS IN THE FUTURE

Establishing and cultivating a healthy relationship with followers is an initial step in developing the ability to influence others. This can be accomplished by ensuring that the three elements of a healthy relationship—trust, mutual respect, and communication—are in place. Understanding the concepts of collaboration and partnership is also important because these describe the nature of the leader-follower relationship.

Collaboration and partnering are terms similar in meaning. *Collaboration* refers to work, or labor accomplished together, and *partner* is derived from the word *partake*, meaning "to share." The essence of a successful leader's relationship with followers and key stakeholders is a combination of collaboration and partnership. Collaboration has become a buzzword in the last decade, found in many journal articles and workshop titles. But like most buzzwords, it is overused and misused without a true understanding of the concept. A good leader may not need to know the actual definition but certainly needs to live the concept in relation with followers and colleagues.

### Collaboration

*Collaboration* has multiple meanings, but the most useful is that of working together, especially in a joint intellectual effort. In referring to leader-follower collaboration, it means interactions between leader and follower that enable the knowledge and skills of both to synergistically influence the decision being made or the work being accomplished (Manion 1989). Synergy is a biochemical term meaning the whole is greater than the sum of its parts. In the leadership context, it means that when the leader and follower work together, they are likely to generate more and better solutions and alternatives than either would by working alone.

Dictionary definitions rarely bring a concept fully to life. To more completely understand collaboration, the relationship between coordination, cooperation, and sharing mutual work must be examined (Baggs and Schmitt 1988). These three ingredients comprise the whole of collaboration.

***Coordination***   Coordination is the summary of individual ideas. It occurs when two or more people come together and share their points of view and their experiences to ensure a harmonious combination or interaction. One executive team meets regularly on Monday mornings for a short time, sharing plans for the week, discussing major issues, and briefly reviewing their members' calendars. Their intent is to coordinate efforts. Another example is a patient-care conference in a patient-care department that is often held for a similar purpose. The individuals from the different disciplines or shifts come together to compare their assessments of patients and to coordinate their efforts. Coordination is based on sharing information.

***Cooperation***   Cooperation implies planning and working together in an actively helpful manner, more than being passively cooperative or simply accommodating. Cooperation as it relates to collaboration means meeting the other person's needs yet being assertive in meeting one's own needs, while being assertive and *un*cooperative is being competitive.

***Sharing Mutual Work***   Sharing mutual work in collaboration means sharing goals, planning, problem solving, decision making, and responsibility. Contrast this with consultation, where sharing occurs during the planning phase but the individual proceeds alone in implementation.

True collaboration requires all three elements in healthy amounts: coordination, cooperation, and mutual work. Too often, a leader will make a decision and then expect others to coordinate and cooperate in its implementation. The leader may honestly feel like he or she is being collaborative because there is a general feeling of cooperation. However, unless the decision was mutually made, it is not collaboration in the true sense of the word. The very basis of any partnering relationship is collaboration.

## Partnership

Successful relationships of the future will be characterized as partnerships, which are forming at all levels in our society. Communities are forming partnerships with businesses and industries. Former competitors, such as Apple and IBM, are creating business partnerships. In a community in the Midwest, two hospitals of competing systems are considering building together a third facility needed in their area. Strategic partnerships are appearing with more regularity in health care, between health care systems as well as individual organizations (Blouin and Brent 1997). Managerial partnerships are found at the executive and managerial level (Manion, Sieg, and Watson 1998). Tomorrow's leader needs to work in partnership with others. It is the very essence of the leader-follower relationship.

The philosophy and approach of "every man for himself" in organization life is gradually going by the wayside. In the past, managers were often rewarded for the size of their turf. The larger their budget, the more direct reports and greater number of personnel in their departments, the greater the status. Organization environments were competitive and predominantly unhealthy. If one manager's request was to be met, it meant another's would be denied. In today's world, the manager who is a leader understands the importance of forming alliances and partnering with colleagues to accomplish results. The effective leader of tomorrow will be one who is able to form collaborative associations with others to reach the organization's mission. This is much more complex than it first appears because an individual, group, or organization may at one time be a competitor, a partner, a distributor, or a supplier. It takes a high level of maturity to balance these complex relationships.

Although successful leaders will be those who are able and willing to be partners to others, it is not as easy as it may seem, because not everyone is suited to being a partner. Partnering may well be the highest level of interpersonal development. Covey, author of *Seven Habits of Highly Effective People* (1989), identifies stages of development and their ramifications in the professional world. As individuals develop, progression occurs from a state of dependence to a state of independence and then to interdependence. Each of these stages of development represents significant progress. In the stage of dependence, the individual relies on others. In the stage of independence, there is more reliance on the self, when the individual has taken responsibility for behavior and ownership of feelings and accomplishments. At this point the individual is capable of moving to the higher interdependence level of development to work effectively with others and share responsibility and recognition.

**Interdependence**    Covey (1989) points out that only independent people can make the choice to become interdependent. So, highly dependent people have difficulty moving into true interdependence. Independent people may choose not to become interdependent and, in fact, may see it as a weakness to relinquish control to others or share decision making. Gordon Sprenger (1996), the CEO of Allina, sees ego and the need to control as barriers to partnering. Charlotte Dison (1996), vice president and chief nursing officer at Baptist Hospital of Miami, emphasizes the importance of a mixture of independence and interdependence as she partners with three other colleagues to lead four previously separate organizations that are now merged. She, too, emphasizes the importance of giving up individual freedom.

This development continuum, as illustrated in figure 2-1, is significant to understanding the leadership relationship. Both Bennis (1989) and DePree (1989), when discussing leaders, describe seasoned, mature people who have recognized the need for—and have consciously chosen—interdependence with their followers. The excellent leader does not "go it alone" but derives energy and ideas from follower-colleagues. In a healthy leader-follower relationship, there is true synergy—more is achieved together than either could achieve alone. Neither leader nor follower exist in a vacuum but function in a reciprocal relationship.

***Collective Responsibility and Accountability***   In any partnership, the members must retain a sense of personal responsibility and accountability. But a new dimension is added in the leader-follower relationship: the sharing of collective responsibility and accountability. For

**FIGURE 2-1.   The Development Continuum**

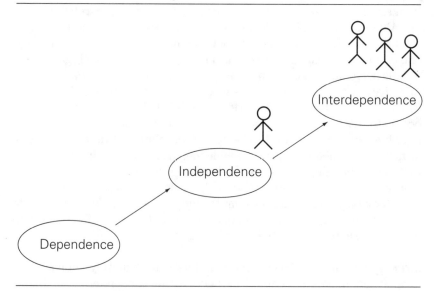

the relationship to thrive and continue to flourish, all elements of a healthy relationship discussed in this chapter must exist on both sides of the partnering agreement. The leader must be trustworthy, as must the followers be. Respect is mutual and communication two-way. Without these things the partnership withers and dies.


## CONCLUSION

The quality of the leader-follower relationship directly correlates to the effectiveness of the leader and ability of all to achieve necessary outcomes. A relationship based on trust and confidence, mutual respect, and honest communication creates a vital association. The nature of the relationship is one of collaboration and partnership—neither of which is easy to attain, but is worth every ounce of effort it takes. Relationships in today's world are "parallel and simultaneous, connected, murky, multiple, and interdependent" (Bennis 1989, 101). Forming healthy relationships is complex, ever changing, and always challenging for the exemplary leader.

# 3

## Building Commitment: Getting Others to Follow

"Compliance is a matter of the mind; commitment engages the heart."

L eadership is more than influencing others to follow a specific direction; it is creating a desire in the followers to do so. With a healthy leader-follower relationship, it is more likely that followers will choose the path indicated by the leader. A healthy relationship, however, is only the beginning. Specific factors that increase the level of commitment felt by followers include sharing the leader's values, appreciating and supporting the leader's purpose, and being able to clearly see a vision of a different future. Peter Senge describes the importance of commitment shared by leaders and followers when he writes about leading learning organizations: "We have seen no examples where significant progress has been made without leadership from local line managers, and many examples where sincerely committed CEOs have failed to generate any significant momentum" (1996, 10). In other words, no leader accomplishes a major change or program initiative alone; it requires a vital partnership with followers, all working in concert to carry out the plan.

## COMPLIANCE

In the past, when formal managers were considered the leadership in the organization and the old command-and-control methodology was still acceptable, compliance seemed fairly easy to attain. Followers were simply told what to do, and they were expected to conform or acquiesce regardless of their own opinions or ideas. Two factors today make mere compliance inadequate. The first is the nature of the workforce. Members of today's health care organizations are older, more mature and experienced, and they feel more involved in their work than ever. Second, the changes occurring are no longer mere tweaks to the system, but are instead fundamental, complex alterations to the very way service is delivered. For this deep level of change to be successful it takes more than mere compliance on the part of those individuals expected to implement these changes. Compliance means conformance. People do what they have been directed or asked to do. There may be very little personal involvement. Commitment is a personal pledge to a position or issue. It is a matter of giving oneself in trust to the issue or solution. Compliance is a matter of the mind; commitment engages the heart.

## COMMITMENT

"Choice is crucial to commitment" (Waterman 1987, 299). The choice is made by followers whether or not to commit to and follow the path indicated. Commitment cannot be forced. This means a leader must face the possibility that followers may choose *not* to follow. "If the most competent and trusted people won't commit, the leader should take another look at the cause itself. It may be ill-conceived or stated in a misleading way" (Waterman 1987, 299).

Superficially, the time invested to obtain compliance appears shorter than the time taken to build commitment. The difference lies in the preparation phase. There is less preparatory work needed if the leader simply tells followers what to do and expects conformance. To gain commitment, there is a long, intense preparatory period that includes collaborative development of the vision and plan, lengthy discussions, open sharing of information, and finally, the internal shift within the follower that indicates a deep level of commitment to the outcome.

The paradox, of course, is that if thorough preparation time is provided and if followers are treated as partners on the journey, the attainment of the desired outcome is actually much faster. In some instances where mere compliance is sought, it is an open-ended process with no closure because there are always some who do not comply. They simply have not "bought into" the concept and do not support it. Unfortunately in many health care organizations today that are undergoing major change, these people may make up the majority of the staff. Sabotage and undermining behaviors are rampant. In other cases, resistant behavior may be covert and not readily apparent. In either case, full compliance and, thus, closure are never attained. (See figure 3-1.) A strong leader understands the difference between compliance and commitment and is seeking to build commitment that supports the desired direction.

## APPROACHES FOR BUILDING COMMITMENT

There are three essential components to building commitment, as shown in figure 3-2:

1. Shared values
2. A mission, or common purpose
3. A clear vision

Shared values, a mission, and a clear vision are three concrete ways a leader builds commitment among followers. The more fully these exist and the degree to which each has meaning for the followers greatly influences the level of commitment. In recent years, at one time or another, each has become a buzzword. These concepts, though simple in meaning, are rarely easy to attain. Implied in each is that the leader first has extraordinary insight into what is personally important in his or her leadership practice and can comfortably and clearly articulate it to others. Then, once understood, it becomes personally relevant to the followers

**FIGURE 3-1.  Compliance versus Commitment in Terms of Time Investment**

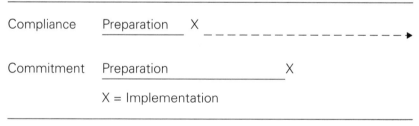

**FIGURE 3-2.  Relationship of Values, Mission, and Vision**

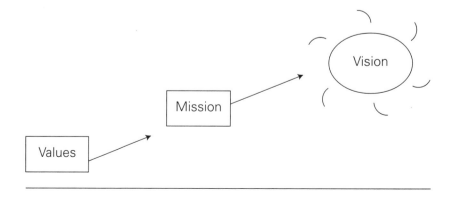

and is deemed important enough that they will commit wholeheartedly to the effort, after which, through the joint efforts of the entire "community," results are attained.

Values, mission, and vision are leadership characteristics rather than skills. Guided classroom activities may help a leader clarify his or her beliefs in each area but cannot develop them if they are not already present. Usually forged by life's experiences and the development of one's personality and spirituality, these elements reveal themselves over time. For optimum leadership effectiveness, these are not only present but are vibrant and vital within the leader's day-to-day practice.

## Shared Values

Essential to developing commitment is the presence of shared values between leaders and followers. Values are pervasive, deep-seated standards that affect all aspects of life. They are beliefs held to be of worth, such as the value of kindness, freedom, or teamwork. There are group and individual values, all of which may exist simultaneously for a person. Societal values are beliefs generally held by most members of a society, such as independence, personal freedom, and choice. Organization values are beliefs held to be important in an establishment, such as service to others, competence, and quality. Family values are beliefs about what's important within the family unit, such as commitment, support, honoring each other, and caring. Personal values are beliefs held by the individual, such as integrity, honesty, challenge, and achievement. In addition to these categories there may also be work values held by an individual, which in the case of a leader become their leadership values. These are the beliefs held for this aspect of their lives. Respect for others, integrity, honesty, and competence are examples of what might be a leader's values.

***Aligned Values***    In an individual who experiences a high level of congruence among the different aspects of his or her life, these values overlap and are in "sync" with one another. High levels of energy and enthusiasm for life are the result. Each arena of life supports and reinforces the others. Personal power and effectiveness are at a peak. Contradiction among values in these different areas creates dissonance resulting in disturbance for an individual. Three choices exist at this point. The individual takes steps to reduce the dissonance or to suppress the uncomfortable and possibly painful feelings. A person of integrity will take steps to change that aspect of life in which there are unacceptable contradictions in values.

***Prioritizing Values***    Life is about choices. An individual with integrity is continually aware of the values that serve as a foundation for their life and recognizes the choices that must be made. Choices, however, are not always seen or experienced with great clarity. In any of the arenas of society, organization, family, or work, stated values may not correspond to the values truly held. It is easy to let rhetoric drown out the truth. A society may say and believe it values personal independence but then institutes a welfare system that encourages dependence. A health care organization may have stated values of service and community when in truth the primary focus of the organization is on the bottom line, profits, and reputation. One organization's slogan of "Patients first" became a source of great dissonance and dissatisfaction for employees as they observed decision after decision based on "Physicians first." The credibility gap grew wider with each new decision and subsequent assurance of "Patients first." It takes courage to examine one's feelings of discomfort, for it may be only intuition that is saying something is wrong. An individual with much invested in the current system may find it difficult to admit that their values are not in alignment.

A person of integrity acts in accordance with his or her beliefs. If the values of the organization or group do not match, the individual first assesses the situation to determine whether it can be changed. Action follows, based on a belief and hope that the situation can be influenced. Perhaps leaders in the organization haven't recognized the incongruent messages their decisions are sending. Honest feedback and open dialogue about a perceived mismatch between a stated value and observed behavior need to occur. If nothing changes, the individual's choice becomes clear: Stay or leave.

In some instances, an individual's assessment of the situation results in a decision to stay so that another highly held personal value may be met. Security and family may be highly held values that result in an individual choosing to remain in an organization even though other values are not congruent. It is hoped that this is a temporary situation; and it is healthier if the individual is able to see clearly the choice that has been made. Too many times, an individual remains in a dissonant situation and suppresses their feelings of rebellion against the differing values. Over the long term they may even lose sight of or change their values, telling themselves these values are not worth leaving for.

Courage to choose a different path can be as difficult when the conflict is between beneficial values. Which is most important? Which choice will be most true to the beliefs held dear by the individual? Jane, a leader in a health care agency, discovered the difficulty inherent in choosing between two seemingly good values. She strongly valued security and stability and had spent most of her professional career in positions that ensured these values were met. Fortunately, these positions also provided her opportunities to meet other values she held dear— challenge and achievement. In fact, these differing values were very compatible for most of her years in health care. With every challenge she met, the more she achieved, the higher rewards and greater financial security and sense of stability she attained. As a vice president at the corporate level in a home health agency, she most enjoyed the new projects and service development aspect of her work.

A new chief executive officer was appointed, and within six months she became aware that the philosophy of the company had changed significantly. Her position became responsible for monitoring and ensuring regulatory compliance and advocating with state legislators. Although Jane was highly skilled in these areas, the challenge and sense of achievement she previously enjoyed no longer existed for her in this role. She tried to negotiate a role change so she would be challenged and excited about work again but was unsuccessful. Instead, to make matters more difficult, her salary was increased significantly by the new CEO, and her sense of security was stronger than ever. Her choice was difficult: Would she stay and be true to her value of security and stability, or would she seek another position full of challenge and the opportunity to grow again? After much soul-searching, she resigned and became an entrepreneur, starting her own business, which over the years became more successful than she dreamed possible. Challenge and achievement were more important than security and stability.

Jane's story illustrates the importance of our values. They guide daily decision making and give a sense of direction in day-to-day existence. Holding the values of security and achievement simultaneously can lead to a crisis point in a career when situations force an individual to make a choice between remaining in a seemingly secure, well-paying job and seeking a new job with greater challenge. When actions are in accordance with held values, events flow more smoothly.

***The Result of Shared Values***     When values are shared among people, the result is a tremendous feeling of connection and synergy. This, of course, first requires that leaders and followers can clearly define their values. They know what beliefs are most important in their lives. However, if these are never discussed, a false assumption may be made— either that values are in agreement or that they differ. Open dialogue about their beliefs benefits both leaders and followers, because when values are shared, people feel united.

The ramifications for a leader who is trying to build commitment to a certain idea are clear. The leader must be absolutely clear about his or her values and how this decision supports these values. If there is incongruity, the leader experiences feelings of dissonance reflected in subtle ways to followers. When the path chosen is consistent with the leader's values and these values are shared by followers, commitment blossoms. Ability to articulate and communicate clearly is critical for this process to succeed. Not only are the technical skills of communication important, the leader also needs the courage to speak from the heart and share his or her deeply held beliefs regardless of the feelings of vulnerability this creates.

## Mission

"The first responsibility of the leader is to define reality" (DePree 1989, 11). In an organizational context, leaders have the task and responsibility of determining both the purpose and the future of their organizations. Beckhard and Pritchard (1992) note that the white-knuckle turbulence of this decade is forcing most leaders to reexamine the very essence of the organization along with its basic purpose; its identity; and its relationships with customers (internal and external), competitors, and all other key stakeholders. In addition to defining the organization's mission, leaders also need a clear sense of their own mission or purpose.

Strong leaders have a clear sense of mission; they know why they are here and are clear about their purpose. Mission is a reason for existence—of the individual, the project, the team, or the organization. A clear mission defines the purpose and gives direction and focus. It enables an individual to decline opportunities that detract from this true purpose. "It's easy to say 'no' when there is a deeper 'yes' burning inside" (Covey, Merrill, and Merrill 1994, 103).

Over time, a person's mission in life is revealed. A person grows into a leadership role by fully experiencing life and learning from its many lessons through extensive reading, talking with and listening to others, travel, trial and error, and observation. People in leadership roles are continual learners, always seeking the lesson in a situation, even when it is difficult or painful. Reflection is a powerful tool the individual can use to better understand motivation behind actions and behaviors, reactions to situations, and what is really important.

*Leadership Mission Statement*    Every leader needs a personal mission statement. An individual's personal mission statement may or may not include a leadership mission statement. For some people these are two different but compatible statements. A leader needs to distinguish between his or her purpose as an individual and as a leader. These written statements cannot be completed in a one- or two-hour period of time. Instead it takes "deep introspection, careful analysis, thoughtful expression, and often many rewrites to produce it in final form" (Covey 1989,129). It means sorting through a great deal of extraneous material to reach the core reason for one's existence and how that purpose is to be achieved. The leadership mission statement usually includes the leader's values, often the means by which the mission is achieved.

A strong sense of connection between leaders and followers results from leaders being open and sharing their personal or leadership mission statements. Vulnerability and embarrassment may be initial feelings because this is a very personal statement. If the leaders are sincere and humble, rather than arrogant and egotistical, this is a powerful way of disclosing more of themselves to the followers. Even if a supporter does not totally agree with or value a leader's personal mission statement, understanding between the two still increases.

An individual without a sense of purpose is like a rudderless ship— buffeted about by every strong wind that happens along. People without purpose do not make good leaders. It is difficult, if not impossible, to lead if the individual has no inner sense of direction or understanding of purpose. And in tumultuous, rapidly changing times such as the present, it is not enough to simply adopt someone else's purpose because it's politically correct or expeditious to do so. There must be a strong inner sense of knowing and a connection to this identified purpose or it does not serve during stressful times.

*Aligning Missions*    This clarity of personal purpose enables leaders to determine whether or not there is a match with their organization. If the purpose or mission of the organization is diametrically opposed to a leader's purpose, he or she may feel it is not possible to carry out his or her mission. If encouraging and nurturing followers to function independently and interdependently is part of a leader's mission statement but the leader is in a bureaucratic, heavily hierarchical organization within which there is no intention of empowering employees, it would be difficult for this leader to feel successful.

Virtually any current exemplary health care leader today demonstrates an abiding sense of personal purpose. Many see themselves as stewards for health care in their communities. This is described by Chawla and Renesch (1995) as a willingness for leaders and managers within health care organizations to be accountable for the well-being of the larger community by operating in service to colleagues, patients, families, and other stakeholders. This enduring sense of operating for the benefit of others and for something bigger than any individual helps create committed partnerships with followers. As described by Robert Greenleaf in the collection of his private writings, *On Becoming a Servant-Leader:*

> The servant-leader is servant first. . . . It begins with the natural feeling that one wants to serve, to serve first. Then conscious choice brings one to aspire to lead. . . . The difference manifests itself in the care taken by the servant—first to make sure that other people's highest-priority needs are being served. The best test, and the most difficult to administer, is: Do those served grow

as persons? Do they, while being served, become healthier, wiser, freer, more autonomous, more likely themselves to become servants? And, what is the effect on the least privileged in society; will they benefit or, at least, not be further deprived? (Frick and Spears 1996, 2)

## Vision

The third way to build commitment among followers is through development of a shared vision. In recent years, "vision" has become a byword in management and leadership circles. Everywhere, managers and leaders are exhorted to "have a vision." Example after example of governments, organizations, and people for whom vision made a difference are shared. And all are impressive. Joel Barker in *The Power of Vision* (1990) raises the question: Does vision come first or does the success of an individual, organization, or government lead to a vision? In each instance he examined, the vision came first, leading him to conclude "vision has the power to change our lives."

All leaders understand vision because of its presence in their lives. It may not be an easily explainable concept, but leaders relate to this idea because they have experienced it. They see the future differently than other people do; leaders see what is possible and dream while others merely predict. The leader's vision of the future is not necessarily accurate, but it is almost always desirable. It is positive. There are three crucial steps followed by leaders who inspire others with a future vision:

1. Define and describe the vision
2. Engage dialogue about the vision
3. Create a structure for the vision

The first involves describing the vision, the second is talking about the vision with others who must help create the new future, and the final step is putting a structure in place to ensure realization of the vision.

**Step 1: Define and Describe the Vision**    A future vision is a picture the leader has of the horizon. The power of vision is in its expectancy—it is a picture of a preferred future rather than a forecast of a predicted future. Alan Kay said: "The best way to predict the future is to invent it." Rather than what might be anticipated, it is a desirable future to be sought. It is an illuminated look into tomorrow based on what the leader believes is possible. Vision takes imagination and optimism. "It is the ability to see beyond our present reality, to create, to invent what does not yet exist, to become what we are not yet. It gives us capacity to live out of our imagination instead of our memory" (Covey 1994, 103).

Some leaders seek or rise to a leadership position because they have a vision of what the future could be, and this vision drives and inspires them to lead. Armed with the vision, it becomes a simple matter to put structures in place to achieve the desired future. Sometimes the position comes first, whether it is a formal leadership position in an organization, appointment to chair a committee or task force, or election to an office. The individual discovers that he or she has the responsibility and obligation to take the lead in a situation. Perhaps there is a clear mission but only a general vision of the outcomes.

The first step is to develop the vision, but this may be more difficult than it sounds. Like the process of creativity, it is valuable to exploit a deliberate intuitive process. The intuitive process starts with preparation by coming to understand as much as possible through reading anything and everything related to the situation, talking with people, and drawing on past experiences. The second step is to let all information and ideas incubate until a spark occurs, leading to illumination, the third step. As the vision becomes clear it is important to create as much detail as possible. Concrete, specific descriptions of a preferred future help others see the vision as well. John F. Kennedy, when speaking of America's space program in his State of the Union address, did not say: "We will be the world leaders in space exploration." Instead, he said that before the end of the decade, America would have a man on the moon and return him safely to Earth. It was explicit and definite.

To be inspiring, the preferred future must be a stretch, a far reach from the present. Martin Luther King Jr. said, "I have a dream that one day this nation will rise up and live out the true meaning of this creed— we hold these truths to be self-evident: that all men are created equal" (Anderson 1990, 11). At the time, in segregated America, this was a tremendous stretch from the reality. Peter Senge (1990) says that once a vision is identified, the greater the distance it is from the current reality, the more creative tension that exists. Creative tension is the pull between the vision and the present. This tension acts like a giant rubber band, pulling toward a new future. During the growth toward a new future, if it seems unlikely that the new future is possible, it is just too distant; Senge says it is better to extend time frames than to compromise the vision. Settling for less is the first step toward mediocrity.

***Step 2: Engage in Dialogue about the Vision***    A leader alone cannot achieve the vision. New realities are created when everyone impacted by the vision works together. In a successful organization or association, in the same way that multiple leaders are encouraged, so are multiple visions sought. These visions are more influential if they are consistent, forming a "cascade" of visions in the organization, as illustrated in figure 3-3. Everyone has their own vision of the future, and a shared vision is created when people dialogue about the vision. The different visions are discussed, explored, and modified based on learning from each other. A shared vision occurs when two or more people have a similar picture for the future and are each committed to having the vision.

Senge writes, "Today, 'vision' is a familiar concept in corporate leadership. But when you look carefully you find that most 'visions' are one person's (or group's) vision imposed on an organization. Such visions, at best, command compliance—not commitment. A shared vision is a vision that many people are truly committed to, because it reflects their own personal vision." When the shared vision reflects these personal visions, there is a deep sense of caring about reaching the future. Senge describes this shared vision:

> A shared vision is not an idea. It is not even an important idea such as freedom. It is, rather, a force in people's hearts, a force of impressive power. It may be inspired by an idea, but once it goes further—if it is compelling enough to acquire the support of more than one person—then it is no longer an abstraction. It is palpable. People begin to see it as if it exists. Few, if any, forces in human affairs are as powerful as shared vision. (Senge 1990, 206)

Shared visions do not happen unless there is plenty of dialogue about the future. There needs to be open give-and-take, honest questioning, and stimulating conversations about the vision. Abraham Lincoln is a wonderful example of a leader who understood and applied this concept. "Throughout the war Lincoln continued to visit his generals and

**FIGURE 3-3.  A Cascade of Visions**

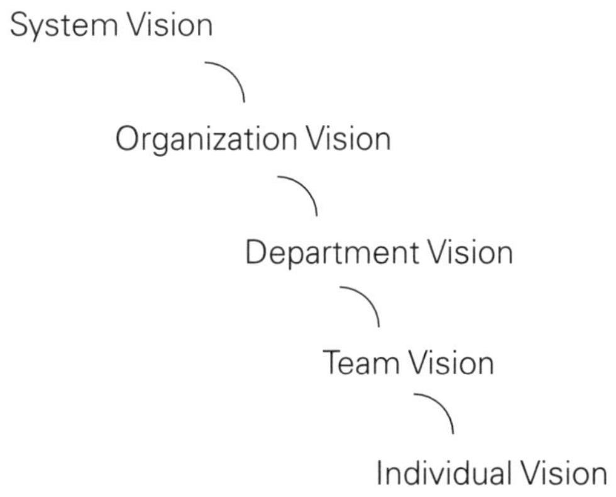

System Vision

Organization Vision

Department Vision

Team Vision

Individual Vision

troops. . . . He always had a kind word for them, frequently telling them his vision of America and how important they were in achieving victory in the cause for which they were fighting" (Phillips 1992, 19).

***Step 3: Create a Structure for the Vision***   Although Martin Luther King Jr. said "I have a dream" and not "I have a plan," it is not enough to have a dream without a structure in place to ensure the new reality is achieved. To quote the Noah principle: "No more prizes for predicting rain; prizes only for building arks!" The ark in this case is the structure that enables attainment of the desired vision. Some people are great dreamers but are unskilled when it comes to implementing those dreams. Leaders need both skills. "Leaders not only have a vision, they work unusually hard to execute it well. Leaders are implementers, not just strategists; doers, not just dreamers" (Berry 1992, 2–3). Structure includes the steps to be taken to create the future. A person can dream of winning the lottery, but if he or she never purchases a ticket, the dream never comes true.

Bennis describes vision as the management of attention, and with this simple statement, he captures the power of vision. With a clearly articulated vision and followers who believe in it, the vision itself focuses the attention of the "vision community." It keeps people focused on the future, hopeful and expectant about its possibilities. "A leader envisions the destination their followers want, they have the superior skill to guide the journey, and they have the belief to drive the group forward in the face of adversity" (Fagiano 1994, 4).

Shared values, a common purpose or mission, and a shared vision together produce the ability to influence others. An individual leader's personal and deeply held values influence the direction or mission chosen. And where there is a strong sense of mission, there exists the possibility of commanding visions powerful enough to forge a new future.

## CASE EXAMPLE 1: CREATING AN INTEGRATED HEALTH CARE SYSTEM—THE POWER OF A COLLECTIVE VISION

Altru Health Systems in Grand Forks, North Dakota, is a fine example of the power of collective vision. In the late 1980s there were seven different independent entities sharing Medical Park, a beautiful campus in central Grand Forks. These entities included an acute-care hospital, a thriving family practice business, a rehabilitation hospital owned and operated by the state, a large primary care/multispeciality, an orthopedic practice, a long-term care facility, and a chemical dependency recovery center. Even in the earliest days, key community leaders foresaw the need to physically locate all community health services on a jointly shared campus.

The original vision for integration was developed through hospital board retreats held in 1989. The retreats included administrative and medical staff leadership as well as the community board members. Armed with this vision, discussions with staff and key stakeholders began. Dialogue revolved around the current reality, future vision, and open discussion about barriers to the achievement of this vision. Initial reactions from regional stakeholders to the possibility of integration of the hospital and clinic were skeptical. These organizations did not want to be acquired; their autonomy was important to them. Although they agreed they needed to plan together and cooperate, full integration was not seen as a desirable option. Many expressed the fear that United Hospital and the Grand Forks Clinic would buy up and close the smaller organizations in an attempt to reduce competition. Both United Hospital and the Grand Forks Clinic assured them that they would not go into their community without an invitation.

From these discussions, the involved leaders developed a strong belief that integration of the facilities in Medical Park would be a necessary first step. If integration could not be successful there, it could not be attained in the region. This helped formulate strategies to reach the vision. Based on these dialogues, formal, concrete strategies for achieving the vision were established in early 1990, with final attainment of the vision projected to be in the year 2000. United Hospital's board of directors held their chief executive officer, Rosemary Jacobson, accountable by requiring from her a thrice-annual review of progress against these strategies.

A persistent win-win approach helped overcome resistance and created increasing buy-in to the vision of a fully integrated health care system for the community. Over the years, barriers were overcome and strategies were successful. Agreement was reached regarding the need to have common governance, a common bottom line, and integrated operations. By 1995 the family medicine and orthopedic practices had been integrated with the Grand Forks Clinic, and the chemical dependency recovery center and rehabilitation hospital were integrated into United Hospital. Final steps were being taken to integrate Grand Forks Clinic with United Health Services. Other entities were asked to join, and Pathology Associates joined in 1996.

The last step to integrating the clinic and hospital was the most difficult to implement. Board and executive leaderships of both organizations were fully committed to the vision, but many physicians at the clinic were skeptical or opposed to the initiative. Both organizations were financially successful, so there were no strong fiscal incentives to pursue integration. Both were concerned about the profound effects of having combined cultures. The boards of directors in each organization were fully committed to their internal staff and were committed to few or no layoffs. There was a clear expectation, however, that cross training, modification of roles, and new assignments would occur as operations became integrated. Few individuals were displaced. Work areas and roles were altered, and working relationships were disrupted. The difference in cultures was measured and found not to be as different as anticipated. The two "new" organizations entered the final eighteen months of negotiation in a state of some stress. Without true commitment to this shared vision, the journey would have been impossible.

These months were difficult and, at times, discouraging. Rosemary Jacobson, then president and CEO of United Health Services, believes that the unwavering support, commitment, and stubborn persistence on the part of executive and board leadership at both facilities were the catalysts for surviving those final months. The chairman of the hospital board attended 99 percent of the integration meetings, and his commitment and openness were instrumental in allaying fears of community control of the clinic and physician practices. Even in the face of direct opposition, the leadership of both organizations stayed true to the collective vision they shared. Potential personal losses were also an issue. Both CEOs realized they had to share the commitment to this vision to ensure good access to health care in their region, or their health care system would be damaged. Today co-CEOs bring experience from both the clinic and hospital side of the business.

Noteworthy throughout this process was the absence of external consultants. Outside attorneys were engaged to ensure all legal ramifications were considered, but the process was otherwise fully managed by organizational leadership. Ms. Jacobson noted: "It took more courage and guts than brains!" Retaining control of, responsibility for, and active involvement in the process created a tremendous sense of ownership on the part of leadership in these organizations.

The closing stages were characterized by starts and stops, intense communication, discouragement, stalemates, and periods of withdrawal from the negotiations on the parts of both parties. Finally a growing momentum resulted in attainment of the vision a full three years ahead of the time schedule. United Health Services and Grand Forks Clinic became officially integrated on July 1, 1997. This accomplishment is even more significant when one remembers that this community was devastated by a cripplingly destructive spring flood, following one of the most difficult winters in the city's history. Even as the community was struggling to cope with its overwhelming losses and restore adequate living conditions, its health care leaders were looking to the future. The power of a shared vision had transformed health care in this region.

Ms. Jacobson credits the successful attainment of this vision to repeated and continual dialogue and communication about the vision, listening and responding to reactions, perseverance in spite of naysayers, and a level of commitment among key leaders to a mission that extended well beyond their own personal interests. The formulation of a shared vision provided the impetus and direction to develop strategies that helped achieve the vision. Ms. Jacobson said of the vision: "It enabled us to make progress, where otherwise we wouldn't have." The leaders of this change were trustworthy individuals serving as stewards for their community. Each leader was absolutely committed to a shared vision of full access to the highest quality of health care services for the community and region they serve. Multiple champions working in concert were essential to the success.

And the work is not yet finished. Although the structural components for the system are in place, internal staff have yet to complete their full transition to this massive change. There remain many issues to work out, relationships to develop and solidify, and day-to-day working arrangements to be established. This system continues to work with other entities that did not join. And, work has begun with regional providers, at their initiation, to develop more formalized networks. This young system now has a new vision: to become a premier health care system in this country.

## CASE EXAMPLE 2: IMPROVING THE DELIVERY OF CARE—A DEPARTMENT LEADER'S VISION

The scope of this case example is more limited than the development of an integrated health care system but no less significant in terms of its impact on the people being served. It involved Joan, a director of maternal-child nursing in a 500-bed community hospital in a western state. Her areas of responsibility included six patient care departments, labor and delivery, postpartum, newborn nursery, neonatal intensive care, and two pediatric units. When Joan was recruited to this organization, these departments were managed in a traditional fashion and were gradually declining in market share because their maternity services were basically unresponsive to the requests of customers.

Joan had been in her position for three years and was well respected throughout the organization for her innovative leadership style. During those three years she had established good relationships with staff in the various departments and had gradually hired new managers who more closely shared her values of participatory leadership and family-centered maternity care. In spite of a traditional medical staff and administration who preferred to maintain the status quo, always in the back of Joan's mind was a vision of a maternity unit where care was organized around the family unit instead of segregated into four different departments.

As Joan and her new managers began implementing innovative programs and services, the hospital's market share for obstetrics began slowly regaining ground. After three years the service was bursting at the seams, and more postpartum beds and bassinet space were required. The closest patient care area available was a rehabilitation unit in the next wing of the hospital. An expansion was planned for an additional ten postpartum beds and a small nursery for newborns to be added to the maternity unit. However, this new unit was so small that staffing would be a significant problem unless staff members were cross trained to care for either mother or baby. Suddenly Joan's long-held vision for a mother-and-baby unit was possible. Commitment to this vision began with frequent discussions with all stakeholders involved. Staff, managers, and physicians were all involved in planning discussions. Major educational sessions were offered to introduce the concept to key stakeholders.

In several instances, commitment was difficult to gain because people involved held values that differed from Joan's belief in maintaining integrity of the family unit. Additionally, this change represented a major impact on postpartum and newborn nursery staff, many of whom believed they could not handle the change. A planning committee of employees and physicians worked out details for the expansion unit. Staff members volunteered and were then selected and trained. The implementation process proceeded smoothly, and within months the unit had a waiting list of expectant parents. Demand for this service was so intense that the original postpartum unit was converted to mother-and-baby care two years later.

This example may not seem remarkable except that it took place in the early 1980s, long before mother-and-baby care was the norm for maternity services. In fact, this was the first such conversion in a several state region and is today continuing to provide truly family-centered care for those it serves. It started with one individual's vision but became possible only when the vision was shared by those within the vision community. Together they created a powerful new reality that improved health care in the area.

## CASE EXAMPLE 3: VISION FAILED

Successful vision attainment creates tremendous feelings of pride and accomplishment for those individuals involved. There is optimism for the future, and people see the direction they are headed. In this final example, however, outcomes were not positive. Judgment errors were made, and results actually damaged the viability of the organization.

This is the story of a large community hospital in the early 1990s. The CEO had been reading about vision and believed a clear vision was needed within his organization. Two interested and capable individuals were assigned as consultants to develop a vision statement. They interviewed the CEO and one or two other key executives to gather ideas and concepts, then worked hard to develop a positive and stretched vision from these ideas. The first draft of the vision statement was beautifully worded and certainly far-reaching, and it seemed to be the direction the organization was already heading. The two internal consultants met with the executive leadership group to share this vision and engage in dialogue about it. This step was only moderately successful because the discussion was somewhat stilted and limited. However, strategies for sharing the vision with staff were identified, with the next step to include holding focus group discussions.

Based on input from these focus groups, there were minor changes made in the vision. But most important was the concern raised by managers and staff alike, relating skepticism and doubt about executive commitment to this vision. This response and concern fell on deaf ears. Advice from the two consultants was disregarded. The final draft was duly prepared and presented to a department managers' meeting, with beautiful overheads and fine rhetoric. Empowered employees and conversion to a team-based organization formed the foundation of the vision. These terms were concretely presented with many fine examples.

Four years later, the organization has undergone repeated crises, internal conflicts, and the stressful effects of a rapidly changing external environment. Where other organizations had been guided through turbulent times by their vision of a new future, this organization emerged weaker and more disorganized than it was before the development of their vision. What was the problem? At least three factors prevented the attainment of their vision. The first was a mistakenly held but strong belief on the part of the CEO that there should be only one vision for the organization. Over the years he and members of his executive group had discouraged the development of multiple visions by individuals and teams, preferring that the only vision used was the organization's vision statement. The end result was a preponderance of individuals and teams who saw the organization's vision statement as just more administrative rhetoric.

A second factor was the unwillingness of executives to consistently model their behavior on the very behavior they expected from employees. Highly visible examples of the old command-and-control approach to management continued to occur; and the executives never got around to developing themselves as a team. The final nail in the coffin was the lack of commitment from internal managers to the vision. Most of the communication about the vision came from the internal consultants rather than the CEO. Even though the vision *sounded* great, the managers were cynical about the possibility of ever attaining it. Over time, those employees who were initially committed to the vision felt betrayed, which caused cynicism that became quite virulent among them about this "bogus" vision statement.

## CONCLUSION

Compliance from followers is not enough during these difficult and demanding times. Exemplary leaders build among followers commitments to a certain course of action. Shared values, a mission common and relevant to all, and a shared vision are three specific ways in which a leader can build commitment among followers who do not just comply with directions set by those leaders but *want* to follow the path. Together these things inspire passion and provide the energy and courage to create a new reality. As Mark Victor Hansen says, "Some things have to be believed to be seen." And, they will not be achieved unless first believed.

# 4

## Communicating with Clarity

"The greatest problem of communication is the illusion that it has been accomplished."

—*George Bernard Shaw*

Closely linked to the other interpersonal competencies of leadership, the ability to communicate clearly is essential to excelling as a leader. Efforts to establish a leadership relationship, build commitment, manage processes, and develop others are futile without superior communication skills. It may sound easy, and some people believe that simply being articulate is enough, yet there is far more than that to proficient communication. Good leaders cultivate openness in their communication; they believe followers desire and deserve information pertaining to their work.

This chapter tackles the issue of sharing information openly and explores several communication techniques for leadership effectiveness. Common barriers to effective communication are reviewed and ideas for overcoming them offered. Special issues in leadership communication are also presented. Many people overestimate the ease of meeting this competency since it appears to be simple—and almost everyone has attended some kind of communication course or seminar. Yet the most common complaints from followers concern communication. "We don't get enough information" and "Nobody is telling us anything" and "Communication here is rotten" are just a few of the complaints heard.

Perpetuating the problem are those individuals who overestimate their effectiveness at communicating. They believe that if they open their mouths and words flow out or they have sent a memo or made an announcement, communication has occurred. This leads to a false sense of security and sometimes an attitude of arrogance. "I've communicated; if they didn't get it, that's their problem." Perhaps nothing can destroy the leader's effectiveness as quickly as a lack of information and miscommunication. Distrust rapidly grows and the leader's credibility shrinks.

## DEFINING COMMUNICATION

Communication is the act of interchanging or imparting thoughts, opinions, ideas, or information by speech, writing, or other signs. It has been
described as the flow of information from a sender to a receiver via a
*channel.* (See figure 4-1.) The channel might be the written or spoken
word, or nonverbal channels, such as body language or the environment. When the receiver gets the message and experiences the same
meaning as is understood by the sender, it is said that communication is
complete. The sender may either perceive a change in the receiver's
behavior or actually be told that the message has been received, and this
feedback closes the communication loop.

## COMMON PROBLEMS

As simplistic as this model seems, there are multiple problematic areas
in the communication loop model. A skilled communicator understands
these potential problems and takes steps to avert them when possible.

### Noise

Noise anywhere in the system can reduce the likelihood of accurate
message transfer. Noise is more than loud or distracting sounds that
impair the ability to hear. It can be anything that reduces the ability to
receive the message accurately, including the state of the receiver's
body (the presence of tension, anxiety, or any intense emotion), elements that cloud the message (jargon, words with multiple meanings,
assumptions, and biases), and attitudes of the receiver toward the mes-

**FIGURE 4-1.   The Communication Loop Model**

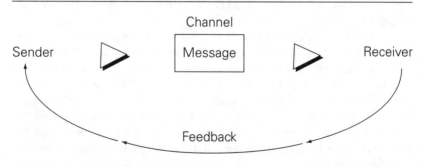

sage (perhaps the message is something the receiver does not want to hear or it has been prejudged).

## Choice of Channel

Another potential problem area is the choice of channel. Announcing major organization changes by memo rather than face-to-face communication may send the wrong message. Changing channels unexpectedly can impact clarity of the message. If the usual channel between sender and receiver is the face-to-face spoken word, switching to a formal written memo can add emphasis. If the message is negative, its tone may be so accentuated by the change in channel that it raises exaggerated emotions in the receiver, making it difficult to correctly interpret that message.

John, the leader-manager of environmental services, and Mary, the leader-manager of a patient care department, found themselves in this kind of situation. John and Mary communicated frequently, mostly talking face-to-face, on issues and problems related to the environmental services function in the patient care area. In the previous year, environmental service workers were deployed to the patient care department reporting directly to Mary. John, frustrated after a particularly bad day, sent Mary a written memo outlining unresolved problems. Because he was irritated, he sent a copy to Mary's supervisor.

Mary felt blasted by the memo, as well as betrayed because it was also sent to her supervisor. The memo actually contained nothing that they hadn't talked about before, but the channel selection accentuated the message dramatically and almost destroyed Mary's willingness to cooperate with John. Even though most leaders are aware of these basic principles, it is still easy to get caught up in a situation and make a poor judgment. Leaders need patience to persevere in the face of these challenges.

## Responsibility

Another potential problem is the issue of responsibility. Although the receiver has some responsibility to respond to the message received, the sender retains full responsibility for the message until the feedback loop is closed. If the sender gets feedback that the message was not received clearly, it is the sender's responsibility to resend the message, perhaps modifying it in a way that increases the likelihood of understanding. If no feedback is forthcoming, the sender seeks a response that is appropriate to the situation. "What did you understand me to say?" "Have you acted on the information in the memo?" "What action have you taken?" Communication is a covenant between sender and receiver and a responsibility that often is only partially accepted.

## Feedback

On concrete, tangible issues, feedback may result from observing the receiver's reaction or behavior following the message's receipt. Perhaps the worst mistake made by the sender, however, is to simply assume that because the message was sent, the responsibility has shifted to the receiver. As a result, the sender does not follow up, makes the assumption that all is well, and then blames the receiver when events do not go as intended.

This problematic attitude can be seen on a regular basis: a written memo or E-mail message is distributed, but only half the people who were supposed to receive it do; the education department notifies potential participants of an upcoming program for which they need to register, but the memo doesn't make it to all intended recipients. Those who do not receive the message may be labeled as resistant or negative because they do not take the required action, or as complaining if they point out that they were left out of the loop. E-mail has contributed to this problem because there is no paper trail. Messages are quickly tapped out and instantly distributed with a single key stroke to multiple recipients. But the old adage "Out of sight, out of mind" holds true. It is difficult to remember to follow up on something if there are no reminders!

If the relationship with receivers is not built on trust, the feedback given the sender may not be entirely honest. The receiver may be embarrassed to admit that the memo, proposal, or vision statement was so filled with buzzwords, jargon, "ten-letter words," highly technical language, or just plain gobbledygook that they really did not understand what it said. It may also be difficult to admit that one did not hear the message the first time because of distractions in the environment. Or perhaps the sender responded in an angry and defensive fashion when negative feedback was given on a previous occasion, and the receiver is not willing to endure such a response again. Trust in the sender is essential for accurate feedback to occur.

When feedback is negative, a common assumption is that there is an attitude problem on the part of the receiver. The conclusion may be that the person receiving the message purposely did not take the intended action and is being obstructive, resistive, or just plain stupid. Instead, to avoid this pitfall, the first question the sender might ask is whether there were technical or semantic problems with the communication. These must be considered first before assuming the receiver has an attitude problem.

*Case Example 1: Miscommunication*    A parenting example makes the distinctions between the different problems of communication clearer. A family expects overnight company during the weekend, and on Wednesday, 16-year-old Sarah is asked to clean her room so the visitors can sleep in it. Friday arrives and Sarah's room isn't cleaned. A typical parental reaction is the assumption that Sarah just didn't get around to it, didn't follow through, or was perhaps being rebellious in reaction to giving up her room or being told what to do (an attitude problem).

If Mom looks back, however, to see how she carried out her responsibility as "sender," she might find other reasons for the miscommunication. For instance, she may remember that when she told Sarah to clean her room, it was just as Sarah was on the way out the door. Also, Sarah had stayed up late studying for a test she was very worried about, and she had overslept and was late leaving for school (internal anxiety—noise in the system). And, as any parent knows, "Clean your room" may mean one thing to a 16-year-old and something entirely different to a parent (semantic differences). To Sarah it meant getting everything out of sight: stuffed under the bed, or in the drawers or closet. To her mom, it meant having a drawer emptied and closet space available, as well as the assurance that the guests wouldn't be disturbed by odors and clutter emanating from under the bed.

*Case Example 2: Mixed Messages*    Similar examples exist in the work world. A 300-bed hospital in the St. Louis area was in severe financial straits. Part of a larger system, the hospital was given six months to reverse these financial problems or the facility would be sold. The director of education purchased modular education that was to be delivered by the managers and supervisors to employees in the belief that this education would assist in the extensive restructuring effort underway. An outside trainer arrived to present the modules for the internal facilitators beginning on a Monday afternoon.

On Monday morning these same internal facilitators (managers and supervisors) were all gathered together to receive the message from the CEO regarding the corporate decision about a likely closure or sale, a planned layoff, and the reduction of management and supervisory positions by half. In the afternoon these same people were expected to attend a learning and development session! Even though these people rallied and concentrated on how they could use the educational modules, the effectiveness of any communication that afternoon was greatly reduced by the presence of strong emotions (a technical problem) following the morning session. If these managers and supervisors were later labeled as resistant or nonsupportive because they had not used the modules, this example would closely parallel the parenting example just given.

*Case Example 3: Inappropriate Settings*    A management development specialist told the story of feedback received from her leader regarding an important project she had been asked to undertake. Their offices were geographically distant from each other, making face-to-face feedback difficult because of inaccessibility. It happened that both the specialist and the leader were attending a seminar together. The specialist decided to use this opportunity to obtain feedback on the project—but the only place and time available was in the women's rest room during a break. As can be imagined, the feedback left a lot to be desired in terms of helpfulness.

How many important conversations take place in the hallway or in the minutes before or after meetings? There never seems to be enough time to communicate thoroughly, and yet hours can be involved in clearing up miscommunication.

## COMMUNICATION AND LEADERSHIP

Warren Bennis and Burt Nanus describe communication as the management of meaning (1985). When Max DePree talks about a leader's role as defining reality, he is referring to the belief that the understanding of the reality is the same and shared by leader and follower. Shared meaning is the very essence of communication. Although complete and totally accurate communication is probably impossible to attain, a more reasonable goal is to accomplish enough clear communication to enable followers to act on ideas or information in a positive and forward-moving manner. The sender of the message retains responsibility until the feedback loop is closed. Following up on feedback, assessing the message for technical, semantic, or attitude difficulties can prevent major miscues.

### Information

Information is one of the most important things transmitted through communication. Information is like a lubricant in the system, and without it the different parts simply do not work well together. In an automobile, if there is not enough oil in the engine, gears grind, friction develops, and overheating can destroy the parts. The same happens in an organization. Margaret Wheatley, in *Leadership and the New Science* (1992), does a beautiful job of exploring the role of information in a system: "If information is not available, people make it up. Rumors proliferate, things get out of hand—all because people lack the real thing. Given the need for constant nourishing information, it is no wonder that 'poor communication' inevitably appears so high on the problems list. Employees know it is the critical vital sign of organizational health" (107).

Part of the problem is that many people regard information as stable, factual, and something that is the same today as it will be tomorrow. Information is instead dynamic and ever changing. Simply sharing it may essentially change the information as it is passed along, much like the childhood game of telephone. "The function of information is revealed in the word itself: in-formation. . . . For a system to remain alive, for the universe to move onward, information must be continually generated. If there is nothing new, or if the information that exists merely confirms what is, then the result will be death" (Wheatley 1992, 104).

Leaders who treat information as something static and fail to appreciate the dynamic quality of its nature end up frustrated by the need to continually communicate with others. Followers who see information as stable have great difficulty understanding why the message today is different from the message yesterday. Some followers conclude that the leader was not being honest yesterday or did not have accurate information, because it is hard to believe that the information could change that quickly. Mistrust grows quickly unless followers understand the true nature of information.

The leader's attitude toward information sharing is crucial to being an expert communicator (Wilson and Wellins 1994). There are at least five rationales, or messages the leader may be playing internally, that affect the amount of information shared with followers:

1. Followers already know the information.
2. Followers do not want to know.
3. Followers do not need to know.
4. Followers cannot understand this information.
5. Everyone is on information overload.

Each of these are explored in this chapter.

***Followers Already Know the Information*** A common misconception that hampers many would-be excellent communicators is the assumption that because the information was shared once, the receiver understood the message. It is a very unusual follower that gets the message right the first time. With so much "noise" in our changing systems and with stress levels as high as they are, it is almost guaranteed that messages need to be repeated multiple times before they are received accurately. In fact, during times of great change in the organization, leaders are counseled to expect to repeat messages at least 7 to 10 times before they are understood by receivers.

Not only do the messages need to be repeated frequently, but using a variety of different channels will increase the likelihood that they will be received. This means using a combination of channels such as face-to-face dialogues, spoken presentations, written methods, and modeling the behavior requested. The greater the frequency and the wider the variety of methods used to communicate messages, the more likely they will get through. Another key principle is to encode the message with what it means for the receiver: why it is important and what the impact is on the receiver's life.

*Followers Do Not Want to Know*   In one organization, a benevolent, paternalistic leader's attitude was: "They don't really want the truth—they couldn't handle it." Even in a supportive, empowering leader, the thought that "the truth will scare them" can be a deterrent to open communication with followers. Some leaders believe it is part of their role to shield followers from bad news. In fact, some followers say: "You take care of that; we don't want to know the gory details." In these cases, followers are giving up their personal power and sense of control to the leader.

This leader attitude displays a lack of respect for followers. From the leader's perspective, it implies that the followers are not strong enough or able to handle difficult news or unpleasant information. "When we shield people we are acting as their parents and treating them like children" (Block 1988, 91). It is better to err on the side of high expectations of others than to continue to weaken followers' self-esteem by keeping them from the truth.

*Followers Do Not Need the Information*   In some instances, the leader's belief is that followers do not need certain information, that it is privileged or confidential. The notion of sharing information openly is the opposite of the military model that "only those that 'need to know' should be informed" (Block 1988, 90). An extreme example of this is seen in a southwestern community hospital. The executive team in this 320-bed facility spends several weeks each year involved in strategic planning. A complete analysis of the organization's strengths, weaknesses, opportunities, and threats is completed, and the steps for action over the next two to three years are plotted out. The team is very clear about their direction and what is needed to accomplish outcomes delineated in the plan.

Interestingly, however, the plan is never shared with employees or managers! The executive team is afraid someone will "leak" it to their competitor, a similar-sized facility in the same community. Employees and managers alike have directly and repeatedly asked over the years to see the plan. Many have reached the conclusion that there really is no plan. How this executive team expects to accomplish their strategic plan in isolation from employees and managers is a true mystery. This situation has led to significant feelings of mistrust in the organization.

Instead, the goal should be to let followers know of plans, ideas, and changes as soon as possible. Plans cannot be implemented without support and involvement of followers, who need to be included from the beginning. Robert Haas, quoted in John Huey's article "The New Post-Heroic Leadership," says: "In a command and control organization, people protect knowledge because it's their claim to distinction. But we share as much information as we possibly can throughout the company. Business literacy is a big issue in developing leadership. You cannot ask people to exercise broader judgment if their world is bounded by very narrow vision" (Huey 1994, 48).

***Followers Cannot Understand the Information***    Admittedly, much of the information concerning the health care environment and community issues can be very complex. However, the workforce today is better educated and informed than ever. When American trade agreements were being debated some years ago in Congress, they were simultaneously being debated on factory-room floors by workers all over this country. To be well informed is as simple as turning on a television set. Increased availability of information through mass media has resulted in well-informed citizens—when they choose to seek the information.

Employees or followers are capable of understanding a great deal more than some supposed leaders give them credit. Increased appreciation for the capabilities of employees has been a wonderfully liberating outcome for organizations that have implemented employee work teams and helped these teams develop to a high level of self-direction and self-management. (Manion, Lorimer, and Leander 1996). Traditional management responsibilities—such as departmental budgeting, interviewing and selecting new team members, planning, and managing supplies and inventory—are often thought to be beyond the capabilities of the average employee. Yet these same individuals leave at the end of their work day and assume these very responsibilities in their homes. They manage financial resources, possibly serve on a church board undertaking a multimillion-dollar building project, help their children select vocational schools or colleges, and manage conflict within the family. The next morning at work brings sudden dependence on a manager to accomplish very similar tasks.

In a Baltimore hospital, executives discovered the power of sharing increasingly complex information with employees. Over the years, great strides were made in creating an empowering environment. Information was shared openly and freely with employees. Town hall–style meetings were held, with executives and employees engaging in direct dialogue about issues of concern. In the early stages of this transformation, the questions employees asked of executives at these meetings included issues such as adequate parking space, health care benefits, and expected structural changes. As months passed and more information was shared, the flavor of employee questions changed significantly. Executives began hearing questions such as: "What's our managed care penetration?" "How is progress going on the managed care contract with _____?" "What is the impact of recent legislative changes on our organization and community?" The more information was shared, the more sophisticated followers became and the broader their understanding was of the organization's reality.

*Everyone Is Already Overloaded with Information*    A common and often justified message playing in a leader's head is that followers are already on overload and too much information is potentially damaging. The leader's concern is that excess information may be overwhelming. There is no question that the overload of information exists and only worsens as each year passes.

No one is immune from the information explosion. The elderly remember days before television when radio was the primary media. Baby boomers remember when only two or three channels were available on television. Now communication is possible virtually anywhere, anytime. Cellular telephones, beepers, fax machines, overnight express mail—all contribute to the immediacy of available information. Computers and mass media in addition to voice and electronic mail have contributed to an information glut. It's no wonder everyone feels overloaded. The flow of information is an unrelenting bombardment that continues throughout nearly every waking hour.

A recent *Wall Street Journal* article reports widespread dismay at the number of messages being sent. "The average person sends and receives a total of about 178 messages each day, according to a recent study of 972 workers at large companies" (Markels 1997, B1). The study also found that this communication barrage causes repeated interruptions of work, leaving people feeling frustrated and overwhelmed. Appreciating this information overload is important, but it should not keep the leader from sharing as much as possible about the project or situation.

## PRIMARY RESPONSIBILITIES OF THE LEADER: INFORMATION AND COMMUNICATION

Because of the glut of information in the environment, an effective communicator knows that messages need to be simple and easily understood. Using a variety of channels helps ensure reception. Analyzing how the information is important to the recipient gives the leader clues about preparing effective transmission. These negative rationales that can affect leaders' attitudes potentially reduce their willingness to impart information

Communication is a full-time responsibility for all leaders. There cannot be too much. It is far better to err on the side of excess information even though it may create its own problems at times. "The fuel of life is new information. . . . We need to have information coursing through our systems, disturbing the peace, imbuing everything it touches with new life. We need, therefore, to develop new approaches to information—not management but encouragement, not control but genesis. How do we create more of this wonderful life source?" (Wheatley 1992, 105).

Three methods of communication—spoken, nonverbal, and written—must be mastered for a leader to be an effective information disseminator. The more versatile the leader is in these three methods, the more congruent the message and the more likely it will transmit clearly. Principles of each method are explored here with ramifications for today's health care leaders. Not all followers are equally skilled as communicators, and the less skilled the follower, the more highly skilled the leader needs to be.

## Spoken Communication

Spoken communication is more than selecting the words. For a leader to influence followers, there must be a way to exchange ideas and opinions, to dialogue about issues, and to share concerns. This is usually done through oral communication. Successful communication includes the following aspects:

- Delivering information clearly
- Creating a message with impact
- Getting the listener's attention
- Establishing commonalities with listeners
- Finding ways to be different
- Using gestures and movement
- Using symbols and graphics
- Using metaphors and analogies
- Storytelling
- Using the environment
- Listening skills
- Asking the right questions

Each of these aspects is examined here within a leadership context.

***Delivering the Message Clearly*** Leaders must be able to order their thoughts, choose words that impart the message clearly, and be comfortable and at ease with the spoken word. Inarticulate leaders often feel self-conscious and are less likely to express their opinions and ideas or engage in conversations with followers. This greatly reduces their effectiveness and results in the loss of synergy between leader and follower.

Expressing difficult or technical concepts in simple ways is essential if the message is going to be received. Some people believe that the larger and more complex the words used, the more intellectual or important a person sounds. This may be true for presenting technical or highly complex information to a homogenous, professional audience, but it does not apply when speaking to or with general audiences composed of varied people. Instead of the communication fostering a connection, the opposite happens: followers feel more distant from the leader. The gap widens and followers focus on how they are different and, perhaps, less informed, less educated, or less intelligent than the leader.

This ability to express complex concepts simply is not always a natural talent. The good news is that it can be learned. At a department head meeting with approximately 70 managers attending, an executive of a 600-bed medical center gave a 20-minute presentation on statistical tests of significance. These managers represented all hospital departments, and less than a handful had any formal research background. Difficult, complex research concepts were explained during the presentation in a way that everyone in the room could clearly understand. When this executive was asked where and how she developed this ability, her response was interesting. In her graduate work, she had a professor who assigned a paper but left the choice of topic up to the student. Once the topic was selected—quality, teams, managed care—the paper had to be written without ever using the word the paper was about. She explained how this taught her to find multiple ways of expressing the same concept. What a gift!

An easy, conversational style of communicating establishes rapport with receivers, whether in a large group or a smaller, more intimate gathering. Ideas flow more freely, and there is less reservation about expressing opinions and disagreements. Bennis (1989) believes a good leader encourages dissent, establishing a climate that encourages expression of contrary ideas.

Body language congruent with the verbal communication substantiates the message sent. If words used by the speaker ring with sincerity but eye contact is limited, posture is stiff, and gestures are reserved, the impact of the message is lessened. Mixed messages are the most difficult to interpret and occur when verbal and nonverbal messages contradict each other. It's confusing to the receiver, who may leave the situation feeling baffled but unable to put a finger on what is wrong. The words sounded good but some sense or intuition tells the listener that the sender did not really mean what he or she said. At one meeting, recommendations from a project team were to be reviewed and discussed. The leader and several members of the project team, all staff members with the exception of one manager, were asked to present their recommendations to the executive team. The CEO started out by saying how important it was to have staff involved in these project teams because of their perspective and proximity to the work and problems being discussed. He also reaffirmed the executive team's commitment to having employees become more involved in major decisions that affected their work.

The team presented their findings while the executives listened politely. A few questions were asked, and then members of the project team were politely thanked and gently dismissed. Behind closed doors the real discussion began, and the executive team ended by discarding all recommendations made by the project team. Feedback to the project team was expressed as "thanks for all your efforts" and "your recommendations helped us clarify the issues and our thinking." Is it any wonder members of the project team had mixed feelings—how to reconcile the courtesy and appreciation expressed by the executive team with their feelings of exclusion and impotence?

Occasionally miscommunication is humorous, as the following story shows: "During his tenure as the director of the Federal Bureau of Investigation, J. Edgar Hoover once wrote in the margin of a draft letter: 'Watch the borders.' He intended only that his secretary widen the margins of the letter; what he got, due to a grand misinterpretation by some overzealous aides, was heightened readiness along the U.S.-Mexico border" (McDonald 1997, 4). Of course, this story is funny only in retrospect. At the time it was a fairly costly miscommunication. Mixed messages can be dangerous because many times they are not consciously recognized. There are vague feelings of discomfort but nothing that can be pinned down and examined. Often they create a sense of discord, and although mixed messages may not lead immediately to a breakdown of trust, loss of trust is an eventual outcome.

The only foolproof way to determine the clarity of the message is for the leader to seek feedback from the receiver. If there is a negative response or if the receiver does not have clear enough understanding to act on the message, another attempt is in order. Ideally, through direct dialogue with the recipient, it may be possible to determine the source of confusion so it can be cleared quickly. In any event, the message can be sent again, perhaps with additional information or a new explanation to increase clarity.

***Messages with Impact***    Clear, concise information enhances the impact of messages. And an effective communicator knows how to emphasize the key points of a message by getting the attention of listeners, establishing something in common with listeners, finding ways to be different, employing gestures and movement for key points, using metaphors and analogies, storytelling, employing symbols, graphics, audiovisuals, and the environment.

Gifted communicators use these methods effortlessly. Although some of these techniques are simpler and easier to use than others, all can become smooth with practice. Mastering these various methods is worth the effort because all will help the receiver to understand the message.

***Getting the Listener's Attention*** Gaining people's attention is an initial step in communicating. In formal presentations or discussions, the communicator or their topic may be introduced to the group by a third party. Most often, eyes and minds focus on the leader because there is a natural beginning point. Just the presence of a known and admired leader may draw the attention of followers who are interested in communicating with him or her. In a few instances, however, the leader may need to specifically draw the attention of followers in order to make a point. Effective ways of accomplishing this include using a hand gesture indicating the desire to speak or simply waiting for silence among the audience.

***Establishing Commonalities with Listeners*** Pointing out commonalities between the speaker and listeners is another way to gain attention and establish rapport or a sense of connection. This is difficult unless the leader knows something about the followers. The more familiarity the leader has with followers and their situation, the easier it is to identify common backgrounds, values, goals, and ideas. If the leader does not know a great deal about the followers, listening closely for "free information" is a useful strategy. This means being alert to information shared during conversations that may not pertain directly to the topic at hand but reveals something about the individuals in the group.

Dialogue between leader and follower often reveals many points of similarity. During the interchange of ideas, thoughts, and opinions or with the expression of concerns and fears, if the leader is in agreement with, has had an experience comparable, or shares the follower's concerns or feelings, these similarities can be used. The leader may say something like: "Yes, I remember when I worked in the night-shift lab, I often felt left out of the loop." Done briefly, without drawing attention away from the speaker, this establishes a commonality and sense of connection. Selected self-disclosure on the part of the leader is a gift of trust extended to followers. Telling the listener "I know just how you feel" is detrimental because it sounds like an empty platitude or cliché. Some listeners may react with skepticism and anger if they do not believe that the person communicating understands. "When I was in a similar situation, I had some of the same feelings or reactions you are expressing" is a more realistic statement and communicates understanding without minimizing the uniqueness of the speaker's experience.

A dramatic example of this illustrates what happens when a leader emphasizes differences. Susan was the project director for a massive work-redesign initiative in an organization where she had been a nurse-manager for years. She enlisted the services of an external consultant to assist with staff training. At the first session, she introduced herself, saying, "I am the hospital administrator in charge of the redesign project." To this audience of nursing staff the message was clear: Susan no longer considered herself a nurse. Many among them were obviously taken aback. Susan's attempt to distance herself from her background was successful—she was so distant from these followers that she was ineffective in her new role.

*Finding Ways to Be Different*    Although it sounds contradictory to the point just made, being different is another way to emphasize a message. O'Dooley writes, "People remember the unusual better than the ordinary." This can be as simple as a leader appearing informally instead of at preannounced, prearranged, and structured times; using overhead transparencies for a presentation instead of slides; or acting out a skit to demonstrate a major point. O'Dooley gives an example from his years selling photocopying machines for IBM, when he wanted customers to remember him over his competitors from Xerox and Kodak. He introduced himself as "Patrick O'Dooley, Reproduction Specialist." It worked in spite of the odd looks he received. "To stand out in others' minds, do things a little differently than everyone else does them" (O'Dooley 1992, 7).

When one large medical center undertook a massive restructuring project, a skit was played out by the senior executive staff to help deliver a message about the importance of the project and the role of employees. The skit included these executives in western garb, on horses, and revolved around a general pioneer theme. The videotape of this skit was powerful—not just the overt message but the impact of seeing these leaders, in blue jeans and cowboy hats, on horses. It was dramatic.

*Using Gestures and Movement*    Accenting key points with gestures, movement, or tone of voice helps anchor the message for listeners. Useful in casual conversations as well as more formal discussions and presentations, movement draws the listener's attention and increases the likelihood that the point will be remembered. Controlled hand and arm gestures can be used to communicate emphasis. Effusive, broad gestures may raise suspicion about the level of sincerity and should be avoided.

Changing the tone or volume of voice can be effective. Either softening or increasing the volume causes the receiver to listen more closely.

**Using Symbols and Graphics**    Enhancing a message with symbols, graphics, and audiovisuals can increase its clarity. A good graphic display often communicates a message in a way that makes words unnecessary. The graphic has to be understandable by the audience, of course. Audiovisuals are useful adjuncts to formal presentations, and there are many sources, especially training journals and materials, that can provide ideas for making them more effective.

Symbols are capable of motivating human behavior. They are very powerful and anything but benign figures of speech. In an article about the use of symbols in health care, Clark (1996) gives some evocative examples:

> A firefighter carries a lifeless toddler from the bomb scene at Oklahoma City's federal building. In the South Bronx, the athletic shoes of youths killed by violent means are hung from fire escapes and clotheslines. In New Mexico, crosses adorned with flowers mark the roadside where a loved one has been killed in an alcohol-related automobile accident.
>
> Mementos left at the Vietnam Veteran's Memorial. The homespun patchwork of the national AIDS quilt. Blouses tied together to signify the women who have been battered and killed as a result of domestic violence. Yellow ribbons as a remembrance of someone missing from home, red ribbons for those who died of AIDS, pink ribbons for the fight against breast cancer. . . . All these images represent the shared experience of Americans, with respect to our health and well-being. (Clark 1996, 20)

Symbolic language or behavior may be used without conscious intent or awareness on the part of the communicator. Termination of employees or announcements of major decisions on Fridays may symbolically distance the sender from receivers of the message by the physical separation over the weekend. Executive offices far from the workers may be practical for executives wanting limited accessibility but create a daunting prospect for employees. The hierarchy often plays out consistently within the executive offices—the CEO is located farthest from the front door, buffered by layers of secretarial staff. In what ways does this symbolize the leader-follower relationship?

**Metaphors and Analogies**    Another way to increase impact is by using metaphors and analogies to help people relate their own experiences and understanding to the message. Metaphors are comparisons in which something is described as if it were something else. Analogies involve a comparison between two cases or things and infer that what is true in one case is true in another. Songwriters and poets use metaphors and analogies extensively. So do effective leaders in health care organizations.

One hospital, which usually had eight labor and delivery rooms available, was undergoing major renovation in that department. It seemed like the entire department was torn apart; and at one particularly difficult time, desk drawers from the central nurses' station were placed on the floor down both sides of the hallway. With ten active labor patients in the department there was absolute chaos. The leader remarked, "This is like having a dinner party for ten while your kitchen is being remodeled!" This humorous observation diffused some of the high emotion and created a picture in people's minds that helped them understand and appreciate their frustration.

*Storytelling*    Storytelling is one of the most effective tools a good communicator uses. There is magic in stories. Throughout history, people have relied on narration and storytelling to express ideas that are difficult to communicate any other way. Abraham Lincoln was a consummate storyteller and is a wonderful example of a leader who was able to use conversation, humor, and stories to make his point and convince listeners of his way of thinking. Phillips, in his fascinating book *Lincoln on Leadership*, says:

> Nearly everyone who came in contact with our sixteenth president heard him relate some kind of yarn. Lincoln, it turned out, had an overwhelming inventory of anecdotes, jokes, and stories; furthermore, he possessed the ability to instantly pull out just the right one for any situation that might arise. Lincoln was a master at the art of storytelling, and he used that ability purposefully and effectively when he was president of the United States. (1992, 157)

The best storytellers collect ideas and anecdotes continually. They are always looking for examples that make a point or can be used to illustrate a complex or emotional concept. And the excellent storyteller practices sharing the tale, over and over again, until it is convincing.

The astute leader knows that successful organizations and teams are "storied" organizations and teams. They listen to the stories circulating and think about what these stories say about the culture. Do the stories reflect positive values and aspirations of the organization? Do they create enthusiasm and loyalty among followers? In one urban tertiary medical center, the organization mission statement and values were beautifully inscribed, framed, and strategically mounted in every office and conference room of the facility. They described a wonderful organization—words with heartfelt meaning that anyone would aspire to reaching. Amazingly, the predominant flavor of stories circulating in the organization was exactly the opposite. The favorite stories, repeated with great fervor, highlighted personal and professional corruption of the executive staff, unscrupulous maneuvering of managers against peers and employees, and malicious whisperings suggesting various reasons for promotions. The stories revealed the true culture of the organization. But stories do not have to be this extreme to have negative impact.

People remember stories longer than they can recall data and facts (Phillips 1992). Students of leadership theory and effectiveness confirm storytelling as a strategy and emphasize the role of stories "as powerful motivational tools that spread loyalty, commitment, and enthusiasm" (Phillips 1992, 158). Peters and Austin (1985) note that "human beings reason largely by means of stories, not by mounds of data. Stories are memorable. . . . They teach" (278, 281). A leader who understands this pays more attention to the role that stories and myths play in communicating ideals, values, and direction.

In a southern 280-bed hospital, a massive restructuring initiative was underway. Teams were developed and functioning in many of the patient care areas. During the most trying week for the newly implemented teams, there was also a serious flu epidemic in the community, and hospital census hit a peak. Staff members had been stretched well beyond their capacity, tempers were short, and absenteeism due to the flu ensured that the upcoming weekend was going to be a calamity. On Saturday, the vice president for patient care services was pitching in and helping out on the patient care units. One of the most pressing needs was cleaning the patient's bathrooms. People in the patient care departments were captivated and heartened to hear the story of how this vice president rolled up her sleeves and began cleaning toilets. The story of this doctorally prepared nurse doing what most needed to be done for patient's comfort and cleanliness still circulates in this organization. People here understand the organization's value of "Patients come first" and teamwork.

During the blizzard of 1996, many health care facilities in the Northeast generated stories that can today tell new employees about the culture in the organization. Executives in jeans and sweatshirts serving food in the cafeteria to hungry staff, employees with four-wheel-drive vehicles who transported colleagues to and from work, and countless other examples exemplified leadership and strong organizational values.

Perhaps some of the most poignant stories come from times of disaster such as the San Francisco earthquake of 1989, Hurricane Andrew in southern Florida, the Oklahoma City bombing, or the 1997 flooding in North Dakota. During these times of crisis, people rise to meet heart-breaking challenges, and leadership emerges. There are hundreds of examples that could be cited. Rosemary Jacobson, CEO of United Health Systems (now Altru Health System) in Grand Forks, North Dakota, describes the disaster faced from the record-breaking spring flooding:

> During the early morning hours of Friday, April 18, the dikes within the city began to fail, forcing mandatory evacuations of several large neighborhoods in Grand Forks and East Grand Forks. The state health officer called me Friday evening and informed me that the water system and infrastructure would fail. I still believed we would be able to keep United dry and open.
>
> It took only a few hours for realization to set in. I knew we would not be able to manage care of 197 inpatients without water or sewer for an extended period of time. Because of this, the decision was made to evacuate all 197 hospital patients and 371 nursing and retirement home residents from Medical Park and the Grand Forks community. This was accomplished within a 24-hour period.
>
> Our evacuation could only have been accomplished with teamwork. We spent many, many hours planning the Altru Health System, and it paid off. We functioned as a team anyone would be proud to know. (Jacobson 1997)

This emergency evacuation was the largest hospital evacuation since Saigon fell to the Viet Cong during the Vietnam War. Stories about disasters endured and calamities shared can strongly bond people together. These stories survive and serve to inspire and hearten, as well as to illustrate the basic beliefs and values of the people in the organization.

*Using the Environment*    Creative use of the environment is another powerful method of making a point. A good example is one clever speaker's presentation to a group of human resource specialists, executives, and trustees about the cost of discrimination when members of minorities are not solicited for governing board positions. Knowing the audience would be approximately 98 percent male, the speaker had interspersed throughout the audience pairs of high heels in front of empty chairs—a visual reminder to this highly homogenous audience of at least one minority underrepresented!

John, CEO of a major health care system, was having trouble with followers who were continually late to the regular meetings established. Punctuality as a team value was discussed repeatedly but to no avail. Finally John decided to communicate the message differently. On the day of his next meeting with the system vice presidents, John went to the boardroom and at the time the meeting was scheduled to begin, he locked the door. Ten minutes later the first vice president arrived and was dismayed to find the door locked. Within twenty minutes all attendees were gathered outside the boardroom where they waited anxiously until the scheduled meeting was over. When John finally opened the door, he told them that if they weren't on time, he would make decisions without them. News of that locked door spread like wildfire throughout the organization. The message was clear and communicated, simply through a locked door.

A different leader having the same problem started her meetings on time regardless of whether anyone else had yet arrived. The impact of coming into a room to find the leader talking to herself, conducting the meeting with no participants, made a tremendous impression, not just on the first follower to finally arrive but on everyone else who was told the story. People got the message.

**Listening Skills**     A discussion of spoken communication would be incomplete without considering the skill of listening. As important as being articulate is the leader's ability to listen. "The common image of leaders is that they are great talkers, charismatic and articulate. Far more important is that they are great listeners" (Berry 1992, 2). Giving attention to other's thoughts, ideas, and opinions allows a leader deeper understanding of the follower. Listening for emotions and feelings ensures that the leader understands a message fully, as these elements are difficult for many people to express verbally. Nothing is so powerful as a leader who has accurate facts and information and realizes that followers are an excellent source of both. Not only does it lead to better decision making, but it increases the shared meaning experienced between leaders and followers. Other notable reasons for developing good listening skills are that the listener can learn new information, that listening provides time to digest ideas and fully attend to the entire message, and that listening communicates respect and caring to the speaker.

*Listening provides new information:*  Exemplary listening skills enable the leader to learn and gather information not previously known. Abraham Lincoln once said, "When you speak you only repeat what you already know; it is when you listen that you might learn something." Not listening to others conveys an attitude of arrogance, intended or not. It is perceived as not needing input from anyone else because the leader feels all-knowing and correct. Listening to others generates ideas, especially for meeting the resistance someone has to the leader's approach. New ideas blend with the leader's ideas and serve as a catalyst for a unique thought or strategy.

*Listening provides time to reflect:*  Listening and thinking happen faster (about three to four times) than words can be conveyed. It is possible while listening to think about what the person communicating is trying to say. Does the individual's body language match their words? Does the message fit previous experiences with this individual? How does their message fit with previous thinking on this topic? Do the ideas expressed stir any other thoughts or possibilities?

*Listening communicates caring:* Listening to an individual express their ideas and thoughts has a powerful impact on the sender. Perhaps nothing else the leader can do communicates respect and caring for the follower as much as showing interest in what the follower has to say. M. Scott Peck, in *The Road Less Traveled* (1978), defines love as "the will to extend one's self for the purpose of nurturing one's own or another's spiritual growth." He goes on to point out:

> When we love another we give him or her our attention; we attend to that person's growth. . . . When we attend to someone, we are caring for that person. The act of attending requires that we make the effort to set aside our preoccupations and actively shift our consciousness. Attention is an act of will, of work against the inertia of our own minds. . . . By far the most common and important way in which we can exercise our attention is by listening." (Peck 1978, 81, 120–121).

*Increasing listening skills:* Communication courses often teach the skill of listening, and leaders with a background in a discipline that emphasizes and requires listening ability, such as counseling or social work, are at an advantage with this skill. The good news is that it is a personal skill and, as such, can be learned and improved with practice. It is common to overrate one's listening ability because it seems so simple. Peck points out, "Listening well is an exercise of attention and by necessity hard work. It is because they do not realize this or because they are not willing to do the work that most people do not listen well" (1978, 121).

The best leaders are great listeners. There are many helpful pointers they have learned as they worked at improving their listening skills:

- *Work at listening and continually attempt to increase listening span.* Good listeners control any temptation to interrupt or draw attention away from the speaker. Some people grapple for the right words to express their ideas and may take longer to finish their thoughts. Being interrupted only extends this process and gives a speaker the clear message that what is being said is not important enough to wait for its full expression. As Peck points out, this attention needs to be conscious.
- *Take the time to listen.* Not everyone is able to speak extemporaneously in a clear and concise manner. Instead they may think

out loud and gradually grope their way to their meaning. Their first statement may be only a vague approximation of what they mean. For the speaker to open up and crystallize the meaning of a message, the listener must convey a feeling that there is plenty of time to speak freely. Some leaders rationalize that they are too busy to listen. A good leader is too busy to *not* listen. Crucial information may be missed and needed understanding never achieved if the leader does not take time to listen. A good listener makes mental or actual notes of items they want to remember.

- *Listen for understanding rather than to reply.* Stephen Covey believes that the single most important principle he has learned in the field of interpersonal relations is to "seek first to understand, then to be understood" (1990, 237). Instead of focusing on preparing a reply to the speaker or thinking about how to make himself or herself understood, the listener actively tries to understand what the speaker is saying. Sometimes by taking on the behaviors of being a good listener, the act of listening may follow. A good listener stays alert, establishes eye contact with the speaker, leans forward if appropriate, shows interest by nodding the head or raising the eyebrows, and encourages the speaker to continue by asking thoughtful and appropriate questions. Jane Fonda once said that putting on her exercise clothes puts her in the frame of mind to work out. In the same way, effective listeners who "don effective listening behavior" may find it leads to that very behavior.

- *Listen in spite of delivery method.* Some speakers are more difficult to listen to than others. The speaker may have been blessed with wonderful ideas and thoughts but has a boring, monotone voice or a face without much expression. Good listeners aren't as concerned about mannerisms or delivery but focus on the message itself. They ask: "What can I learn from this speaker?" They know that not everyone is a brilliant, witty conversationalist.

- *Listen in spite of content.* If the content of the message is one that evokes strong emotion in the listener, it can be very difficult to not respond in an emotional fashion and interrupt the speaker. The listener can become excited or upset, especially when pet peeves are ignited or personal convictions or prejudices are challenged. It is easy to judge the speaker's comments too hastily and this can close down further communication.

- *Remove external distractions and resist internal distractions.* Distractions create "noise" in the system and make communication an even tougher job for both speaker and listener. If this is an especially important conversation, move the dialogue someplace where distractions are at a minimum, even if it means delaying it. A good listener recognizes and admits internal distractions and suggests alternate times for the speaker to return.

Participants at a national conference were taking a break in the middle of a three-hour session. The speaker had just discovered she had left her purse in the rest room earlier that morning. As the speaker was leaving the conference room in a panic, a participant approached her and attempted to engage her in a discussion. The speaker listened politely for a moment and then explained her present inability to listen. She told the participant she would be back soon, when they could then talk. But the participant tried to continue the conversation, at which point the speaker said, "You don't understand. I cannot hear a word you're saying because I am upset about losing my purse. Let's talk when I return."

This is the same conversation a leader needs to have with a follower if the time just is not right to listen. With the emphasis on an open-door policy and total accessibility of the leader, it may seem to be contradictory to ask the person to come back at a better time. However, if distractions are just too great, it is better to be honest than to pretend and risk missing an important message. Of course, the listener must make certain that the follow-up time occurs.

- *Restate or paraphrase the message.* When the speaker is finished, it is very affirming to have the listener restate what they heard and understood as the message. This also allows the speaker to clarify, if the message received was inaccurate. This very powerful technique is often referred to as reflective listening because it reflects back to the speaker on major points of the message.

These suggestions can help increase listening effectiveness, but probably even more important is that the leader-listener continually evaluates his or her level of listening ability. Is it improving? Do followers believe they have been heard and understood? How often are miscommunications occurring as a result of poor listening? In addition to using these principles, effective listeners understand that there are several levels of listening.

*Levels of listening:* In *The Seven Habits of Highly Effective People* (1990), Stephen Covey identifies several different levels of listening. The lowest level is ignoring; basically the person is not listening at all. This describes the listening—or lack of listening—that occurs when we tune someone or something out totally. Pretend listening is the second level, when the "listener" may nod and behave in a manner that connotes listening while not hearing a word. The standard example of this is when one's spouse is reading the paper or watching a favorite sports event on television and distractedly responds to questions that he or she does not even hear. Selective listening is hearing only chosen parts of the conversation. The leader who is interested in agreement from followers may hear only positive elements of feedback and ignore or discount more unfavorable segments.

The fourth level is attentive listening, in which the listener pays attention and focuses energy on the words being said. The fifth and highest level is empathic listening, which involves understanding not only the words of the message but the emotion and meaning of the message as well. Whether called active, reflective, or empathic listening, it is the only form of listening that focuses completely on the listener. Its purpose is to fully comprehend what the speaker is expressing, and it goes even further by adding the feedback loop to give the speaker a response that reflects this understanding. The power of this communication technique is that it gives the speaker the opportunity to correct misperceptions or misunderstandings at the time they occur. When a listener uses reflective or empathic listening, the speaker feels understood and validated.

Use of this technique requires judgment and skill on the part of the listener. Reflecting back the speaker's words and perceived emotion is a direct invitation to the speaker to continue. If the listener does not have time to follow through fully, use of this technique may send a mixed message. Practice and refinement of this skill are necessary so that the listener is not just parroting the speaker's words (an irritating and foolish thing to do!). The listener may say something like: "Let me check this out. I thought I heard you say _____," or "Are you saying _____?" or "It sounds like you're feeling _____. Am I right?" Until this is a natural part of the listener's repertoire it may feel uncomfortable, but the benefits are tremendous.

Using empathic listening helps a listener stay actively in the listening mode and focus solely on the speaker. If the listener has to repeat the essence of the message to the speaker, it focuses his or her attention tremendously. It puts the listener in the speaker's frame of reference and increases the listener's understanding of the speaker. Virtually no other technique is as helpful in building a solid relationship. The disadvantage is that the listener has no sense of control or efficiency. So, although this method is effective, it may not be efficient.

A signal to the leader that he or she is not using empathic listening occurs when a follower or speaker conveys the same message repeatedly. The leader may not have provided any feedback indicating that the message was received. An example of this occurred in a team of executives that had formed to attend a long-term learning program together. Members of the team were handpicked and were required to commit to attending a series of four three-day sessions over a year's period of time. As part of the selection criteria, all agreed that they would not miss a session. After two sessions, Cal told his other team members that he would be missing the next session. His team members were justifiably angry and gave him that feedback. One member, Jill, told him directly that she felt he was letting the team down and she was very disappointed in him. He showed no response.

In another week the team met again to discuss what they would do with Cal's decision to miss the next three-day session. Again, Jill gave Cal the same feedback and he showed no response. The team was having difficulty dealing with this dilemma and met one last time to decide whether Cal should remain on the team after the missed session. Again the teammates expressed their concern and anger, with Jill again directly telling Cal how she felt. Cal became very angry in return and said to Jill, "You've said that three times now; will you stop beating a dead horse? I'm getting tired of hearing this." Jill was surprised and replied, "I didn't think you ever heard me because you showed no response."

Followers who believe they have not been heard do one of two things. They may stop trying, believing that the leader does not care or is not interested in their opinions or ideas. If they are more persistent, however, they may continue to repeat a message until it is acknowledged. To be effective listeners, good leaders pay attention; and if they are hearing the same message repeatedly, they ask themselves: "Why am I hearing this again? Have I acknowledged this message?"

Listening is a skill that takes time to develop and continual attention to keep improving. The payoff is tremendous. One of the most remarkable benefits of listening to others is that it becomes a reciprocal process. If leaders want to increase the probability that others will listen to what they have to say, they will start listening (Campbell and Inguagiato, 1994).

***The Art of Asking Questions***   Few people consider asking questions an art form, and yet it requires a much higher level of skill than most people think. Questions can be used by the leader to gain information, to obtain a different point of view, and to show respect for followers and make them feel important and valued. And there is another benefit, as described by Ed Oakley and Doug Krug: "Smart communicators ask questions not only so they can hear the answers, but so the person asked can hear their own answers and thereby gain clarity for themselves or internalize something they have grasped only intellectually" (1993, 150). They go on to describe questions as a gift to the person being asked, just as answers are a gift to the asker.

Tips for more powerful questioning techniques that can increase the skill of the individual asking the questions include the following:

- *State the reason for the question.* Letting the person know why you are asking the question can eliminate resistance or the feeling of unwarranted curiosity. "Help me understand this better," or "I would like to understand the factors you considered when you made this decision."
- *Make it enjoyable for the other person.* Be enthusiastic and the person being questioned will feel positive.
- *Show interest in what is being said.* Through body language show an attentive attitude. This includes good eye contact, nodding or tilting the head, and appropriate facial expressions.
- *Use open-ended rather than closed questions.* Closed questions can be answered with a yes, no, or other one-word answer, which does not provide the breadth of communication desired. It is the difference between saying: "Do I have your support on this project?" versus "What parts of this project can you support? What elements will you have difficulty supporting?"
- *Avoid creating the feeling of the third degree.* Giving followers the third degree puts them on the defensive, even if they were feeling open in the beginning. One question after another, delivered in a rapid-fire manner is certain to raise a negative reaction in most people.
- *Ask for their opinion.* A very powerful question is one that simply solicits the person's thoughts about a particular issue or situation: "What do you think about _____?" Of course, the person asking the question has to be truly interested or will risk sending a mixed message.
- *Repeat key words from answers and summarize thoughts.* This indicates to the person responding to the questions that he or she has been listened to and heard.
- *Share appreciation of responses.* Let the speakers know that you appreciate their thoughts and the time they have given to answer your questions. "Thank you for going through this with me so I can understand it better."

Sometimes leaders are afraid that if they seek opinions from others and listen carefully to the answers and ideas, this communicates implicit agreement with these ideas. This is one reason feedback to the speaker is important. It is possible to listen attentively and yet clearly tell the individual when there is disagreement on an idea. Good questioners continually monitor other people's reactions to their questioning techniques. Does their technique facilitate the flow of information? Do people open up more, or are they becoming quieter and more reserved? This feedback gives the questioner direct information on the effectiveness of his or her technique.

## Nonverbal Communication

Intertwined closely with spoken communication is nonverbal communication, sometimes referred to as body language, although nonverbal communication is a broader term and can include the use of time, space, and the environment as well as body language. Verbal and nonverbal messages must match or they create confusion and frustration. Of these two channels of communication, nonverbal language can be more potent, as demonstrated by the childhood game of Simon Says. Simon gives rapid oral instructions while demonstrating the requested behavior. Participants follow the leader's movements, and the unlucky players who continue to follow the leader even in the absence of a stated "Simon says _____" lose the game. The point, of course, is that people are more likely to emulate behavior than to follow words or directives.

The potential power of nonverbal language compels the effective leader to observe and understand the significance of certain body language and to continually examine their own nonverbal communication for the messages they send. Leaders who are sensitive to these messages have greater control over their ability to communicate with clarity. In the same way, a leader becomes more skilled at interpreting the messages of others by tuning into nonverbal cues. Important nonverbal messages can be conveyed through the following:

- Use of time
- Touch
- Use of space
- Appearance
- Body motions and posture
- Choice of words and voice tone
- Eye behavior

*Use of Time*   The leader's use of time communicates a clear message about what the leader believes is important. This relates back to the concept of visibility and accessibility in the discussion of trust. Are followers able to reach the leader? Is there time to dialogue on important issues and concerns? With whom does the leader spend the most time? Who doesn't get any of the leader's time? Allowing enough time in a busy schedule to periodically have coffee or lunch with followers is a practical way of keeping in touch with what is happening. This can be difficult for more introverted leaders for whom casual, spontaneous conversation does not come easily. Sometimes scheduled, structured meeting times, even though the meeting itself is informal, can ease the way for this leader.

*Touch*    In this country, the issue of touch is more complex because of the increased focus on sexual harassment. Anything that could be construed to be of an intimate or sexual nature is unacceptable. Even if it doesn't result in litigation, it leads to distrust between leader and follower. Casual contact can actually improve the relationship because it connotes acceptance and caring. A famous research study involved a librarian who was asked to lightly touch students on the arm when checking out books to them or answering their questions. The students in the experimental group who were touched rated the librarian as more helpful, intelligent, and personable than the students in the control group. The librarian was the same individual and otherwise treated the students identically.

There are other cultural differences that influence the use of touch (Morris 1979). North Americans and northern Europeans are considered to have noncontact cultures, which means that body contact and touch are not common except in prescribed arenas. Arabs and Latins, however, are high-contact people and would consider North Americans and northern Europeans reserved, cool, and downright uptight. Family differences can also account for touch being more or less acceptable. Some people come from affectionate, demonstrative families and even in the workplace hugs are common. Other people are uncomfortable with hugging even in social situations as this behavior is reserved only for those on an intimate basis. Paying close attention to a follower's reaction to touch alerts the leader to its appropriateness.

*Use of Space*    Both space and spacing are issues to consider when evaluating nonverbal messages. Space can connote status: the person with the best and most space usually has highest status. A corner office with windows is often touted as the highest-status executive space. The size and location of the work space send a message indicating value and worth. Is there space allotted in the organization for classrooms and adequate room for employee lounges? Is there a special physician dining room? Is there reserved parking space for executives and managers? In the same way, reserved parking for "Employee of the Month" indicates value and esteem. What messages are being sent by the organization's leadership?

Another issue related to space is that of territoriality (Morris 1979). Humans are highly territorial, and this translates to an inherent compulsion to possess and defend space perceived as their exclusive property. Participants at a meeting or a conference choose their chair and put up boundaries to indicate to others where their space begins and ends. A coat on the chair, a notebook and coffee cup strategically placed all indicate possession of space. In the workplace, employees carve out their space and may then feel violated if they return to find someone else in "their" chair, at "their" desk, using "their" telephone or computer.

Respect for an individual's space is an important issue because there is often a complete lack of regard or concern for an employee's space, especially the frontline staff's. Departments are relocated, offices moved, and space invaded, often without any acknowledgment of the impact on the individual. To build trust between leaders and followers there must be care and respect shown for one another's work and personal spaces.

Personal space is another concept the excellent communicator understands. North American adults who are interacting in a professional or business capacity generally have four basic and distinct distances of interaction (Morris 1979):

1. Intimate zone: ranging from actual physical contact to about 2 feet
2. Personal zone: ranging from about 2 to 4 feet
3. Social zone: extending from about 4 to 12 feet
4. Public zone: stretching from 12 feet to the limits of hearing and sight

If an individual's space is violated by someone coming too close, the result is increased tension and distrust. Common cues are that the individual reduces eye contact, moves away, or puts something (like a chair, table, or desk) between him- or herself and the speaker. Leader-follower relationships usually begin in the social zone, and after trust has been established, they move into the personal zone.

Seating arrangements at a meeting send a message. When the leader joins others in the break room for a cup of coffee and always chooses to sit at the head of the table, it may send a message that he or she expects to always be in charge. In a formal meeting, sitting straight across from someone tends to increase conflict between the two parties. A too-crowded conference or meeting room can increase hostility. Power is also ascribed to the person on whose "turf" the meeting is taking place. Does the leader go to where followers are, or do followers always come to the leader? Especially in resolving conflict, power is equalized if a neutral territory is used.

*Appearance*   An individual's dress and appearance send a message to others. Like it or not, physical appearance makes an initial impression on others within the first five to seven seconds of contact. Although this is not about "dressing for success" or how to impress your followers, it is a reminder to consider the importance of the leader-follower relationship and the need to establish rapport and trust with those followers. Rapport is built by others perceiving sameness rather than difference. If the leader is trying to impress upward, the old dress-for-success model is appropriate. Impressing horizontally, or downward, is more likely to occur if the followers can see what they have in common with the leader. Some of these issues become clouded if there is formal hierarchy involved in the leader-follower relationship. A peer- or employee-leader is more likely to dress in a similar manner to followers. If followers are in scrub clothes and uniforms, a leader in a navy blue business suit may inadvertently emphasize differences.

***Body Motions and Posture***    Body motions and posture send distinct messages. Passive, aggressive, and assertive behavior are clearly communicated through posture and gestures. Slumped posture indicates passive behavior. Restricted hand and arm movement, hiding the hands, gripping one arm with the opposite hand, and holding hands rigidly at the side reinforce an impression of a nonassertive individual. Aggressive behavior is suggested by clenched teeth, jaw jutted forward, tight lips, flushed cheeks, flared nostrils, thrusting arm with a pointed index finger, pounding of fists, hands on hips, or clenched fists. The assertive leader uses more moderate and less frequent facial movement that expresses emotion congruent with the communication. Hand and arm movements are fluid, with hands held open and in view.

Leaders who sit in relaxed positions are able to effect greater influence on followers and are seen as more persuasive and active. They are generally better liked than those who sit in a tight, closed manner. Standing over others is seen as dominance; although it is appropriate in some settings (giving a formal speech), it would be too intimidating in others (at an informal or spontaneous meeting).

There are some gestures that are considered universal signals: hands over head for surrender, saluting, shrugging the shoulders, and blowing a kiss. However, leaders who understand cultural differences are aware of the importance of accurately assessing the body language of the followers; otherwise signals from one culture may be misinterpreted in another. Every culture has its own body language, and children learn these nuances as they grow up. A North American who had traveled in Japan related this story: He and his wife were very impressed with the politeness of the Japanese schoolchildren who would stand by the side of the road and wave at cars going past. On their third day they commented to the hotel desk clerk about how polite the children were. Imagine their chagrin when he told them that Japanese children stand at the side of the road and wave to indicate that they want to cross the street!

Leaders need to understand the significance of cultural behaviors of their followers. In Japan, for example, workers despise being surprised at meetings. Each worker-follower expects the leader to take him or her aside to privately deliver word of any upcoming changes. The ramifications for the leader are significant. Anticipating and understanding cultural differences allow a leader to communicate more effectively. People do not hear the intended message if they are embarrassed, insulted, or intimidated.

***Choice of Words and Voice Tone***     This chapter has explored the effect of metaphors and use of language to evoke meaning. Health care is liberally sprinkled with military metaphors. People talk of "doing battle" with disease, patients are given "shots" or endure "invasive" procedures, and employees "on duty" are "in uniform." In emergency departments patients are "triaged," and surgery is carried out in the "operating theater." "When we use language like this, the force of the metaphor powerfully conveys our values, past experiences, and what we consider legitimate. . . . The truth lurks in the metaphor" (Henry and LeClair 1987, 23). For this reason, leaders need to be very careful about the words they use. Referring to unconscious patients as "vegetables," to people who cannot pay their bill as "write-offs," to employees as "bodies," and to "FTEs" (full-time equivalents) and "drones" communicates the way the leader values people. One health care manager was well known in her organization for joking about needing to "lobotomize" employees so they would be more compliant. Even though this conversation almost always occurred behind closed doors, it certainly affected her leadership ability and reflected how she valued people.

Voice tone and volume also communicate congruence or discrepancy with the words being said. An assertive tone of voice is usually described as having moderate volume and emphasis on words—an adult-to-adult tone of voice. Aggression is communicated with a loud voice, a heavy emphasis on certain words, and a parental tone. Nonassertive, or passive, voice is usually a soft, perhaps inaudible, monotone and a childlike delivery.

***Eye Behavior***     Eye contact is culturally determined. North Americans are very careful about how and when they meet another person's eyes. An honest person looks another straight in the eye; shifty eyes connote dishonesty. North Americans avoid eye contact when walking down the street in a large city, when they are uncomfortable, or sometimes when they ask a question. In contrast, Israelis stare at each other on the street, not breaking eye contact until they have passed each other. In many Eastern cultures, direct eye contact is considered impolite. In England, polite listeners will fix the speaker with an attentive stare and blink their eyes periodically as a sign of interest.

Direct eye contact in North America is considered assertive, usually meaning the individual is comfortable with looking another straight in the eye. Too piercing a stare can be intimidating, and narrowing the eyes is often considered aggressive. Eyes flitting back and forth between objects can give an individual the "scared rabbit" look. Not looking a person directly in the eye causes the listener to wonder what the speaker is hiding.

Understanding the nuances of nonverbal communication not only enables the effective communicator to transmit clearer, more congruent messages but also assists in interpreting signals they read. This process often occurs in retrospect, after miscommunication has occurred. Continually evaluating the effectiveness of one's communication leads to better results later.

## *Written Communication*

Studies of leaders who hold managerial or executive positions reveal that approximately three-quarters of their day is spent in spoken communication with others (Mintzberg 1980). But ideas are not exchanged exclusively by word of mouth. Although oral communication skills are more often used, writing skills are just as pivotal in a leadership practice. The ability to choose words carefully, express thoughts in writing, and create a document that serves followers in understanding a message leads to better communication. Clear and confident expression of the written word is an asset for any leader.

Of the three methods of communication—spoken, nonverbal, and written—the written form is most troublesome, if only because of its formal nature. "It is received cold, without the communicator's tone of voice or gesture to help. It is rigid; it cannot be adjusted to the recipients' reactions as it is being delivered. It stays 'on the record,' and cannot be undone. Further, the reason it is in fact committed to paper is usually that its subject is considered too crucial or significant to be entrusted to casual, short-lived verbal form" (Fielden 1981, 42). For these reasons, an effective leader needs to be able to communicate effectively through writing.

The written word can be used to emphasize the importance of a message and serve as a record for future reference. Some people are visually oriented and prefer to see the message in writing to anchor it more solidly in their minds. The written means used by leaders today can include memos, letters, announcements, bulletins, newsletters, reports, and E-mail. The purpose and importance of the message determine which means are used. Because it is impossible to retrieve the written word once it is published, important written messages require a lot of thought and consideration. Considered one of the best leader-communicators of all time, Abraham Lincoln not only wrote his own speeches, he was an eloquent public speaker and wrote "thousands of letters and notes to anyone with whom he felt he needed to communicate" (Phillips 1992, 145). He believed in thorough preparation, often writing his thoughts over a long period of time and refining them later. This is still good advice today.

Important messages deserve the necessary time to ensure that they are well written and communicate the desired meaning. Being overly cautious, however, can result in an unreasonably prolonged communication process. In one organization, the executive team decided that a written letter was needed to communicate with staff members about several significant upcoming changes. The members of the team were so litigious conscious that by the time the document was reviewed multiple times by various attorneys and team members, it was months later—so late it was virtually useless. Not to mention that most of the intended audience could not understand what it really said. The need for accuracy, clarity, and caution must be balanced.

**E-Mail**   Electronic mail is the newest method of written communication and has grown in importance over the past five years. There are many advantages to E-mail, including speed and ease of sending information. It enables closer and more timely contact between leaders and followers because it allows direct access to the leader. On the downside, E-mail has replaced face-to-face communication in some organizations precisely because it is so easy. A major disadvantage is that there is no tone of voice or body language to help the receiver interpret a message, and miscues can be serious. It is so easy to tap out a message, hit the send key, and it is gone! This spontaneity has some disadvantages because there is less thinking time. The final disadvantage of E-mail is also one of its benefits: there is no paper trail. Follow-up is more difficult to remember and yet more critical. Ross Perot's advice is to be cautious of using E-mail: "Treat e-mail like you would a snake. Don't let anybody communicate with you by e-mail. Have people come in and talk to you face to face, eyeball to eyeball" (Perot 1996, 7).

**Improving Writing Skills**   Fielden (1981, 42) identifies four categories to consider when writing:

1. Readability
2. Correctness
3. Appropriateness
4. Thought

The relative importance of each of these categories differs with the writer and situation, but considering each will increase a writer's effectiveness.

*Readability:*  Readability depends on a clear style of writing. The leader needs to know the audience for whom the material is being written in order to write clearly. The more general the audience, the simpler the sentences and the less use of jargon, or "shop talk," makes a document readable. Liberal use of paragraphs, each beginning with a topic sentence, makes it easier for readers to grasp content quickly. Using simple language increases comprehension of the material.

Another aspect of readability, as identified by Fielden (1981), is the ability to lead the reader in an intended direction. The effective writer develops a skeleton structure first, which is later fleshed out with descriptive words. Clearly identifying the purpose and using transition sentences between paragraphs increase readability. Staying focused on the main points of the communication takes less effort if the writer has clearly thought through what needs to be said.

*Correctness:* Correctness is a second category to consider when writing. This refers to much more than grammar and punctuation. Coherence and the ability to correctly position sentences and paragraphs increase the smoothness of the communication. Sentences logically flowing from one to another result in clearer understanding. An easy way to evaluate coherence is to ask someone with no knowledge of the topic or situation to review the document and give feedback.

*Appropriateness:* The third category, appropriateness, is related to how content is presented. A leader writing a memo or announcement of a major initiative must first clarify in his or her own mind the intent of the communication. Diplomacy is important; if the reader feels insulted or that the tone of the document is condescending, acceptance of the message is impaired. Giving enough information and using "straight talk" is better than employing flowery, convoluted language that passes for communication but is really just semantics.

*Thought:* Thought content of the communication is the last category to consider when writing. Content must be accurate and well organized. "Much disorganized writing results from insufficient preparation, from a failure to think through and isolate the purpose and the aim of the writing job. Most writers tend to think as they write; in fact, most of us do not even know what it is we think until we have actually written it down" (Fielden 1981, 46). A carefully considered outline is of tremendous value to producing logical, well-presented information.

Careful analysis, bias-free evidence, and identification of working assumptions are all components of the content of the written communication. If facts are part of the document, they must be carefully analyzed; and the conclusions drawn must be supported by these facts. The writer may experience a tendency to state conclusions without sharing any of the relevant facts with the reader, perhaps fearing that the reader would not draw the same conclusion. Supporting evidence that is logical and clearly presented serves to guide the reader in the direction sought by the writer. Personal opinions can be shared if they are identified as such and not considered "hard" evidence for a particular argument.

It is also the writer's responsibility to succinctly state any assumptions that are operating in the situation. This gives the reader the opportunity to agree or disagree with assumptions made and prevents potential disagreements with the actual content. A curriculum team was asked to develop a proposal for meeting the education needs of employees during a planned cultural change in their system. When the proposal was presented, one of the first sections included the assumptions under which the team worked:

- People will not make cultural changes without new learning.
- Becoming something different is as important a goal as dealing with day-to-day issues.
- Leaders must model the desired behaviors.
- Expectations of employees must be clearly communicated and understood.
- The investment in employee education is an investment in the future.
- The most cost-effective approach must be found.

Simply identifying these assumptions generated tremendous dialogue with the executive team. As they talked though each assumption and examined the current reality of their system, they achieved an increased clarity of issues and needs. Both groups became more realistic about what the project could achieve.

Leaders communicating through written words need to avoid an effusive "con man" presentation meant to manipulate others. Simple words that ring with conviction, and enthusiasm for an idea and for understanding the reader's point of view go further to convince readers of important points than an excess of flowery language. Keeping these four areas in mind—readability, correctness, appropriateness, and thought content—results in clearer written communication.

## Summary

Effective communicators are skilled and versatile in all three of these modes of communication: spoken, nonverbal, and written. Judgment is applied in each situation to determine the appropriate means of sending a message, and outcomes of every communication are continually scanned to evaluate effectiveness of the message transfer. Exemplary leaders know that the highest impact of message delivery occurs when the message is congruent among all three modes.

## SPECIAL COMMUNICATION ISSUES

Today's leader faces many challenges in attempting to communicate with clarity to all followers that need information:

- Communicating during change
- Communicating long-distance
- Communicating with teams

### Communicating during Change

Health care is undergoing tremendous changes, in some instances almost cataclysmic in nature. The basic principles and techniques of good communication become even more important during times of rapid change because people seem to have an almost insatiable need for information at these times. Principles especially applicable during change include the following:

- Be available and accessible
- Find multiple ways of describing a concept
- Articulate complex concepts in as simple a way as possible
- Repeat key messages at least seven to nine times
- Share stories that communicate desired key values
- Make certain that the metaphors being used fit what needs to be communicated
- Scrupulously avoid mixed messages—they are deadly in times of change
- Ask for feedback to ensure the message was received
- Remember people are in a state of high emotion, which creates "noise" in their systems
- Separate resistance from learning and seeking information.

In addition to these principles, a key strategy during change is to develop specific communication approaches for key stakeholders. In *The Empowered Manager* (1987), Peter Block does a beautiful job of describing this strategy. He points out that a stakeholder is anyone who is needed for the success of the project or who can influence the project significantly. The first step is to identify the issue or change project targeted and any key stakeholders impacted by this initiative. Stakeholders are assessed as "key" by the degree to which they agree with the project and the level to which they are trusted. Level of agreement with the project cannot be assumed. If not known, evaluation occurs after the leader sits downs with the stakeholder and talks about the vision, purpose, or goals of the project or endeavor. Through this dialogue, agreement is either confirmed or denied.

The leader then determines where the stakeholder fits into a specific matrix (figure 4-2), depending on the level of trust in and agreement by the individual, both of which influence the communication strategy and effectiveness of message transfer. Opponents differ from adversaries only in the area of trust, but this difference dramatically impacts the selection of communication strategies for each. A strategy for working with opponents is to keep communication lines open and to engage in frank and honest dialogue with them. Opponents are important because they value and trust the leader—they just do not agree with this particular initiative. With adversaries, however, there is not only a lack of agreement, but there is a lack of trust. Dialogue is not particularly helpful because the leader cannot believe the adversary will be honest. A common error in judgment must be highlighted in using this model. This error occurs when a leader makes the assumption that anyone who disagrees is an adversary. If opponents are treated like adversaries, they may in fact convert to this less desirable category. This happens when a supposed leader sees opposition as negative and all resisters as untrustworthy. A summary of appropriate strategies for each category is provided in figure 4-3.

Some difficulties are inherent in using this model. It is not a static but a dynamic model. Through ongoing interchanges with stakeholders, continual reassessment both of their status on the matrix and of the effectiveness of a particular communication strategy selected is critical. Something in the environment or within the individual may have

**FIGURE 4-2.  The Stakeholder Matrix**

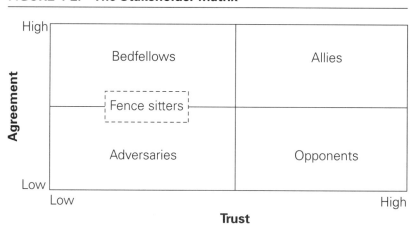

Reprinted with permission from *The Empowered Manager* © 1987 Jossey-Bass Publishers.

changed that alters their placement on the matrix. One manager whose organization was converting to a team-based structure was resistant to the idea of employee teams in his department, the business office. He was identified as an opponent according to Block's matrix. His daughter visited over the holidays and told him about her experiences with employee work teams at her bank. She was enthusiastic, and after that

**FIGURE 4-3.   Strategies for Categories of Key Stakeholders**

*Allies*
- Treat them as "one of us."
- Ask them honestly what they believe and see happening, and listen to what they tell you.
- Continually discuss the project, vision, plan, and so on.
- Reaffirm the quality and importance of the relationship, especially that you appreciate their honesty.
- Acknowledge the doubts and vulnerability you feel.
- Ask for advice and support.
- Have regular meetings and ask them how they perceive things are going and what they need.

*Opponents*
- Reaffirm the quality of the relationship and the fact that it is based on trust.
- State your position; keep communication lines open.
- State in a neutral way what you think their position is.
- Engage in some kind of problem solving.

*Bedfellows*
- Reaffirm any agreements.
- Acknowledge the caution that exists.
- Be clear about what you want from them in terms of working together and ask them to do the same.
- Try to reach some agreement on how you will work together.

*Fence sitters*
- State your position.
- Ask where they stand, encourage them to express their opinion without judging them.
- Apply gentle pressure.
- Encourage them to think about the issue and let you know what it would take to give you their support.

*Adversaries*
- State your vision for the project.
- State in a neutral way your best understanding of your adversary's position.
- Identify your contribution to the problem.
- End the meeting with your plans and no demands.

Reprinted with permission from *The Empowered Manager* © 1987 Jossey-Bass Publishers weekend, he was an ally! All it really took were concrete examples from a similar business, and he could see the possibilities. It also helped that he trusted his daughter explicitly.

A second drawback relates to accurately identifying where the stakeholder fits on the matrix. Some groups of stakeholders are so large that it is difficult to determine where each individual falls. To use this model, the leader must be able to dialogue directly with each stakeholder to determine agreement and choose a communication strategy based on this knowledge.

A cardiopulmonary leadership team in one organization used this model successfully for communicating with key physician stakeholders during a massive change initiative in their care center. The team consisted of the care center leader and managers reporting directly to her. First, all key physician stakeholders were identified, and the team placed each on the matrix. In one or two instances, no one had enough current information to make an accurate determination, so those physicians in question were each assigned to a team member. The team member's responsibility was to then engage in a dialogue with the physician to determine that physician's understanding of the change being planned and level of support.

Once all physician stakeholders were located on the matrix, an appropriate communication strategy based on levels of trust and agreement was determined for each. All key stakeholders were each assigned to a member of the leadership team for purposes of primary communication regarding this change initiative. This spread the responsibility of physician communication among all members of the team and allowed for a more individualized strategy for each stakeholder. The project was implemented with greater support from more physicians than this team had previously experienced.

## Communicating Long-Distance

Today's leader has a new challenge: leading people from afar. Recent mergers, acquisitions, and consolidations of health care facilities have resulted in fewer stand-alone organizations (Blouin and Brent 1997). With each passing year, the likelihood of geographically distant leaders increases. Leaders are managing and directing projects with representatives from multiple sites, which may or may not be within the community; more executives and managers today have responsibility for multiple facilities and departments; and the ascent of the virtual office coupled with the dejobbing of health care all combine to create the need for leaders who are effective in spite of geographical distance from their followers.

Geographical distance from followers creates significant barriers to applying any of the interpersonal competencies. It is difficult to form and nurture a quality relationship if two people are not physically proximate at least periodically. Dialogue over a computer or telephone line is not the same as face-to-face interaction. Communication is made more difficult and complicated by distance. Just as the price for a long-distance telephone call is higher than for a local call, so is the price exacted in a relationship when conducted long-distance. The Pinchots (1996) articulate this issue very well: "As organizations become more complex, more geographically distributed, it becomes harder to create enough common vision and community spirit to guide the actions without increasing reliance on the chains of command. When people are separated by distance, vast differences in power and wealth, and conflict over resources and promotions, political struggle often replaces community. As the power of community is stretched thin, the chain of command becomes more prominent, and sense of community declines further" (18).

The savvy leader applies the basic principles of communication and pays special attention to them when the situation is complicated by distance. In *Knights of the TeleRound Table*, Kostner (1994) shares insights for executives who must manage from afar. Many of the principles she identifies are equally applicable to long-distance leaders. She points out that "the key way to build high performance across distance . . . is to build trust. Be obvious that every word, every action, every initiative on the virtual team builds trust" (169). The paradox is that in these virtual relationships trust is more difficult to build long-distance but is even more important.

Other especially important principles in long-distance leader-follower relationships include the following:

- Use strong symbols as a way of uniting people who are not in the same workplace
- Establish ways to help people learn more about each other so they collaborate even when distant, such as on-site visits, kick-off meetings for key projects, and teleconferencing
- Use technology to link people across distances (a computer network, E-mail, and teleconferencing)
- "Be scrupulously fair in treating all team members, near and far, equally. Even appearances or suggestions of favoritism break trust" (Kostner 1994, 171)
- Rely equally on followers whether on or off site (there is often temptation to rely more fully on those sharing the same geographical location)
- Expect high performance equally from followers, not allowing distance to impede dealing with performance issues

Leading from a distance is a growing challenge in today's workforce. The importance of good communication cannot be overstated.

"Miscommunication, inequities of information, and unequal access to information are significant trust-breakers. . . . The impact of these remote problems may not show up for months, but will always negatively impact productivity and profits across distance" (Kostner 1994, 172). Continually flowing communication and diligent sharing of information can counteract the "out-of-sight, out-of-mind" syndrome.

## Communicating with Teams

In organizations that have converted to a team structure in their departments, leaders face the challenge of communicating with teams in addition to communicating with individuals or groups. The leader must be sensitive, in each situation, to the question: "Is this an individual issue or a team issue?" If it is a team issue, the leader must decide carefully how to communicate and with whom. Executives, especially, need to be careful about not usurping the team's responsibility and authority. There is often a strong tendency to access previous lines of communication and simply pick up the telephone and contact the manager to whom the team is responsible. Most managers willingly follow up and attain information or take action requested. Results are speedier and it appears—on the surface at least—that communication is simplified. However, the team may end up resenting the fact that the manager intervened in what the team members consider their work. An astute manager may put the leader directly in touch with the team so that the communication is as direct as possible.

When working with a group of individuals who have been selected as representatives of their teams, a good leader makes certain they are clear about their role. Too often, team members participate on ad hoc problem-solving teams or committees within the organization and forget that their role is to represent the interests and ideas of all of their teammates. A simple reminder at each meeting helps these people focus on their need to return to their team and communicate with their colleagues. When issues are discussed in the group, asking attendees about the thoughts and ideas of their teammates also reinforces their roles as team representatives.

Communicating with teams can complicate matters in an organization. The increased feeling of ownership and responsibility, as well as improved outcomes attained by teams, usually outweighs the difficulties. However, there is a strong tendency on the part of leaders to want to simplify reporting and communication relationships and to stay with those methods that have been used in the past. A vivid example of this was observed in a large medical center that was four years into the process of converting to a team-based structure. Employees in the risk management department had begun working together as a team. They were cross trained, self-directed, and self-managing. The director, Sammie, had been asked to report on a particular problem, and she had turned the project over to the team. These highly seasoned team members investigated the issue thoroughly and produced an outstanding report. Each proudly signed their name to the work and asked to present it to the executive team. The executive team declined the team's request to present the report and instead asked Sammie to "do the honors" instead. Then, unbelievably, the executive team refused to accept the report with the team's signatures and insisted on the department director's signature only. Their reasoning was that the department director was solely accountable in case of any future problems. This demoralizing blow to an excited, enthusiastic, fully engaged team was devastating. It created a tremendous ripple of distrust and cynicism throughout the organization that went totally unrecognized by these executive leaders. Employees in this organization no longer believe that executive leaders understand what it means to be on a team.

## COMMON BARRIERS TO EFFECTIVE COMMUNICATION

Understanding common barriers, such as gender and style differences, communication preferences, and tribal language, helps the leader increase communication effectiveness.

### Barrier 1: Gender Differences

It is obvious to anyone who can see that there are differences between the genders. Not so visually apparent, however, is one profound manner in which men and women differ: communication. Differences in this area have resulted from effects of the cultural environment and how each were socialized as children. Sometimes, however, these disparities are downplayed in the workplace when attempting to emphasize similarities. Lack of appreciation for the uniqueness of each gender only brings trouble for a leader attempting to communicate and establish relationships. In recent years a plethora of popular books have discussed these differences. Any leader interested in improving his or her communication skills is encouraged to include several of these books on their reading list. Only a few examples are identified here, with leadership ramifications briefly examined. None of the following observations are considered absolutes for either gender but are meant to stimulate awareness and thinking about these differences.

*Giving an Answer versus Talking It Over*     Young boys are socialized to give an immediate answer or solution to a problem. Young girls talk things over to solve their problems. It does not mean that the young girl wants an answer to the problem, just as it does not mean that talking the issue over once is enough. "Problem talk" becomes great conversation for two women. But when a woman starts talking over an issue with a man, a common initial reaction is for him to give her an answer (Tannen 1994).

John Gray, who wrote *Men Are from Mars, Women Are from Venus* (1992), substantiates this. He says that men "go to the cave" when they have a problem. A man likes to work things out for himself, while a woman likes to talk things over. In the workplace, a leader-follower relationship can be strained by these two different approaches. One way to avert this problem is to state clearly at the beginning of the conversation what is desired. A woman might say to a male listener: "I don't need an answer, I just want to talk about this, and I need for you to listen." A man might ask a woman: "Do you want a suggestion here? Or do you just want me to listen?" On the reverse side, a woman who understands these differences will not take offense if a man does not want to discuss an issue in depth. And when a woman steps in to help a man (which may be normal and expected coworker or team behavior), he may be insulted and believe she thinks he cannot handle the situation himself.

This was clearly demonstrated in a surgical services leadership team. The team was composed of six women and one man. Jim was the manager of the inpatient surgical unit. He had previously been director of respiratory therapy. This leadership team was formed when the organization underwent a major restructuring and work-redesign initiative. Jim's department was in the midst of major reengineering, new roles were being defined and implemented, cross training was initiated, and business and service associates were transferred to his responsibility. The department was large, and with the restructuring, he had over 120 employees reporting directly to him. Needless to say, there was a great deal of confusion and more work than any one manager could possibly handle. To exacerbate the situation, Jim had never managed an inpatient department before.

At a leadership team retreat, the discussion revolved around the reengineering efforts in Jim's department. Team members were rapidly identifying problems, talking through issues, and suggesting solutions—including ways that they could help Jim with his workload. The team grew more enthusiastic as the conversation continued, and Jim grew more and more reserved. The retreat facilitator finally remarked on his behavior and stopped the process. When he was asked how he was feeling about the offers of help he replied, "It feels like they don't trust me to do my job." The female members of the team were aghast and hurried to assure him. Their typically female response to help had been misconstrued. After discussing the two different gender approaches, they sat back and asked Jim what he would like from them.

**Separation versus Attachment**    In her book *In a Different Voice* (1982), Carol Gilligan reports the results of a longitudinal study of boys and girls that revealed some fascinating gender differences. These children were studied over many years. Each observation was completed at five-year intervals. Gilligan points out that most children are still raised in their early years by female caregivers. For little boys, when they reach the age at which they become aware they are physically different from their caregiver, they learn to separate. So over the years, they become skilled at separating. Little girls do not have to separate from their same-sex caregivers so instead become very good at sustaining relationships.

This plays out in the workplace in potentially significant ways. Women are more likely to work hard at nurturing a relationship and working out issues in it, while men may be more likely to terminate a relationship rather than try to work it out. Another effect this can have is the ease with which men separate work from their relationships— there can be a bitter battle in the workplace and the men involved will still go out and play golf together. For women, a major disagreement can destroy a relationship.

**Direct versus Indirect Communication**    Men are more comfortable making requests, while women are more likely to use indirect methods of communication. Many little girls are socialized to get what they want and need by hinting, indirectly asking, or using innuendo. A recent comic strip showed a wife asking her husband: "Ted, do you want to take my car to work today?" Ted then turns to their daughter and says: "What she really means is—it's low on gas, would you fill it up for me?"

In the workplace, a woman who says: "I think the report is still out there on the desk" may actually mean: "Please bring it in." Women may inadvertently hide the real message in so many words that a male coworker never gets it. There is usually no problem if two people who are direct, or two who are indirect, get together. The problem arises when the two different types get together.

**Body Language**    Body language may be different in the genders as well. Men talk most comfortably shoulder to shoulder, while women like to talk face-to-face. Deborah Tannen (1994) concluded that men may find a woman's direct face-to-face interaction to be flirtatious or intimidating. Gray (1992) found that when a man nods his head during a conversation, he means "I agree," while a woman nodding means "I'm listening." There's quite a difference between these two signals.

As stated earlier, none of these are absolutes. Cultural differences also impact each of these categories. However, if a leader does not understand these distinctions, significant miscommunication can occur. Exemplary leaders are translators, and the more they are aware of nuances in communication, the greater their effectiveness.

## Barrier 2: Communication Styles and Preferences

A common barrier to effective communication is a lack of understanding or appreciation for differing communication styles and preferences. The excellent communicator pays close attention to a listener's style and adapts their own style accordingly. Some listeners want specific details and endless facts to support an idea or solution. Others get impatient with what they perceive as overkill and just want to get to the bottom line. Some followers are chatty and long-winded, others are reticent and seem unwilling to share more than one sentence at a time— delivered with a lot of effort! Some listeners are severely affronted and take it personally if their opinion is questioned or their arguments are challenged. Others shrug off contradictory ideas and go about promoting their own opinion regardless of anyone else's viewpoint. None of these approaches is inherently right or wrong; they are simply different. The more the leader understands a follower's communication style, the better able he or she is to avert problems.

A relatively recent communication technique that can help a person read another with greater sensitivity is called *neuro-linguistic programming*. It is based on research findings that people can be visual, auditory, or kinesthetic; and application of these findings to communication issues is obvious: a visual person better receives a message that is encoded with visual terminology; an auditory person, auditory terminology; and a kinesthetic person, kinesthetic terminology.

The trick is to listen to an individual for clues as to which of these is preferred. "One of the ways you can know this is by listening to the kinds of process words (the predicates: verbs, adverbs, and adjectives) that the person uses to describe his/her experience" (Bandler and Grinder 1979, 15). A visual person's conversations include comments such as "I see what you are saying," "Draw me a picture or map so I can see it," and "Do you see what I mean?" From an auditory person comments such as "I hear you," "That rings a bell," and "Let me hear it from your lips" are common. A kinesthetic individual may say "I really feel for them," "I can handle that," or "It feels right to me."

Sophisticated communicators pick up these clues and begin to mirror the three preferences by including appropriately similar references in their messages. Rapport is more easily established if there is commonality in language. All three of these sensory sources may be used in a consequential communication. Transmitted both in writing (for visuals) and orally (for auditory), important messages should also be delivered with feeling.

## Barrier 3: Tribal Language

In her book *Tribal Warfare in Organizations* (1988), Peg Neuhauser presents the concept of *tribes* as a source of major conflict in many organizations. For a leader, this has special ramifications. "In today's hospitals with their many specialized groups, each with its own vocabulary, executives who engender willing cooperation and build cohesive groups may well be the most highly skilled at speaking many special languages and at translating ideas captured in specialized, sometimes esoteric vocabularies into a common language that all organizational constituents can understand" (Henry and LeClair 1987, 21). The highly effective leader has to be fluent in a multitude of languages in order to communicate constructively with followers.

In today's health care organizations some of the tribes include but are not limited to those of administration, nursing, radiology, pharmacy, business office, environmental services, physicians, and security. Not only does the language vary from tribe to tribe but so do the primary and important values, rules of the game, training and background, and thinking patterns (Neuhauser, 1988). These differences lead to conflicts and a lack of connection if they are not understood and taken into account by the leader when communicating.

Examples are common. Members of the laboratory tribe value accuracy over speed, while members of the accounts receivable tribe value speedy turnaround for bill payment. Rules of the game pertain to how the tribal members get the job done. Caregiving tribe members may believe that honesty with patients and families is the only wise policy and criticize what they perceive as political doublespeak by physicians or administration. The rites of passage for each tribe are very different as is the education or training required. These rites for obstetric nurses may include passing state boards, working nights, or their first unassisted birth or patient death.

Lack of consideration for tribal differences leads to problems. For example, security officers need to be customer oriented, while they also play a primary role in an organization's safety and security. Whereas a caregiver or a receptionist may see the security officer's role as making people feel comfortable and welcome in the environment, the more urgently needed role in a large urban medical center may be to provide an intimidating presence in the emergency room. One organization, attempting to create multiskilled employees, encountered numerous problems in cross training security officers to also be transporters and care providers in its emergency department.

Language is a primary way in which tribes differ and one of the first things to cause trouble. A code in the medical records department is very different from what is also called a code in the intensive care unit. Each tribe has a language specific to its own culture. In the management information systems department (MIS), there are bytes, memory, and megahertz. Simply calling the help line in MIS gives one a clue as to how different the languages are. If a leader does not understand a tribe's language, it is easy to inadvertently halt communication. Neuhauser (1988) describes this as the 15-second phenomena: A member of one tribe meeting a member of another tribe usually insults the other within 15 seconds. The impact on communication is obvious—it shuts down. The internal message played by the listening member of the "other" tribe is: "He or she just doesn't understand us" or "He or she is different from us." Referring to people from finance as "number crunchers" or "bean counters" can be demeaning. Telling patient caregivers that something is "not in the budget" is like waving a red flag. In the same way that becoming fluent in a foreign language allows one to communicate in another culture, so does understanding the many languages of the different health care tribes.

Health care tribes are so complex that the task of communicating without insulting requires tremendous effort. An individual may be a member of multiple tribes. Take, for instance, a nurse. Although there is general nursing language, it is complicated by the specialty in which an individual practices. Obstetric nurses have different lingo from surgical or intensive care nurses. Home health and long-term care nurses have their own jargon. It may even differ by shift! Educators, regardless of original discipline, have their own language. Although it can seem overwhelming, a good leader makes the effort to become aware of these differences and works to understand each tribe.

## CONCLUSION

This chapter has addressed one of the most crucial issues for any leader: how to communicate effectively. Without this skill the other leadership competencies are virtually inoperative—relationships are not healthy, it is impossible to gain commitment to a cause, processes cannot flow smoothly, and the leader is unable to develop and nurture others. To be an effective leader, one must understand the various facets of spoken, nonverbal, and written communication and the barriers that must be overcome. Every day brings a leader numerous opportunities to improve his or her communication skills, as well as new challenges in creating shared meaning with followers.

# 5

## The Art of Effectively Managing Processes

"Solutions . . . reside not in the executive suite but in the collective intelligence of employees at all levels, who need to use one another as resources, often across boundaries, and learn their way to those solutions."

—*R. A. Heifetz and D. L. Laurie*

E xemplary leaders are skilled at guiding key processes in order to obtain synergistic, extraordinary outcomes. Process management is a critical competency for a leader because of the increasing complexity of today's work and the accelerating competency of workers. The old command-and-control approach to leadership and management was effective in the past when workers did not have the scope, skills, or ability to make decisions other than basic ones directly influencing their work. Today's workforce is better educated, more sophisticated, and increasingly interested in being involved in planning and making decisions that directly or indirectly impact their work. Ramifications for the present-day leader are significant. Good leaders gather input, involve others, guide discussions, build commitment, empower others, and recognize when a decision needs to be a group effort and then gain consensus. In short, they are capable and skilled at facilitating a variety of processes.

Managing processes as a leader is not as easy as it might first appear. In the past, managers were often rewarded for a "get it done" mentality and approaches that were decisive and outcome oriented. How a result was achieved mattered less than the fact that it was achieved. In fact, individuals who focused on the process involved in achieving outcomes often reached those results more slowly and were thus judged less effective. The current business climate adds pressure to managing processes in that it reinforces the need for quick action, decisive leaders, and an outcome-oriented approach. Courage is a necessary asset in a leader who is pressured for a decision but believes better results can be obtained when a collective and collaborative decision is made.

This chapter explores several key tenets underlying the leadership skill of managing processes. The first is to understand and respect the process involved. The second tenet refers to the role of leaders in persistently seeking to improve current situations by continually challenging the process. The final tenet establishes the leader's role in facilitation. To illustrate, numerous fundamental processes are examined as they relate to current health care leadership practice. These include empowering others, problem solving, decision making, resolving conflict, creating teams, and managing the processes of change and transition.

## TENET 1: UNDERSTAND AND RESPECT PROCESS

This tenet is twofold: Not only must leaders understand basic processes that are operative in particular situations, but they must also respect the processes, allowing them to unfold in their own natural time frames. Both elements of this tenet are important. First, it is necessary to recognize the process involved and demonstrate knowledge of it through the application of logical, methodical, or other appropriate steps. A major cause of an ineffective process is skipping or eliminating an important step, which is illustrated in the exploration of specific processes in this chapter.

Leaders need not always apply the steps to these processes in exactly the manner they are outlined here. Through experience, trial and error, and continually evaluating outcomes, a leader gains experience and may develop his or her own processes. However, most processes have a structure that when consistently applied will improve outcomes.

Process requires patience. More time may be spent in preparatory groundwork, but when decisions are made or solutions are formulated, those involved are thoroughly committed to carrying them out. With the command-and-control approach, after a decision is made or solution determined, time is spent convincing others to comply—a never-ending cycle of explanations, persuasion, and monitoring of behavior.

Respecting the process means that the leader understands how long a normal process should take and allows the proper time for the process to unfold naturally. This requires a significant amount of judgment because there are times when a little nudge or push may be required to get things back on track. When people express an aversion to processes, it likely comes from having had the too frequent experience of involvement in a process that was never ending. People inexperienced or unskilled in managing processes sometimes let them drag on and on, never bringing closure or producing needed results. Following a process for process' sake is mind deadening and demoralizing. The purpose of managing process is to make it meaningful; and to be considered meaningful, a process must result in effective and beneficial outcomes.

Respecting process is similar to understanding and respecting the principles involved in any situation. Best-selling author Stephen Covey, in *Principle-Centered Leadership* (1990), describes principles as abiding laws of nature that never change. To explain, Covey uses the principle of farming as an example. A farmer cannot take it easy in the spring and summer—procrastinating and not planting—and expect a bountiful harvest in the fall. The farmer must plant the seeds in the spring and cultivate and fertilize the fields during the summer to be rewarded with a crop in the fall. Unable to hasten the growth of the crop or to control all the external elements that affect the crop's bounty, the farmer respects and awaits the unfolding of the process. In the same way, a leader who understands and respects the natural flow of a particular process does only what he or she can to influence results but knows that the process cannot be accelerated unnaturally or controlled completely.

## Disrespect of Process

Examples demonstrating a lack of respect for process are common in today's health care organizations. Unfortunately, the external climate creates a sense of urgency and need that can easily affect the leader's ability or desire to patiently let a process unfold. Take, for example, the formation of a healthy relationship between followers and leaders. Establishing and maturing this relationship is a developmental process. It cannot be rushed or developed suddenly when there is a crisis generating a need for it. Yet, observe what happens in an organization where employees threaten collective action through a union-organizing attempt. Consultants are hired to coach managers about what they can and cannot say. Overnight, managers are available and visible to employees, listening to what employees are saying, and asking for input. It is often a matter of too little, too late. This sudden flurry of relationship building on the part of managers is often received with cynicism by employees. Worse, the behavior being reinforced is "Threaten union formation and administration listens!" Issues are more likely to be resolved to the parties' mutual satisfaction if healthy relationships built on mutual trust and respect have been established over the years. Leaders have always been listening to employees, and employees and managers work together as full partners. When a volatile or critical situation develops, trust will be extended to a leader who has built a trusting relationship over time.

Numerous examples exist in the area of empowerment. One mid-size hospital brought in consultants and paid hundreds of thousands of dollars for a reengineering and restructuring project. The project was believed to be essential for the organization's survival. Employees were cross trained and placed in teams and expected to assume responsibilities not only for their own work but for that of management and supervisory positions that had been eliminated. All of which might have been reasonable except that the organization had never invested in employee or management education and development. Neither employees nor managers were prepared in any way for the tremendous change this project represented. The organization needed these people to be empowered yet had never taken time nor allotted resources to develop them. Instead of empowerment for strengthening the organization, the initiative failed miserably and the hospital went on the market and was later closed. Earlier investment in its people's development could have been the turning point for this organization's survival.

## TENET 2: CONTINUALLY CHALLENGE THE PROCESS

Leaders do more than simply understand the operative process and allow it to unfold within its natural time frame. Leaders continually question the process, looking for opportunities to improve it and methods that increase its effectiveness. "Challenge is the opportunity for greatness. People do their best when there's the chance to change the ways things are. Maintaining the status quo breeds mediocrity. . . . [Leaders] motivate others to exceed their limits. They look for innovative ways to improve the organization" (Kouzes and Posner 1987, 29).

Challenging the process is accomplished by continually evaluating the effectiveness of outcomes and identifying lessons learned from the manner in which the outcomes were obtained. What went well and what actions created problems? Did the process flow smoothly or drag on too long? Did the leader intervene at appropriate times? Was enough time allotted? Did members of the group or team participate fully?

Questioning the status quo results in opportunities for improvement. Too many times the ways in which things are done in an organization are simply because "they have always been done this way." A leader challenges this thinking. Traditions are questioned: Does it make sense to continue doing things the old way? Is there a better way? Leaders are always on the lookout for something that is not working well or something that can be improved. Kouzes and Posner describe this role of the leader clearly:

The root origin of the word *lead* is a word meaning "to go." This root origin denotes travel from one place to another. Leaders can be said to be those who "go first." They are those who step out to show others the direction in which to head. They begin the quest for a new order. In this sense, leaders are pioneers. They are people who venture into unexplored territory. They guide us to new and often unfamiliar destinations. People who take the lead are the foot soldiers in the campaigns for change. (1987, 32)

Another way a leader challenges a process is to encourage risk taking. This is accomplished by taking risks themselves and growing from the lessons learned and accomplishments achieved. Leaders also encourage risk taking when they talk about their own failures and mistakes and treat these as opportunities for learning. Followers are supported when they make errors and are expected to learn from their mistakes. The overall attitude in the organization is similar to the sentiment expressed by actress Mary Pickford, who said, "If you have made mistakes . . . there is always another chance for you. . . . You may have a fresh start any moment you choose, for this thing we call 'failure' is not the falling down, but the staying down."

A risk is simply the act of seeking to achieve a goal that exceeds the usual limits. Risk is inherent in any change initiative or innovation. Exemplary leaders and followers are familiar with risk taking because it is part of their very nature. Uncertainty and danger are a normal part of this process. Taking a risk is central to everything worthwhile in life. A person cannot grow without taking a chance. In every risk there is an unavoidable loss, something that has to be given up to move ahead. Not risking is the surest way of losing. If an individual or organization continually shuns new experiences or experiments because they are risky, the result is a person or organization that is comfortable with fewer and fewer experiences. Not taking risks is a sure way to become stagnant and ill prepared for the future.

Part of a leader's role is to understand and become comfortable with risk taking. Although careful planning reduces risk considerably, no one is ever completely prepared to take a big risk. But nothing can be gained if nothing is ventured, of course. One of the most needed changes by today's managers is "to cultivate the imagination and courage to innovate—that is, to question received wisdom and constantly look for a better way. Too many managers are still afraid of innovation" (Kanter 1997, 7).

Unfortunately, this is not only true of managers and employee leaders but is seen throughout many systems. Difficulty letting go of the hospital mentality and traditional modes of service can lead to an aversion to risk sharing among physicians, community agencies, and hospitals.

Board members may also be averse to risk taking. Alan Gauthier suggests that board members have traditionally focused on narrow financial concerns and must now refocus and reorient themselves toward expressing the voice of the community (Chawla and Renesch 1995). Their role is changing, and speaking for the community may mean accepting higher levels of risk for the system.

## TENET 3: FACILITATING PROCESS

In addition to understanding and challenging the process involved, the leader has a role in actually intervening to facilitate the process flow. Facilitation skills such as managing and leading group process, addressing difficult or negative group behavior, getting participation from everyone involved, asking the right questions, and guiding a group to consensus are necessary. These are self-evident. However, there are additional techniques a leader might use to facilitate process. Teaching others the logical steps of a process is one technique. Rather than assuming followers or participants understand the process involved, the leader encourages followers to learn the sequential steps and what is expected. This smoothes the process because followers become knowledgeable enough to actively support the process and can work in partnership with the leader.

Another subtle but critical manner in which a leader facilitates process is by providing the time needed to fully engage the process. The leader must be patient and thus encourages patience in others. The leader does not look for results too early, yet urges progress based on realistic time frames and gives feedback that is reassuring and reinforcing. If the leader is a manager, this support can be very concrete, such as allotting time for staff members to work through a process while being clear about expected outcomes. In a laboratory department, for instance, a staff action committee was working with another department on solving a particular problem. The manager not only approved employee time away from the laboratory department but assisted in finding replacement help for committee participants.

Removing barriers in the department or organization is another way a leader facilitates effective processes. This may be as simple as providing any training that is needed. Being clear about parameters, expectations, and levels of authority also reduces barriers. The leader may need to communicate and pave the way with other leaders or managers in the organization. Again using the example of the laboratory department, when the staff action committee was initiated, the leader made certain that several members were skilled in using an established problem-solving model. The first meeting was used to teach other members of the committee the same model. Expectations and levels of authority for carrying out their responsibilities were established at the second meeting. The lab manager also contacted several peripherally involved department managers and introduced committee members to them, asking the managers for their support and assistance should committee members call on them.

The final way to remove barriers has already been discussed briefly, which is to reduce risks involved in the process, using trial periods and properly measuring results. Expecting and planning for mistakes and "stops and starts" provides an opportunity for damage control. Modeling accepting behavior when mistakes occur and helping sort out reasons for the mistake and how to correct it removes yet another barrier.

These three tenets, or principles, can be applied to all types of processes. The specific processes necessary for today's leader to master include empowering others, resolving conflict, problem solving and decision making, creating teams, and managing change and transition. All are key elements to increasing a leader's ability to influence others in a manner beneficial to the organization and people involved. Each process is examined in some detail and illustrated by current real-life examples to show its importance, as well as common pitfalls. The reader is encouraged to review other references for greater detail.

## EMPOWERING OTHERS

One of the most important processes undertaken by any leader today is the empowerment of others. Unfortunately, it is also one of the least understood of the key processes. Empowerment became a buzzword in the late 1980s and early 1990s, but for many, the concept never went beyond lip service. The term today is often met with cynicism and horror stories that seem to substantiate the ineffectiveness of empowerment. However, for leaders who found ways to operationalize the implied promise of empowerment, results have been dramatic.

The definition of *empowerment* is "to be given the legal authority to." The word *power* means "the ability to act or to produce a result." These two definitions combined are "to be given the legal authority to act or produce a result." Gibson defines empowerment as "a social process of recognizing, promoting, and enhancing people's abilities to meet their own needs, solve their own problems, and mobilize the necessary resources in order for them to feel in control of their lives" (1991, 351). This is very similar to the definition of leader provided in chapter 1.

Empowerment is both a process and an outcome. As a process there is a sequential order to the steps that ensure greater likelihood of success. Empowerment is dynamic because it is transactional, meaning it occurs as a result of interaction between two or more people and cannot, therefore, be completely predictable. Empowerment is a developmental process because it is directly influenced by the increasing ability of an individual to accept higher and higher levels of responsibility.

The importance of empowering people in organizations cannot be overstated. Empowered employees are fully engaged in their work, contributing at a much higher level than their counterparts who see their work as simply a job. With the constantly shifting business climate and increasingly challenging external conditions facing health care, every organization needs the ability to respond rapidly. Quick response is virtually impossible from a workforce that has to constantly be told what to do, that is basically uninformed and unused to making decisions, and that has never participated in collaborative planning. On the other hand, organizations that have dedicated resources to the continual development of their people and treat their employees as intelligent partners in the delivery of services are much more likely to have individuals who are able to respond quickly when external and internal conditions change. These employees are not dependent on the manager or leader for direction or decisions; they can function independently and interdependently when needed.

In many organizations it is not just frontline employees who are not developed and empowered, but also first-line managers. This creates a tremendous ripple effect in the organization. Rosabeth Moss Kanter is a professor at Harvard Business School and has been on the frontier of management and leadership for nearly twenty years. She points out the dangers of not empowering managers in the organization:

> Managers with power accomplish more because they have greater access to information, resources, and support in the company. Being busy, they pass the information and resources to subordinates. Thus, powerful leaders are more likely to delegate responsibility and reward talent.
>
> Powerless managers who can't easily get access to resources and information are frustrated and weak. The result is often petty, dictatorial managers who wield the only power they can: oppression of subordinates. It is powerlessness, not power, that corrupts. (Kanter 1997, 6)

Empowerment does not occur simply because a leader says "You are now empowered; go perform!" There is no magic wand to wave so that people suddenly begin behaving differently. "Empowerment takes planning, patience, trust, and time. It's not something you can do overnight. If you want it to work, you have to commit to it. You must be willing to invest in it, support it with systems, and approach it in a logical, determined way" (McCarthy 1997, 7).

## *The Process*

As a process, empowerment begins with an understanding of four inter-related concepts:

1. Capability
2. Responsibility
3. Authority
4. Accountability

The sequential application of these four concepts leads to empowerment. (See figure 5-1.) First, the meaning of each of these terms must be clarified.

***Capability***    Capability refers to the ability, knowledge, and willingness of an individual to carry out the task, assignment, or responsibility. Ability is not only personal competence comprising skill and experience but the availability of needed resources. An individual may be willing to accept a particular responsibility but simply not have the time, equipment, or resources necessary to do an adequate job. Or vice versa. The person may have ability, in terms of both personal competence and

**FIGURE 5-1.    An Empowerment Model**

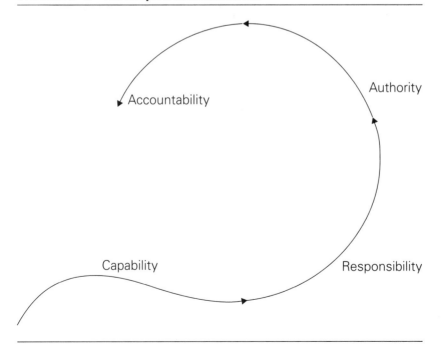

resources, but lacks willingness. All must be present or empowerment fails.

**Responsibility**    Responsibility is the clear allocation or assignment of a task or piece of work that needs to be accomplished. Responsibility also implies acceptance of this allocation by the individual involved. The person to whom the task or assignment has been given must accept ownership before this responsibility has truly been transferred. For instance, a team accepts responsibility for carrying out its work, monitoring and controlling work flow, and making necessary decisions within their scope of responsibility and authority. They are responsible for maintaining an acceptable standard and for continually searching for ways to improve their processes and outcomes.

**Authority**    Authority is the right to act in an area for which one has accepted responsibility. For responsibility to be carried out, an individual must have a commensurate level of authority. There are four commonly accepted levels of authority:

Level 1:    This is the authority to collect data or gather information. No action is taken on the data or information, and decision making is retained by the person assigning the responsibility and granting the authority.

Level 2:    Once the data is collected or information gathered, the individual involved in the gathering also reviews it and makes a recommendation based on his or her assessment and previous experience. Decision making is retained by the person assigning the responsibility and granting the authority, but the gatherer's recommendation is considered in making the final decision.

Level 3:    At this level, the individual collects and reviews the information, makes a recommendation and discusses it with the person assigning the responsibility. After their discussion and upon agreement, the individual proceeds to carry out the action.

Level 4:    This is the highest level of authority because it represents independent action. It is the right to gather information, determine what needs to be done, and take necessary action. The person accepting the assignment is authorized to act in the place of the delegating individual.

In addition to these levels of authority, the individual's responsibility or authority may be limited by constraints or parameters of a particular situation. For instance, the individual is given responsibility for making a purchasing decision with a level 4 authority but within the constraints of an established dollar amount. Or a person may be given the responsibility to make a decision and determine necessary action but only after getting agreement from certain key stakeholders.

*Accountability*     Accountability is the retrospective review of decisions made or actions taken to determine if they were appropriate. Were desired outcomes, in fact, achieved? If results were not satisfactory, what corrective action is needed to remedy the situation? This attitude of continual review is characteristic of a lifelong learner, a learning team, or a learning organization.

## Applying the Process

When a leader applies this empowerment process sequentially, it goes something like this: Before a follower is expected to take on a responsibility, the individual's ability and willingness are assessed. Does the person have the knowledge to carry out this responsibility? Are necessary resources, such as information and time, available? Has training or education been provided? Once it is determined that capability is present, the leader clearly defines and communicates the responsibility. Assumptions are not enough; the assignment must be clear to both the party accepting the responsibility and the other people who may be affected by this assignment. A discussion of applicable parameters is held, and agreement on the appropriate level of authority is reached. And, last, outcome measures are determined to monitor success.

The significance of empowerment as a developmental process is now clear. As an individual becomes more capable and highly skilled, he or she can be given more responsibility. The level of authority is gradually increased following successful performance of a responsibility. Parameters and constraints may be expanded as comfort with an individual's performance increases. It would be highly foolish, and even dangerous, to give a novice performer a level 4 authority and no constraints the first time he or she takes on a responsibility.

Using this process appears simplistic, yet there are many pitfalls and potential missteps in any health care organization today. When situations arise in which people feel disempowered, this process can be used to assess the source of the problem and to give guidance for correcting it. Here are some of the more common examples of pitfalls with each of these elements of empowerment.

*Pitfalls: Capability*     Job requirements change as a result of new needs in the organization, yet people stay in their position even though they are no longer able to do the work required. This leads to an environment of entitlement rather than earning. New expectations in the workplace can be communicated, education and training provided, and employees given time to adjust and meet new standards. However, at some point, these individuals can be expected to develop the abilities required or face a change in roles.

Another problematic situation occurs when individuals accept responsibility for something they are not capable of doing. Perhaps they believe they have the skills, but in reality they do not. This creates frustration for both parties, the individual and the leader. It also results in lengthy and potentially costly delays in completing the task.

Some individuals are simply unwilling to accept more responsibility. This creates an admittedly difficult situation for a leader or manager. With reductions in staffing levels and downsizing of organizations, everybody simply has to pull their own weight. The highest level of performance is needed from every individual, and shortfalls from those not contributing fully can simply no longer be absorbed by others. Acceptance of responsibility can be made a requirement of the job, which if not met means job loss.

Also, there may be insufficient resources for people to capably accept certain responsibilities. Time, equipment, money, education, training, or coaching may not be available, although individuals may be willing to accept additional responsibility. Today's organizations that are converting to team-based structures are good examples. Redesign of work is accomplished and team structures are determined. Employees are then assigned to these teams and expected to carry out their work in a new way without preparation in the form of education or training; and they are reporting to managers incapable of coaching a team. This creates a no-win situation.

*Pitfalls: Responsibility*    The most common pitfall with responsibility is that it is not clearly communicated but is instead assumed to be understood. For instance, a manager-leader makes the mistake of assuming that the job description clearly defines what the employee is expected to do. Nevertheless there are numerous other responsibilities for which an individual is held accountable, and these must be clearly articulated. For instance, individuals may be told: "You are responsible for maintaining healthy interpersonal relationships with your coworkers as well as with your customers." This means individuals are responsible for resolving conflicts in a positive manner and having open, honest, and direct communication with coworkers. How many employees have been clearly given this expectation?

Another problem with this element occurs when there is a significant overlapping of responsibility. In one organization the chief operating officer (COO) was a cautious individual with a bad habit of asking multiple managers to do the same tasks. A manager asked to investigate and follow up on a problem would discover that others had been asked to assume the same responsibility. This was irritating and demoralizing to the managers to find they were duplicating one another's efforts. In some rare instances it makes sense for several people to share a responsibility. But in order to avoid a disempowering and discouraging situation, the involved parties need to clearly discuss who is doing what. Few people appreciate it when they waste time in this manner.

In some instances, individuals have an exaggerated sense of responsibility and take ownership beyond what is intended. This can also lead to frustration and discouragement for all involved. In one organization, a team of internal trainers was created to provide the education and training for conversion to employee work teams. In the beginning, the team mistakenly believed that their role was to lead this initiative. They felt responsible for the success or failure of employee work teams. It did not help matters that managers in this organization abdicated their responsibility for developing the teams to the trainers. Conflict and difficulties were significant until the responsibility of each was clearly defined.

***Pitfalls: Authority***   Problems occur most frequently with the concept of authority. This area also causes the most confusion for people. Many individuals believe empowerment only occurs when they have level 4 authority and that anything less than independent action is disempowering. Nothing could be further from the truth. The level of authority has to be high enough to carry out the responsibility, and when these two are commensurate, empowerment results. Even a CEO or system president does not have level 4 authority for every aspect of his or her work. In any role, there are some responsibilities that rightfully entail a lower level of authority.

A second source of confusion around authority comes from the mistaken, but commonly held, belief that lower levels of authority are not as important. Many mistakes and poor decisions are made in today's organizations because of this misconception. Individuals are asked for their opinion or to gather information, but because they are not making the final decision, they do a halfhearted job of collecting or giving the requested information. The individual making a final decision is disadvantaged because of poor-quality input. Each level of authority is critical, and responsibilities with each level of authority must be taken seriously.

Levels of authority may be falsely assumed by both performers and leaders unless they are specifically discussed and agreed upon. Conflict occurs when it becomes apparent that there is disagreement. Quality or problem-solving teams often run into this situation. In one organization this occurred in the nursing department with a very visible employee team that had been asked to develop a clinical career ladder for the department. The team worked diligently for months and created an entire program based on extensive research from other hospitals.

On the verge of implementation, they were stopped by the corporate human resource department because of compensation issues and a need for equity across the entire system. Home health and long-term care had not been included, nor had any other professional departments. This team had unwittingly exceeded their level of authority, and as a result, a significant amount of resentment and frustration developed among the hospital nursing department, corporate human resources, and the rest of the system.

Changing levels of authority in the middle of a project is sometimes necessary but should be avoided if at all possible. A leader or manager may have given a responsibility and agreed upon its level of authority, only to recall or decrease the level of authority when the individual or group does not carry out the work in the way the manager-leader expected. There are, however, multiple ways of achieving necessary outcomes, and a confident leader recognizes the need to relinquish control and let followers find their own way. If the project or assignment is snatched away midstream, the result leaves a bad taste for the followers and an unwillingness to accept further responsibility.

New authority-related problems are appearing today with the major structural changes in the workplace. In the past, managers were clearly delegated a certain level of authority and reporting relationships were delineated and unambiguous. For many people in today's health care system, this has changed completely. Take, for example, the role of the nurse executive in today's hospital who is responsible for the nursing function throughout the organization. The responsibility has become increasingly difficult to carry out now that it is dispersed among a variety of leader-managers, some of whom have no professional nursing background and may report directly to a different executive. Communicating the essence of nursing issues and ensuring quality standards in the absence of line authority requires strong leadership skills.

A final problem related to authority is the reversal of authority. This occurs when a leader undermines the work of an individual or group or simply shows a lack of respect for the final decision. The most frequent cause of this behavior is that the leader neglected to identify key parameters up front and the decision made was based on incomplete information. Less frequently, the leader may have had no intention of relinquishing control but wanted others to feel as if they participated.

In the early days of the quality movement, this lesson was frequently learned the hard way. One quality team worked for six months on a specific problem. Their recommendation cost $200,000 to implement and included the addition of several full-time-equivalent positions to the annual personnel budget. No one thought to tell the team that any recommendation could not exceed the current budget. Unfortunately, their experience led them to conclude that administration was not serious about involving employees in decision making and that quality was not a primary concern. Although members of the team were selected because of their interest and commitment, they became unwilling after this experience to participate in any further projects. Sadly, these budget constraints would have been acceptable if they had been identified in the beginning stages of work.

Sometimes group members attempt to undermine decisions. A medical clinical affairs committee discovered this in one organization. The director of medical affairs (DMA) was given the authority to solve a problem within a certain dollar amount. Two weeks later he reported on his actions. Two physicians who had not been present at the previous meeting began questioning and second-guessing his decision. The chair of the committee firmly reminded them that the DMA had been given the authority to solve the problem and that his decision would be supported.

*Pitfalls: Accountability*    Although problems with authority are the most common, issues concerning accountability are often the most serious. This element is potentially the weakest link in the chain. If people are not held accountable for their behaviors and actions, whatever may be done through the first three steps can be quickly negated. One reason so many things go right in organizations today is because many employees and leaders feel a high level of personal accountability, continually reviewing their outcomes and learning from them. People who are continual learners demonstrate a high level of internal accountability. Nevertheless, there are many problems with external accountability, or the formal, traceable lines of accountability in the organization.

Most organizations have only limited systems of accountability. It can sometimes be very difficult to ascertain what went wrong and why. Increasing numbers of part-time staff and per diem or temporary employees have made determining who is responsible when a problem occurs rather complicated. Assignments of staff are not consistent and many "handoffs" from caregiver to caregiver and department to department increase the difficulty of tracking.

The recent move to create employee work teams is one way to increase accountability. When patient care work teams are clearly responsible for specific patients and assignments are consistent, the team can be held accountable for patient outcomes. A seasoned, mature team can even become case managers and responsible for patients' lengths of stay.

Another issue hampering accountability is the tendency of managers and leaders to protect employees. When an individual or team makes a mistake or poor decision, the real role of leader is to coach and support them in their efforts to correct the situation. Too often the manager steps in and takes responsibility for correcting the problem. Take, for example, a situation in which a physician has a complaint about a team and goes to the manager. If the manager takes care of the problem, the team has learned little except that it is not capable of resolving its customer service problems. On the other hand, if the manager coaches the team to work directly with the physician to resolve the issue, both the team and the physician benefit. The manager's behavior is sometimes motivated by his or her satisfaction in solving problems or, in some cases, by expectations within the hierarchy. Many established bureaucracies have only limited tolerance for these situations and simply want them resolved in the quickest fashion possible.

The final major pitfall for accountability is that the consequences of mistakes or poor judgment are too often punitive rather than corrective. Many organizational climates today are characterized by blame and accusation when things go wrong. These negative, punitive responses are probably the fastest way to squelch responsibility acceptance. People are quick learners; and they also watch what happens to their colleagues and coworkers. Swift retribution designed at extinguishing poor performance, in reality, extinguishes all performance. People are not willing to take risks in a harsh and unforgiving environment.

## Summary

This process for empowering others is key to effective leadership. It creates mechanisms for delegating responsibility and developing people. Without leadership's astute application of these skills, people in the organization are less likely to contribute at their highest potential.

# CONFLICT RESOLUTION

Conflict in the workplace is on the rise as major change disrupts comfortable routines, accelerated expectations require greater job performance, and the workforce shrinks as a result of work redesign and downsizing. People going through change and transition experience a wide range of intense emotional reactions, heightening the potential for conflict.

## Common Reactions to Conflict

Most people react to conflict in a negative manner for a variety of reasons. These include early socialization patterns, when parents admonished children for being angry or fighting with siblings, or past negative experiences with conflict. Perhaps the individual remembers how it felt as a child to hear his or her parents argue and fight with each other. If the arguments and conflict ended in physical abuse or divorce, the message imbedded in the child may be that conflict is bad. On the other hand, if a child never saw or heard his or her parents disagree or argue with each other, the result may be that the child believes conflict is to be avoided at all costs. The child may never have seen steps taken for healthy conflict resolution and concludes that conflict does not exist in healthy relationships. Another factor influencing an adult's reaction to conflict is the normal need to feel in control of situations. Intense conflict is frightening for many because of its unpredictability and the sense of control that is missing.

To effectively assist in the resolution of conflict, leaders with insight into their own reaction to conflict are an asset. Each leader has specific skills that are more highly developed. For instance, one leader may be especially skilled at mediating, while another may be a skilled negotiations coach. One may stay calm under attack, while another needs time away to separate emotions from interventions. Knowing and tapping into one's own strengths increases the ability to assist others.

Understanding and accepting one's limitations are also vital. Very few people actually enjoy being involved in open conflict, but a strong leader recognizes that it is part of everyday life in any organization or workplace—every relationship has within it the elements of potential conflict. Conflicts are often avoided because emotions run high, egos respond to attack, people feel hurt, and solutions seem elusive and difficult to reach.

### The Positive Side of Conflict

When conflict is considered a normal part of the environment, it takes on a more positive aspect. Teams, for instance, go through a normal stage of development called *storming* in which the predominant characteristic is conflict. Members argue about everything, disagree with the team leader and each other, and resist even good ideas. Healthy teams learn how to resolve conflict from these experiences as they work out these issues together. The team becomes stronger by confronting and addressing differences and conflicts rather than avoiding or ignoring them. What is true for teams is also true for individuals. Too many people believe that avoidance is the best approach for dealing with conflict, but all it does is delay the inevitable confrontation.

Conflict can serve as a positive, driving force for change and improvement. It often exposes true feelings, which leads to a better frame of mind and increases the likelihood that resolution will occur. When one party shares true feelings, it allows others to understand how strongly that individual feels. Open conflict can save time in an organization because excessive politeness and courtesy may mean that nothing is accomplished. When there is conflict over procedures, policies, or systems in place, it forces examination of the status quo. Maybe something needs to be changed to prevent a serious problem later. An honest dispute often engenders a greater mutual respect among individuals and a clearer understanding of the positions of both sides. Seeing others disagree and work out conflicts encourages the more timid to express their opinions, which they might otherwise have never shared.

The benefits of open conflict were demonstrated clearly by a clinical information systems team in a midsize hospital in the South. For the first six months, they worked beautifully together, becoming a strong team and establishing their purpose and working approaches. At this point, however, a major conflict about working approaches erupted during a team meeting in which the external leader-manager was not present. The team had agreed on a specific procedure for documenting "help calls" received from customers that would allow the team to measure outcomes and evaluate their service. One team member, the computer systems person for the laboratory, continued to document her help calls in the manner to which she had been accustomed, thus creating problems for the team in tracking their outcomes.

When open conflict exploded between this individual and other members, the team spent the entire meeting trying to work through this issue. Weeks later they still expressed negative feelings about the conflict and believed that they should have handled the situation better. In exploring these feelings, the leader asked the team to identify what they had learned from the situation. They came up with thirteen specific things that were positive about either the way they had handled the conflict or what they had learned from the experience. This discussion immediately shifted their perception from "conflict is bad" to "conflict can help us grow."

## The Leadership Role

In organizations where employees are empowered, they assume responsibility for having healthy relationships with others in the workplace, which means being responsible for effective resolution of conflicts. In team-based organizations, team members are responsible for resolving conflicts that occur. In both instances, however, employees need a leader to coach them as they learn these nontraditional skills and at times to serve as mediator. The role of a leader is to develop others in their conflict resolution skills and intervene only as necessary. Leaders use a variety of approaches for conflict resolution and should avoid those that are only partially effective.

## Ineffective Methods of Conflict Resolution

These are strategies that seem effective over the short term, but because the solution is not mutually beneficial to the involved parties, all are not committed to supporting the solution. Strategies that appear to solve the conflict but instead produce frustration, distrust, and a feeling of being treated unfairly include

- Competing
- Coercion
- Intimidation and dominance
- Persuasion
- Procrastination and avoidance
- Coalition building
- Accommodation

*Competing*    Competing is an ineffective strategy for resolving conflict because it encourages a "scarcity mind-set" in which there is never enough (time, resources, financial support) to go around. It creates a win-lose situation rather than win-win. The sense of sharing for mutual benefit is not even considered when individuals or teams are pitted against each other; for one to win, the other must lose.

*Coercion*    Either overt or covert coercion seems to settle the matter quickly, too, but actually results in resentment. Leaders must be careful when serving as mediators not to use coercion. Simply the influence held by the leader expressing an opinion can feel like coercion to others. If the leader is also a manager, this is doubly important. The legitimate authority of a managerial position can give unfair weight to the manager's opinion. Coercion can also occur among peers. One individual may feel coerced into accepting a disagreeable point of view in the interest of preserving harmony among the group.

*Intimidation and Dominance*    Similar to coercion, these are pressure tactics based on power relationships. In the short term they may seem to be effective, but many people find them distasteful. Intimidation and dominance can destroy trust in a relationship because of use of unfair advantage.

*Persuasion*    Persuasion is a strategy commonly used by articulate, charismatic people. The problem with persuasion is that the persuader ends up psychologically superior to the persuaded individual. When persuasion is used, it becomes more and more difficult over time to keep people focused on the solution. Greater "doses" of persuasion are needed as people begin thinking for themselves and questioning the solution they were persuaded to accept.

*Procrastination and Avoidance*    Putting off any real resolution of the disagreement or conflict is the basis of this strategy. It usually causes the conflict to feed on itself and become worse with time. A short delay in dealing with the conflict is often used to see if it will work itself out. Although this is appropriate and effective in some instances, delays in addressing conflict should be used judiciously and not allowed to interfere with effective resolution of the conflict.

*Coalition Building*    Alliances, in the positive sense, are often needed to get something accomplished. As a means of resolving conflict, however, building coalitions can be negative because it forces people to choose sides. This increases the likelihood of head-to-head battles. Unfortunately, this is one of the more common approaches to resolving conflict in health care today. Employees who feel unable to obtain what they need through their own efforts talk to physicians in an attempt to engage them in the cause. Department managers in conflict with one another often talk to other managers in an attempt to build support for their positions. This has actually been viewed as effective executive strategy: getting all the "ducks in a line" before a key meeting. Purposely talking with others to bring them to a certain point of view is building a coalition, which may work well when the group is planning or making a decision. But it is ineffective over the long haul in resolution of active conflict.

*Accommodation*    Accommodation is a strategy that is helpful at times, but it tends to be overused. It means that one party is giving up its rights or desires and allowing the other's rights or desires to take precedence. In some instances this may be appropriate in order to benefit the whole. One problem with accommodation is that it tends to be the same individual or group that allows this and they eventually grow to resent the situation. Accommodation can result in perceptions of uneven status and foster long-term resentments. Individuals who usually seek harmony may begin to feel that others are taking advantage of them.

## Effective Methods of Conflict Resolution

Although in the real world, a perfect solution to conflict simply does not exist, there are several potentially effective strategies that can be attempted. These enable the parties involved to deal with the conflict in an open, positive manner while limiting the conflict's negative impact. Effective methods of resolution include:

- Appeal
- Mediation
- Superordinate Goals
- Peaceful Coexistence
- Negotiation

***Appeal*** This strategy allows any party to take a decision to a higher level or to someone who is not emotionally involved with the situation. Appeal is powerful because both parties in a conflict realize that a decision can be appealed, which inspires them to seek resolution more honestly. The grievance procedure that exists in most organizations is a good example of an appeal process. However, it can be more informally used within a team or between individuals by simply agreeing to take the decision to an uninvolved third party for a decision. When appeal is used, both parties must agree to support the decision rendered.

***Mediation*** Although similar to appeal because a third party is involved, mediation is different. It requires the involvement of a knowledgeable and trusted third party to act as an intermediary for all involved in the conflict. The objective viewpoint of the mediator can often diffuse emotions and serve as a catalyst to reach a mutually agreeable solution. When the leader serves as a coach for conflicting parties in a team, this is an example of mediation. In some instances, each party has their own coach.

***Superordinate Goals*** Finding a goal that transcends the special interests of both parties is an excellent strategy for resolving conflict. This is a *superordinate goal*, which leaders use frequently, perhaps without even realizing it. Asking people to forgo minor differences and stay focused on the overriding purpose and vision is an example of this approach. The urgent deadlines and immense challenges facing a work group often pull them together and facilitate the speedy resolution of conflicts that arise.

***Peaceful Coexistence*** This strategy is useful in selected situations when the parties in conflict can stay "on their side of the fence" without negative impact. If two team members, for instance, find each other abrasive, they can still agree to work together peacefully if there is some separation, such as working different shifts or in different departments or not having a significant amount of interdependent work to do. The leader gets the involved parties to agree to the old adage of "I don't have to like you to work well with you." This approach works only if there are clear expectations set and the involved parties agree to work within them. The level of productivity of the work group must not be affected by these attitudes.

**Negotiation**    Probably the most effective strategy for resolving conflict is negotiation. This strategy is based on a win-win problem-solving approach in which no one involved has to give up anything that is essential to him or her. Negotiation is a process of mutual agreement. It is approached from a win-win stance and takes place with a spirit of cooperation rather than conflict. It is the most powerful strategy for conflict resolution simply because in any work situation, the parties involved are likely to interact with each other over the long term. If win-win solutions are found, each party will be committed to supporting these decisions. If one of the ineffective strategies is used, such as coercion, a subsequent conflict among the same people will be much more difficult to resolve. The party who lost in the first round is likely to be waiting for the next opportunity to get even.

Nierenberg and Ross (1985) outline a specific process for negotiating that they refer to as a negotiation map. On this map, the steps for negotiating a conflict are:

1. Define the issue
2. Clarify objectives
3. Gather all relevant information
4. Identify alternatives
5. Select strategies

*Step 1: Define the issue:*  The need to define the real issues in a negotiation may seem to be self-evident, but a good negotiator makes no assumptions. For example, when a team and manager are experiencing conflict about a decision made by the manager, the real issue may not be the outcome or decision but the fact that the manager made the decision rather than allowing the team to do so within its clearly identified parameters. These are two very different issues; the real issue may be the team's decision-making authority.

The first step is to determine that both sides of the dispute share an understanding of the issue. This requires honesty and the ability to disclose hidden agendas. Both parties must trust each other enough to share information openly, without fearing that the other party will use the information in an adversarial manner. Hidden agendas and personal issues can destroy the ability of individuals to effectively negotiate.

One newly formed executive team was in the process of negotiating their assignments when a hidden agenda blocked their progress. Five new executives had been appointed but not yet assigned to specific care centers. In a meeting to determine division of responsibility, one of the new team members, Lynette, was operating with a hidden agenda. She did not want to be assigned to a particular care center. Throughout the discussion, every comment and suggestion Lynette made was based on her avoiding taking an assignment to that particular care center rather than focusing on what was best for the organization. The meeting ended in a stalemate with Lynette in tears. Her teammates were flabbergasted because the decision was not emotional in nature to them and they were not sure what was happening. The team decided to think about the possibilities over the weekend and return on Monday to further discuss it prior to making a decision.

When the facilitator talked with Lynette and discovered the important personal agenda she was keeping hidden, Lynette was advised to be open with her teammates and share her strong feelings. When she did so, the team was able to rapidly reach a decision that was good not only for the organization but for each team member.

*Step 2: Clarify objectives:* In this second step on the map, each party determines what is desired. This sounds somewhat simplistic but people often limit themselves by limiting their objectives. Thinking broadly about objectives may extend the possibilities to be tried in negotiation. Each side may have a range of objectives that would be satisfactory.

An example of this arose during the annual performance appraisal of an excellent department secretary in a home health agency. Renee was a superbly skilled secretary but functioned more as a direct assistant to the leader of a special program. During her annual review she requested that she be promoted to an executive assistant position. The manager knew this was impossible in the current setting because there could only be one executive assistant position in the agency. In talking with Renee, the manager asked why she was interested in the promotion. Was the title important? The increase in pay? The type of work included in the job? Renee's response was interesting. She had noticed that the executive assistant was the only clerical person who attended workshops and seminars at the company's expense. Renee valued continuing education and wanted the same opportunity. Fortunately this was something that the manager could provide, so once this objective was identified, a win-win solution was easily achieved.

*Step 3: Gather all relevant information:* This next step includes gathering any relevant facts, identifying operative assumptions, and determining needs of the involved parties. Facts are important because they determine how negotiable certain positions are. The more facts shared between the parties, the more successful the negotiation. Checking out the assumptions of all parties is absolutely critical because more people make decisions based on assumptions than on facts. Both before and during an active negotiation, both parties sharing openly what they need increases the likelihood of a successful win-win negotiation. Priority needs should not be confused with peripheral needs. For negotiation to have lasting results, both parties must have their needs satisfied so each has a stake in the continued success of the solution.

When a laboratory manager was asked by a physician to have lab results available for early morning rounds, she discovered that to draw the lab specimens early enough, patients would have to be awakened at 5 A.M.! Most patients would be highly dissatisfied by this early awakening. Furthermore, although the request had been made to sound as though many physicians had wanted it, investigation revealed that only one or two other physicians had been involved in the request. Another false assumption was the physicians' belief that this would be a "budget neutral" request. Also, in terms of needs, it initially appeared to require a major shift in the lab staff's schedule. But when the facts were checked out, the manager discovered the only day this was really needed was Sundays, when the physicians involved wanted to attend early church services and therefore to make rounds earlier than usual.

*Step 4: Identify alternatives:*  In this step all possible alternatives are considered. As when identifying objectives, widening the range of possibilities makes it more likely a mutually acceptable solution will be found. After brainstorming to uncover all options from both parties, it is appropriate to begin to whittle them down to acceptable alternatives.

In the previous example of the lab manager and the physicians requesting earlier lab reports, numerous ideas were considered. Was there a technological fix? Was the lab already considering newer, faster equipment? Could schedules be changed easily by floor or lab staff? Was no change actually best for all involved? Could lab services be decentralized or redeployed to smaller, more local labs nearer the patient units?

From the list of possible alternatives, at least two, and preferably three, reasonable alternatives must be generated. Locking onto one acceptable alternative can be a trap in negotiation because it results in an ultimatum. Multiple alternatives allow for true choice.

*Step 5: Select strategies:*  Once acceptable alternatives are identified, action must be determined. Strategies are the actions to be taken both during and after the negotiation and include the type of climate to set for an effective negotiation. Climate should be fluid and dynamic in every negotiation. Nierenberg and Ross (1985) believe that the party controlling the climate has more influence over the negotiation, and positive climates are generally accepted by the other party, while negative climates are resisted.

The lab manager in the previous example, for instance, thought through the information she had and how to present it to the physicians.

Part of her strategy may have been to discuss their needs more fully and to share the assumptions she discovered. Sharing the facts she had collected may have helped if these physicians were logical thinkers. She probably also considered strategies for establishing a positive climate. Would the discussion take place in her office, the physician's office, the dining room?

This negotiation map works best when it is treated as a dynamic process. To prepare for a negotiation, each individual works through the map first from his or her own perspective and then from the perspective of the other party. The most effective negotiators are those who are clear about their own positions and not overly accommodating, yet flexible when the other party has a valid point. This role is most easily assumed when each step of the negotiation process has been fully considered. Clear expectations between the parties for obtaining a win-win situation can result in effective negotiation. In the integration case example in chapter 3, the law firms for the parties involved were both told they must find a win-win solution. This powerful message clearly avoided the development of adversarial positioning.

***Pitfalls of Conflict Resolution***     The most common pitfall related to conflict resolution is a tendency to avoid dealing with it. Although few people approach a conflict situation with enthusiasm, there are some individuals who absolutely abhor conflict of any kind and thus greatly reduce their effectiveness because they simply won't deal with it. Modeling this behavior as a leader sends the wrong message to followers, who will think: If the leader cannot effectively deal with conflict, why should we bother?

One health care entrepreneur is a good example for this pitfall. A visionary head of his own company, Bob had attained great success. However, his Achilles' heel was an inability to deal with conflict. In his organization, he had retained several costly employees who consistently underperformed, yet he dreaded a confrontation over their lack of performance. Not only did they contribute significantly to a high overhead, but the company lost several excellent performers who were not willing to continue to work hard to cover the salaries of the nonperformers.

Bob worked diligently to expand the company's services, and one strategy involved partnering with other companies. These relationships began with great enthusiasm and high hopes, but at the first sign of any conflict (and what relationship is without it?), Bob would withdraw his support and sever the relationship. Needless to say, the company's reputation began to deteriorate. The source of all of these problems was Bob's intense discomfort with conflict.

A second common pitfall exists when a leader is so emotionally attached to an outcome that it becomes difficult or impossible to objectively identify possible alternatives. Too often these situations reach an impasse at which point an ultimatum is delivered. This is rarely, if ever, a healthy way to resolve conflict. An example of this was averted in a midsize hospital in the Southwest. Liz, the vice president of patient services, was trusted explicitly by the CEO, to whom she had reported for years. John, the CEO, supported her decisions and valued her judgment. On this occasion, a recruiting process for a new director of preoperative services was underway. There were no viable internal candidates, from her perspective, and recruiting efforts had brought forth only two external possibilities. Suddenly a couple of the anesthesiologists decided they would recommend one of the staff nurses for promotion. The suggestion fell on deaf ears—Liz felt the individual was not qualified for this promotion for a number of valid reasons. When the physicians were unable to achieve their goal through Liz, they immediately bombarded the CEO's office. John sent the physicians back to Liz but also talked to Liz directly about the recommendation. Liz's immediate response was concern that if John told her she must hire this individual, she would have to resign. She did not believe she could continue in her position if he interfered in such a way with her authority.

After discussing the situation with an objective colleague, several alternatives were identified that helped prevent the situation from escalating into an out-and-out conflict. Liz set up an interview process that included staff members, other managers, surgeons, and anesthesiologists. Selection criteria were identified ahead of time, and each candidate was evaluated against these measures. As a result, the anesthesiologists realized for themselves the limitations of their personal favorite.

The final major pitfall with significant consequences is seeing conflict only in a negative light. This creates an organizational culture where disagreements are not expressed openly because of fear they may damage a relationship, conflicts are repressed, and people do not express their honest reactions to ideas or events because of possible repercussions. When this is the organizational culture, managers and leaders have little experience using the effective methods of conflict resolution because conflict is viewed as something to be avoided at all costs.

This described the organizational culture in one eastern seaboard medical center that was part of a large system. One of the system's four hospitals underwent a major reengineering initiative. Planning took two years, with employees and key stakeholders heavily involved. Implementation of the new design began on the first two units and, as would be expected during major change, multiple conflicts arose. Implementation did not proceed as smoothly as anticipated and physician and patient complaints increased. The conflicts were seen as a sign that the change was not working, and the COO pulled the plug on the entire project! Years of work and hundreds of thousands of dollars were lost because the conflict was interpreted as failure rather than a normal step along the process.

## PROBLEM SOLVING AND DECISION MAKING

Problem solving and decision making are two key processes guided by knowledgeable leaders. Often these two terms are used interchangeably, but they are not synonymous. All effective problem solving results in decisions. In fact, unless decisions are made and actions implemented, problem solving is a misnomer and would more accurately be called problem processing! And, most effective decision making involves some degree of problem solving. Decisions, however, can be made with no problem solving.

### *Problem Solving*

In hierarchical, top-down organizations, problem solving is limited in terms of both who is involved and the kinds of problems around which groups meet. Group problem solving is a "bottom-up" process requiring a visionary leader—a leader who can relinquish control sufficiently to create an environment for employee empowerment. When problem-solving groups are prevalent in an organization, it is a good sign of employee involvement. And knowledgeable leaders understand that it is difficult for individuals to feel empowered if they have no tools with which to solve pressing problems directly affecting their ability to do their work.

Most effective problem-solving processes include some variation of the following five steps, as outlined in figure 5-2:

1. Problem identification and analysis
2. A desired future statement
3. Solution generation
4. Analysis of options
5. Action planning and implementation
6. Evaluation

Regardless of what these steps are called, a skilled leader understands that this process must be both sequential and methodical. All steps must be included, and in the appropriate sequence, in order to obtain a quality outcome. Often what passes for problem solving is some spontaneous, inconsistently applied brainstorming technique that follows no proven methodology and misses one or more important steps.

**FIGURE 5-2.   The Problem-Solving Process**

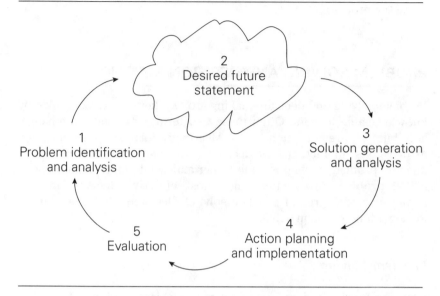

The following problem-solving process can be used effectively by either individuals or groups. Group problem solving is the format considered for purposes of this discussion.

***Step 1: Problem Identification and Analysis***   In the first step of a problem-solving process, the group describes and, ultimately, defines and analyzes the problem. The discussion typically begins with descriptions of symptoms or other evidence of a problem as it affects various members of the group. In many instances, initial statements of the problem are vague and confused. Sometimes additional information is needed before a problem statement can be written.

It is important to surface as many characteristics of the problem as possible at this point and to avoid jumping to hasty conclusions. Psychologists who have experimented with thinking for over 70 years have discovered that once a person offers an explanation, they have difficulty revising it or dropping it, even in the face of contradictory information. In experiments, subjects were shown an out-of-focus 35-millimeter slide of a fire hydrant. The psychologists found that if a person wrongly identified the object when it was out of focus, he or she often could not identify it when it was brought sufficiently into focus so that another person (who had not seen the blurry slide) could easily recognize it. Their conclusion was significant: More evidence is required to overcome an incorrect hypothesis than to establish a correct one. Individuals who jumped to a hasty conclusion were less sensitive to new ideas and information (Adams 1986).

Questions often help to define the problem more fully. What are signs and symptoms of this problem? Who is it impacting? Directly or indirectly? What is the frequency of occurrence? What are all possible causes or factors involved? The group may determine that more information or data are required.

During this first step, another important issue to consider is ownership. How have the group or individuals within the group contributed to or created the current problem? This is critical to determine because those alternatives over which the group has control bring a higher rate of success. This is difficult for many groups, who may begin by believing that the fault for the problem lies elsewhere. By pushing themselves, however, they usually begin to see how they have helped created the current situation.

Caregivers in one organization were angry because they often did not have enough clean linen in the morning to complete changing the patients' beds. They clearly attributed the problem to the linen services department. When forced to look at their own role in creating the problem, they were clueless. They continued to insist that it was the fault of linen services. But with persistent prodding, they gradually began to come up with ideas. "We stopped attending the liaison meeting with linen services because we didn't think they were listening." They also recalled being told that over $200,000 in scrub clothes were replaced during the year because of employee theft. That money could have helped pay for a higher-capacity washing machine that would process linens faster. The final contributing factor that they identified was their common practice of hoarding linen and stashing it in all kinds of places so that it would be available when needed. This practice had made it impossible to get an accurate inventory count, which caused planning by linen services to be based on inaccurate figures. Once these issues were identified, the group began to work more effectively on the problem.

The problem statement is a concise description of the problem. Novice problem-solving groups sometimes actually put a solution into the problem statement. One group, for example, came up with "The problem is inadequate staffing." So stated, this limits problem-solving creativity because the solution becomes "Get more staff." When the problem statement is changed to "There is more work than the current staff can handle," multiple possibilities become apparent, including eliminating some of the work, changing the way it is being done, and temporary adjustments in staffing levels.

Once the problem is clearly identified, the group determines its level of authority in solving the problem. Determining the level of authority at this point is crucial so that everyone's expectations are appropriate. Necessary communication and involvement with others in the organization can be planned. Just because a group has a low level of authority does not preclude this group's working on a particular problem; and clarity about authority levels will prevent misunderstandings later, when it is time to implement decisions.

Compare these two groups: Both chose to work on a problem for which they had only level 1 authority. The issue was employee benefits. The first group was very aware of its level of authority. The members spent their time investigating the problem and gathering information, and based on their findings, they made recommendations for the human resource department to consider. Their work focused on a desired future that included the successful presentation of their information and specific steps aimed at their strategies for delivering the recommendations.

The second group had not clarified its level of authority. The members proceeded with enthusiasm throughout the entire process, developing a future vision that included employee benefits, offered in a "buffet-style" approach, from which employees could select. Their action planning revolved around the implementation of the new benefits. They were excited and eager when they finished the problem-solving process only to become frustrated and angry when their work was never acted upon. The members of the group cynically observed that it was the last time they would volunteer for a problem-solving task force, never realizing that they had exceeded their level of authority.

*Step 2: Desired Future Statement*    A common mistake problem-solving groups make is to focus almost exclusively on the problem and its causes rather than on what they would like to build or create for the future. Russell Ackoff, the creator of interactive planning, has demonstrated clearly that solutions are more creative if the focus remains on desired outcomes rather than on details of the current problem (Ackoff, Finnel, and Gharajedaghi 1984).

This step involves asking the question: "What would this look like if there were no problem, if it were solved?" The group then writes a description of the ideal situation. So, for example, if the group's problem statement is "Communication between hospital and home health personnel is poor, creating problems in delivery of quality patient care," a desired future statement might be "Communication between hospital and home health personnel is free flowing, timely, and accurate." In another system, a group was working on coordinating community services for seniors. Their desired future statement read: "Community services for seniors are coordinated and easily accessible to participants, with information flowing freely and fluidly between agencies for the benefit of our customers."

Focusing exclusively on the problem statement leads to more limited solutions. A clear, desirable future statement creates a picture for those involved and generates more imaginative and original ideas, as well as a broader scope of possibilities.

***Step 3: Solution Generation and Analysis of Alternatives***    This stage is both creative and analytical, and it is critical that the two phases of this step are separated. The group first generates all possible solutions. Analysis, discussion, and critical thinking about the solutions are withheld until all solutions are identified. Nothing impairs creative flow faster than criticism or an analysis of the ideas as they are presented. Several creativity techniques are useful for generating ideas:

- Nominal group technique
- Mind mapping
- List making
- Attribute analysis
- Storyboards

Described only briefly here, they can be reviewed in more detail in the many books available about innovation or creativity.

*Nominal group technique:*  This method is often confused with brainstorming, which is unfortunate because most people think of brainstorming as a loose, free-flowing process with few guidelines. Nominal group technique involves a specific process that results in successful outcomes (Delbecq and VandeVen 1971). The nominal group technique combines quiet, individual thinking time with a structured yet free-flowing sharing of ideas, a technique that is especially useful when group members vary in verbal and other expressive skills.

First, the leader asks a question about the problem, to which group members will individually respond in a specific way. For instance, if the desired future is to have communication between two agencies to be free flowing, timely, and accurate, the leader may solicit responses regarding characteristics required to achieve this state. The group members then individually write down all responses that come to mind after the leader either specifies either how many ideas (say, 5 to 10) each participant should list or the time frame in which the list should be completed (perhaps five minutes).

Next, the leader provides these guidelines for sharing the ideas:

- Taking turns, every participant will give one idea at a time.
- No one is to react in any way to the ideas as they are being presented, which means no clarification or discussion of any kind at this point.
- If a group member runs out of ideas, they can pass until their next turn, when they may present another idea if they have one.

The leader lists each idea on a flip chart or board, with no rewording of the idea, until all ideas from the group have been written for the group to see. Once the ideas are gathered, the facilitator leads a discussion of the ideas to clarify, elaborate, defend, dispute, or add to the items. The list is reviewed and categories are identified. Some items may be combined or eliminated.

*Mind mapping:* This technique is similar to the nominal group process but the recording of ideas is done in a circular fashion. In a box or oval drawn in the center of the chart or board, one or two words that capture the essence of the issue are printed. From the previous example it might be "communication between agencies." As the thoughts and ideas on this topic pour out from the members, the facilitator prints the key words of those thoughts around the essence statement and then connects them to the box with lines. As ideas are generated that relate to one of those branches, the idea's key word is printed and then attached to the branch with a line. Even totally unrelated ideas are captured and printed because they may spark an idea for someone else. Wycoff explains, "Two things happen when you allow yourself to put the idea down—the first is that the mind is freed to go onto other ideas, and the second is that associations are made with this idea. This is where the best ideas come from" (1991, 48).

*List making:* List making is a commonly used conceptualization technique. It uses the construction of lists as a method of forcing alternative thinking. A simple and effective approach, it starts simply with a question or issue, and then the group members generate a list of ideas to address the subject. The value of list making lies in the fact that checklists require a person to consciously control his or her thinking in order to focus on alternatives that the unconscious mind might ignore in trying to simplify life (Adams 1986).

List making was used in a head injury rehabilitation center to discover ways of improving the environment for clients (Manion 1990). Groups of staff members were asked to think about things that they would miss or want if they were confined by a head injury to a rehabilitation facility for the months that recovery would require. Lists were generated and then used to guide changes in the environment at the center. Items generated included the following:

- Pictures of family and friends
- The feel of sun or rain on my face
- The feel of sand between my toes
- The smell of coffee in the morning
- My hair and makeup done every day
- Shopping trips

- Favorite television programs
- Favorite music
- My children staying overnight with me
- Surprises
- Sleeping late in the morning
- Popcorn
- Ability to make my own decisions
- My pets

*Attribute analysis:* If the attributes of a situation are considered, problem solvers come to different conclusions than if operating with generalized stereotyping. Attribute analysis involves breaking the common tendency to frequently use generalization. The three steps for this process are:

1. List the attributes of the situation.
2. Below each attribute, list as many alternatives as possible.
3. When completed, make many random runs through the alternates, selecting a different one from each column and assembling combinations of entirely new forms of the original subject.

This approach was used by the staff of a new outpatient surgical center wanting to design a user-friendly system with correspondingly "friendly" processes. They began by listing attributes of a user-friendly system: easy access to the building, convenient parking, comfortable waiting facilities for family or friends, speedy admission processes, simplified discharge procedures, a pleasant atmosphere, and procedures scheduled for the convenience of the client. They then listed the specific attributes under each of these characteristics. Below convenient parking, for example, was listed "covered, inexpensive or free, safe, and not far from the door or shuttle service."

By listing these various attributes and going through the lists several times in different ways, the staff generated several unique (at the time) approaches that enabled the new center to quickly capture a large segment of the market. These approaches included valet parking, procedures scheduled for the convenience of clients (after-work hours were in high demand), discharge prescriptions available prior to surgery to eliminate a stop at the pharmacy on the way home, comedy videos in the waiting room, beepers for family members so they can be called back to the waiting area, and snacks or meals for waiting family members.

*Storyboards:* The storyboard was created by Walt Disney as a planning method for his animators (Vance 1982). It is used to develop and record the creative thinking process. In this context, corkboards or wallboards are used, and cards with ideas are attached to the board. When ideas are visibly recorded, it is often easier to see their interconnections. One idea often ignites others, and participants can add cards as they come up with ideas. The advantage to using cards is that they can be easily rearranged or discarded. This is a useful technique for stimulating and recording ideas between meetings of the problem-solving group.

One executive team adopted this idea to use during their strategic planning. In developing a group vision, members were each given a pad of Post-it notes and asked to write down one idea per note that described an element of their vision. Individuals generated as many as 25 items each. These were then shared and stuck on large pieces of paper around the room. As the notes were discussed, categories began emerging, and subsequent ideas were placed on appropriate pages. It proved a speedy method of generating and recording a wide assortment of ideas.

***Step 4: Analysis of Options***    The first part of step 4 is to analyze all the solutions generated in step 3. Once all of the possible alternatives have been identified, the group can begin to converge regarding the most viable options. A series of helpful questions for sorting and categorizing feasible alternatives include the following:

- Are some alternatives very similar; do they overlap?
- Can certain solutions be combined?
- Do any alternatives need to be rearranged?
- Can any be eliminated? (If yes, are there any worthwhile applications or characteristics of this option that need to be considered?)
- What is good about a solution?
- How would it solve the problem or help create the desired future?
- Are there any possible unexpected consequences of this option?
- If anything goes wrong, what would be the course of action?
- What is the group's degree of control or level of authority over this option?
- Are there key stakeholders that need to be involved to make this option a success? Are stakeholders likely to support it?
- What resources would be needed to implement this solution and are obtainable?
- Are more data and information needed?

Although this is a lengthy list of questions, each question is important. However, the group needs to think about the answers and get ready to move on. There is no perfect solution for the problems in organizations today, and it is better to implement something than to be caught in a spiral of data collection. If the selected solution does not work, at least the group has more knowledge and information on which to base a new decision.

At the end of this step the group should have identified at least two or three viable solutions. Stopping at only one solution is dangerous. If it is not accepted or cannot be implemented, the group members feel demoralized and as though they have wasted their time. Also, research has demonstrated that problem solvers are dominated by pressure to solve the problem and that adopting the first solution may reflect this pressure. Forcing the group to develop at least a second alternative results in more creative solutions because focus is on the desired future as opposed to the need to find an answer.

Deciding among the alternatives requires knowledge of decision-making approaches. There are several types of decision making, including voting and reaching consensus, which are explored later in this chapter under the heading "Decision Making."

***Step 5: Action Planning and Implementation***    Determining specific actions to be taken, the time frame within which they are to be completed, and responsibility assignments for each action must be specific and realistic. Once identified, the steps to be taken are prioritized. In many instances, they must be sequential, as some are dependent on completion of others.

Once the plan is reasonably complete, both current practice and recommended alternatives are costed out. Spending money or time in order to save money or time can be a compelling incentive to adopt a new practice. In some instances, no more money is needed for an alternative, but quality of service is positively impacted. At this stage, a communication strategy is developed based on who needs to know about this plan and who must be included in developing additional expectations. How and when to present the results of the problem-solving group are decided.

During implementation, the plan must be monitored closely to maintain momentum. This monitoring function is assigned to an individual who can also reinstitute the group if further work is necessary.

***Step 6: Evaluation***    The final step in the problem-solving process is to establish criteria for evaluating success and determine who will be responsible for the evaluations. The parties involved in implementation must know up front how success will be measured. This evaluation criterion should be as precise and objective as possible, which in some instances is fairly simple. A percentage error rate, the number of patient falls, and staff productivity figures are a few examples of easily obtained objective measures. Others are more difficult to quantify, such as improvement in relationships between teams or departments, satisfaction levels of key customers, or more subtle changes in the quality of service.

Specific review dates are established, and plans are made for celebration of the completion of this phase of the group's work. Results must be monitored and necessary corrections made. Divergence from expected outcomes will mean that the cause must be identified and another workable solution found. The second and third solution alternatives formulated earlier in the process are helpful in this case. At this point, the group may need to be encouraged and reminded that even if the first recommendation or solution did not work exactly as planned, the solution is now closer than it was before.

This problem-solving process was used effectively in a hospital in the U.S. sunbelt. An annually recurring problem of a lack of patient beds during the winter months when the "snowbirds" came south created conflict between staff and physicians, all scraping to come up with needed resources. Finally, during the summer months, administration initiated a problem-solving team composed of staff, managers, executives, and physicians. This process took several months, but the result was a plan that increased the number of available beds during the winter months and clearly identified backup contingency plans. For the first time in years, the winter season was managed without key stakeholders coming to blows over beds.

***Pitfalls of the Problem-Solving Process***    The most common pitfall occurs when the group includes a suggested solution in the problem statement. This limits the variety and creativity of alternatives the group identifies. Then it is "the same old answer" one more time. Not only is the solution ineffective, but everyone involved ends up disenchanted.

A second pitfall relates to the group's level of authority. Steps for action must fit the level of authority and the problem. Too often groups develop grandiose action plans that go way beyond their authority and any reasonable parameters. The previously mentioned quality problem-solving team that came up with a solution costing over $200,000 annually and adding another four full-time equivalents to the personnel budget is a good example.

Hidden agendas and personal platforms make up the next pitfall. Some group members may have a personal strategy they want to promote, even if it has little to do with the issue at hand. This cannot be allowed to interfere with a fully explored problem-solving process.

Time frames and people responsible for each action step often are not determined. These are critical to the implementation stage, at which point it is easy for the group to lose steam and neglect to carry out agreed-upon steps. Monitoring and follow-through are essential.

Following the process sequentially is difficult for many groups. The process is a blend of both right- and left-brain activities, and some groups have trouble with one or the other, or simply switching between the two. Problem identification, analysis, and determining action steps and evaluation measures are all examples of logical left-brain thinking. Establishing a desired future and generating all possible options are right-brain thinking, requiring creativity and spontaneity. Moving from one stage to the other may be facilitated by taking a break between them or actually carrying out each step in separate meetings. This creates boundaries between the two types of thinking processes and helps members make the transition.

Not respecting the problem-solving process as a methodical, sequential process leads to several common problems. The most common is called the Band-Aid approach, often a knee-jerk reaction, when the group moves straight from problem identification to action planning without taking the time to think through a desired future or develop a full range of creative options, as illustrated in figure 5-3.

Another common problem, called analysis paralysis (figure 5-4), is experienced when the group stays in the problem-identification phase so long that paralysis sets in. It seems as though there is never enough data to make a decision, not all the facts have been collected, or there is not enough information with which to move ahead. The goal here is to reach a happy medium between gathering the information and coming to a

**FIGURE 5-3.  The Band-Aid Approach**

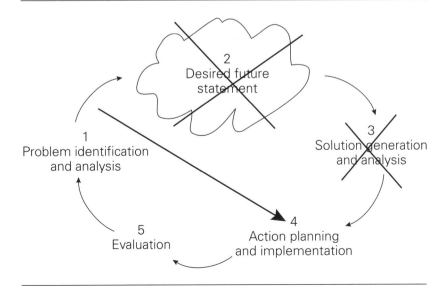

**FIGURE 5-4.   Analysis Paralysis**

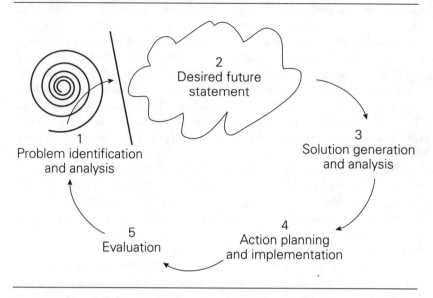

decision. Collect enough data to provide information for adequate analysis through a specific agreed-upon process and agree to an acceptable time frame for the problem at hand.

Some groups have an exaggerated sense of responsibility and take on too much ownership for the problems. This can often be avoided by asking the important question: What is our level of authority for solving this problem? They may discover that they do not have an adequate level of authority for implementing a solution to the problem and can therefore accept that it is not their responsibility to do so. In some instances, they may realize that they are trying to solve a problem for a key group not represented and change the membership of their group.

## Reasons Groups Bog Down in Process

It is imperative that both individuals and groups develop effective problem-solving skills. Most groups process problems rather than solve them, continually discussing the symptoms or effects—anything but the root causes. In many instances, the problem itself escapes during the discussion, without ever having been defined. There are at least three reasons groups engage in unproductive processing:

1.   The group uses voting to determine plans of action, which forces group members to pick sides. Once a person takes a side

and another opposes it, the two opposing stances become even more adamant and continue to grow further apart.

2.  Groups neglect monitoring the group process. Although members may observe unproductive process, they are too often unwilling to address it. The nonparticipatory member is not asked to contribute, apathy is ignored, and disruptive behavior tolerated.

3.  The group does not recognize or understand its patterns of behavior, which may include closing discussions prematurely or reaching decisions without fully analyzing the problem. Members may not recognize "groupthink" or behavior that is so polite and courteous that no one dare talk about the real issues. When the group's solutions or alternatives are not accepted, too often the group blames those with authority rather than reviewing their own process and truly evaluating the quality of their work.

Groupthink is a phenomenon "whereby team members become afraid of offering ideas that might conflict with the group's policies and actions. New ideas are often offered weakly and withdrawn quickly if opposed" (Chaleff 1997, 4). Groupthink can destroy creative initiative and even cause people with opposing views to be forced out. The remedy for groupthink is continual self-evaluation of the group's patterns and outcomes.

Leaders who understand problem solving also understand its relationship to decision making. The two are closely interwoven and highly interdependent. Good problem solvers make decisions and good decision makers use a problem-solving approach.

### Decision Making

A decision, in this context, is a choice among alternative courses of action that may lead to the desired result. If there are no alternatives, there is no decision to be made. Leaders and followers alike assume responsibility for the consequences of their decisions. This can be frightening at times because many decisions are made under conditions of uncertainty.

Decisions are evaluated based on their results or consequences, which are often unpredictable. An individual or group does not have to be right all the time, only *most* of the time. A sign in a printing shop provided this profound piece of wisdom: "Good decisions come from experience. Experience comes from wisdom. Wisdom comes from making bad decisions." If an individual or group has difficulty dealing with uncertainty, they either postpone decisions until all uncertainties are resolved or they make poor decisions because they aren't comfortable coping with the uncertainties.

Good decision makers combine a logical, systematic approach with their intuition. They sort and classify information; differentiate between the valuable, worthless, and redundant; prioritize; and are able to integrate the whole into an accurate picture of reality. As the amount of information available increases, the complexity of decision making also increases. A leader who is a good decision maker evaluates and recognizes what type of decision is called for from the situation. There are at least five types of decisions:

- Individual decisions
- Minority decisions
- Majority decisions
- Consensus decisions
- Unanimous decisions

Each is appropriate in selected instances, as discussed below.

**Individual Decisions**    These decisions are made by one person, a leader, a manager, or an individual with the responsibility and authority to decide. Others involved are expected to abide by this decision. This type of decision is used when there is no choice, the decision is not important, or the group does not want to make a decision. One example of this is called the "plop," a suggestion that gets accepted without any discussion. The plop can be offered by any member of the group.

Individual decisions are sometimes seen as an imposition or a mandated solution directed by someone with the authority to impose such a solution. Impositions are justified when the issue is truly nonnegotiable in terms of responsibility, when a group does not accept responsibility for the solution, or when the decision is a low-impact decision.

**Minority Decisions**    Minority decisions occur when a few people involved in a situation meet to consider the matter and make a decision. If a group decides that minority decisions are appropriate, expectations must be clearly articulated between the individual or group delegating the responsibility and the minority group accepting the responsibility. The decision of the minority group is considered binding for everyone involved.

This approach is often used by teams. A subset of the team examines an issue and makes a decision for the team, which can be a very effective method of decision making when it is difficult for a larger group to come together and take the time to navigate the entire process together. It requires a high level of trust within the team or group. Team members with a vested interest in the decision are expected to be part of the subset and are not allowed to later sabotage the decision.

*Majority Decisions*   When more than half of the people involved in a situation make a decision, it is considered a majority decision and is often referred to as a "majority rules" vote. The resulting decision is binding on all. This type of decision is problematic because it may mean that not all team members support the result.

A significant disadvantage to majority decision making is that it forces people onto one side or the other. Often the best solutions are found somewhere in the middle. The more firmly one argues for a certain side or solution, the less likely he or she will support an opposing solution if it wins. This form of decision making can be useful when the decisions involve minor issues that do not require 100 percent support to implement or when large numbers of people are involved and there is no forum or structure for resolving minority positions.

*Consensus Decisions*   A consensus decision results when the entire group or team addresses a problem with all group members, who fully present their views. Consensus is said to exist when each group or team member can honestly make these three statements to every other member:

1. I believe I understand your point of view.
2. I believe you understand my point of view.
3. I believe the decision has been made in an open and fair manner, and I am willing to support the decision whether or not it's my first preference.

In true consensus, no "majority rules" voting, bargaining, or averaging of votes is allowed. The process takes more time to achieve but results in active support and prevents sabotage and undermining of decisions made. Consensus is especially useful when full team or group commitment to the decision is essential for implementation. In an organization, for example, major decisions such as whether to embark upon a major reengineering initiative or to purchase another facility should be decided by consensus of the entire executive team. If the decision is made in any other manner, support may not be present during implementation, when it is required from the entire team.

*Unanimous Decisions*   In a unanimous decision, when each group member fully agrees on the action to be taken, there is a higher level of commitment. This may be needed when the decision significantly affects each member.

*Group versus Individual Decisions*   Although moving up the decision-making scale from individual to unanimous decisions increases the level of commitment, it also increases the difficulty in arriving at the agreement. A leader may be responsible for deciding whether to use individual or group decisions, for which there are at least five factors to consider:

1. *The nature of the problem or task.* Some problems are more easily solved by a group and others by an individual. In creating a new alternative or doing independent tasks, individuals often surpass groups. A project such as creating a new crossword puzzle is a good example. When tasks are convergent or integrative and require various pieces of information be brought together to produce a solution (such as solving that crossword puzzle), then a group is better. Most goal setting is also more effective in a group because it increases the variety of contributions and level of commitment.

2. *The importance of acceptance of a solution.* When people participate in the process of reaching a decision, they have more commitment to the decision. They work harder and have a greater interest in making the decision successful. When an individual solves a problem or makes a decision, two things must happen: others must be persuaded that this decision is best, and others must agree to act on the decision to carry it out. Not all decisions require commitment, and these can appropriately be made by an individual.

3. *The value placed on the quality of the decision.* If a leader is concerned with acceptance of a decision and with empowering others, he or she may accept a decision of somewhat lesser quality because it has widespread acceptance. Decisions made by a group in the beginning of their skill development simply may not have the same quality as an experienced individual's decisions. If the quality of the decision is paramount, an individual expert in the field might be used.

   For example, if a group's members are having communication problems among themselves, they may produce and decide on the problem-solving alternatives to implement. If the outcomes are not beneficial, the group goes back to the drawing board and engages in additional problem solving. Getting it right the first time is not critical. However, if there are significant computer hardware problems with a particular application that could significantly affect the organization's information systems, a decision to bring in an external expert to solve the problem may be the prudent choice.

4. *The characteristics of individual group members.* Effective leaders consider the expertise of the various group members, the stake each has in the outcome, and the role each is likely to play in implementing the decision.

5. *The operating effectiveness of the group.* It may be a better choice to ask an individual to solve a problem or make a decision than a group who is too new to make the decision or who cannot seem to work together. The skills of the group facilitator have an impact as well.

On the upside, group decision making represents greater total knowledge and information. Each group member brings a different perspective, resulting in a greater variety of approaches. Group decisions may have better acceptance and fewer communication problems. Implementation is likely to be smoother and to require less monitoring. On the downside, there can be strong social pressure to conform in a group setting. Groups also tend to err on the side of quick convergence, perhaps settling prematurely on a decision that seems to have support. High-quality ideas introduced late in the discussion have a limited chance of serious consideration. A dominant individual can prevail because of status, verbal skills, or stubborn persistence. Hidden agendas create problems in group decision making. Unless these are surfaced, they result in skewed and sometimes unfair or poor decisions. A significant problem for group decision making is that it simply takes longer for a group to decide.

## Pitfalls of Decision Making

The most common decision-making pitfall is approaching decisions without due consideration of the various types of decision making. Without careful analysis of the situation or sufficient thought given to outcomes, a leader may miss opportunities for effectively engaging others in the decision. Followers can fall into the same trap. There are appropriate occasions for all types of decision making, but if followers expect to participate and reach consensus and the leader is making an individual decision, the follower's expectations will not be met.

In one urgent care business, Ellen, the CEO, decided to reorganize and restructure the leadership and management ranks. Several managers were furious because they were not included in any discussion but were instead simply told what the new structure would be. Ellen elected to make an individual decision, which was her right as CEO. Unfortunately, however, she had been preaching empowerment for some months, and her individual decision was therefore seen as a slap in the face to those committed to empowerment in the company. An open discussion about how decisions would be made and which were to be individual and which were to be group decisions may have prevented some of these hard feelings.

The second most common pitfall is a lack of understanding of consensus. Consensus has become an overused and misused buzzword in recent years. If a decision truly needs to be made by consensus, there can be no assumption that the conditions of mutual belief, understanding, and support have been met. Because reticent or disagreeing group members may not come forward or openly oppose the decision, the leader needs to actually ask each member of the group to state his or her commitment to the decision.

A statewide ad hoc committee, whose task it was to recommend a new organizational structure for the state hospital association, spent long hours debating this hot political issue. When the group finally settled on a recommendation, the leader asked for consensus. Every group member was individually asked: "Do you believe you understood everyone else's point of view?" and "Do you believe your point of view was fully expressed and understood by the others?" and "Can you support this decision?" Each stated his or her agreement. At the annual meeting, however, one of the committee members had second thoughts when realizing members from a special interest group of which he was also a member were upset about the committee's final recommendation. This member began talking with key association members, trying to engender support for an alternative and basically undermining the committee's work. During a public discussion of the issue, the committee chairman reminded association members that the recommendation had been reached by consensus and reviewed exactly what consensus means. When reminded that he had agreed to support the decision of the committee, the individual ceased his efforts to overturn the recommendations.

Not carefully considering the various factors in group versus individual decision making can be a major pitfall for a leader. A healthy combination of the two is important. In some instances, it is also appropriate to explain why one or the other is used.

Decision making is closely related to problem solving but involves its own special issues. Exemplary leaders are good decision makers but they also are able to relinquish control and engage others in decision making when circumstances warrant. Shared decision making can strengthen any organization as long as it follows careful consideration.

## CREATING TEAMS

Creating and developing high-performance teams is the fourth key process that today's leaders must master in order to be effective. "Teams make sense in today's world for many reasons: the increasing complexity of our work; the changing values of the workforce; the increasing need for immediate organizational response to difficult external marketplace changes and internal challenges; and our desire to create a healthy, satisfying workplace for employees" (Manion 1997, 31). Exemplary leaders understand the concept of team and determine when a team can do a better job than an individual. Even more important, effective leaders have the skills to facilitate a team's development.

*Team* and *teamwork* are two terms often confused and used synonymously by people who do not understand the difference between the two concepts. The word *team* is overused in today's world, loosely applied to exhort others to perform in a particular manner, usually through teamwork. *Teamwork* is a way of working together, and it may mean different things to different people. For most, it implies cooperation, open communication, and pitching in to help each other out. A team is a structural unit, a designed group of people drawn together to complete certain prescribed work. How they carry out the work can be described as teamwork. As adapted from Katzenbach and Smith's definition in *The Wisdom of Teams* (1993), a team is "a small number of consistent people with a relevant, shared purpose, common performance goals, complementary and overlapping skills, and a common approach to its collective work. Team members hold themselves mutually accountable for the team's results and outcomes" (Manion 1997, 31).

In organizations today there are several types of teams. Primary work teams are permanent structures organized around the primary work of a department. In a business office, the teams may be organized around business functions, such as credit verification, billings, and collections. Teams in a patient care department are organized around patient care. In a laboratory, teams are often designed around specialized functions, such as microbiology, hematology, and chemistry. Ad hoc teams are temporary teams created to perform a particular piece of work, and when the work is completed, the team is dissolved. Quality and project teams are good examples of ad hoc teams, which can last for years and yet not be considered part of the permanent structure of an organization. Leadership teams are formed to provide collective leadership for a project, department, service, or organization.

Leaders today may need to create a team for a specific purpose, may actually redesign their department into teams, or may have responsibility for guiding the conversion of the bureaucracy to a team-based structure. The implementation of teams in health care is discussed extensively in other sources (Manion, Lorimer, and Leander 1996; Manion 1997; Lorimer and Manion 1996; Leander, Shortridge, and Watson 1996; Manion and Watson 1995). Exemplary leaders who understand the concepts and language of systems thinking often form diverse teams that use systems thinking to focus on critical issues. These teams outperform individuals because systems issues require multiple approaches, a variety of experiences, and diverse thinking patterns.

### Step 1: Define the Work

Prior to selecting team members, the expected work of the team must be defined. The individual initiating a team delineates what the team is expected to do by considering certain questions. Is this a problem-solving team focusing on a specific issue, or a project team formed to design and implement a new service or system? Is providing collective leadership for the organization the work of the team? Is systems thinking required to challenge mental models and initiate breakthrough thinking? This step can be difficult, but it forces the leader to be very clear about his or her reasons for initiating a team.

### Step 2: Select Members

The most effective teams are those with a small number of consistent team members. Teams of more than twelve members simply run into more logistic problems than do smaller teams. In larger groups it is easier for members to disengage and remain anonymous. Finding a common time to meet is more problematic with larger groups. Consistency of membership is critical. Frequent changes in team membership directly impact the synergy of the group and the quality of work completed. When team members leave and have to be replaced, the team usually regresses in its effectiveness until the new member is brought up to speed. Consistency of membership also refers to consistent attendance at team meetings. Frequent absenteeism directly affects the team's ability to produce high-quality outcomes.

Based on the work of the team, potential members are identified. Members are selected based on their potential contribution to the team's work. The team member may represent a particular part of the system or have certain skills needed by the team. In some cases, it is impossible to obtain all the skills needed by the team, and members may be selected for their skills potential. Perhaps no one in the organization has the skills needed, but the team, through its work, can develop those skills.

### Step 3: Define the Team Purpose

Once team members have been identified and the team comes together for the first time, the initial work of the team is to define their purpose. Although the leader may have given some preliminary direction to the group (based on his or her thoughts from step 1), it is critical that the team actually writes its own mission statement. This describes what the team does and for whom they do it. It clarifies the reason for the team's existence. Teams that are handed a completed purpose statement, or are simply told by the leader why they exist, never develop the same level of ownership as those teams who actually do this work. If the team is given a mission statement describing its work, one way to ensure relevancy and identification with this purpose is to have the team modify it to fit its beliefs. Even small modifications increase a feeling of ownership. Team members simply do not engage with the team if they do not find the team's purpose relevant.

It is important for the leader to stay involved with the team during development of this mission statement in order to prevent the team from heading in the wrong direction. The team's purpose must support the organization's or department's purpose. If the two are incongruent, the team is headed for trouble. An actively participating leader does not mandate their purpose but is involved in guiding and setting the general direction.

## Step 4: Establish Common Working Approaches

Once the team is clear about its mission and reason for existence, the next step is to determine and agree upon approaches it plans to use in doing its work. "A common approach means that team members discuss, delineate, and agree on ways they are going to work together to accomplish their purpose. *Common* refers to the collective effort that is required, not an approach that is ordinary or average. There is nothing common nor ordinary about a highly effective team" (Manion, Lorimer, and Leander 1996, 64).

Some examples of early decisions needed about working approaches include the following:

- *Logistics of team meetings.* How often will the team meet? When will it meet? Where? Will an agenda be circulated? Who facilitates the meeting? Will minutes be needed; and if so, taken by whom?
- *Methods for communicating.* This includes both formal and informal methods of communicating. Is there a need for frequent team "huddles"? Are team members readily accessible to each other? Do they need to be? Is everyone on E-mail?
- *Problem-solving approaches.* How will the team tackle problems? Is there a quality process to be followed?
- *Decision making.* What types of decisions will be made by the team? What are the boundaries in regard to the team's work? Which will be individual decisions, and which should be made by the entire team? Will majority decision making be used, or will consensus? When would minority decision making be used?

Roles and responsibilities within the team also need to be discussed. Are there specific roles that need to be filled by team members to ensure work is completed? Examples of these include meeting coordinator or facilitator and process person. Some teams identify a celebrations role to ensure that key events are recognized and cheered. If there are any needed roles, the specific responsibilities of each need to be defined clearly. Some teams identify the role of challenger. The challenger is "the team member who openly questions the goals, methods, and the ethics of the team, who is willing to disagree with the team leader, and who encourages the team to take well-considered risks" (Parker 1997, 8). This role is critical for most teams because the challenger is honest in reporting team progress and identifying problems. This individual, however, does back off if his or her views are not accepted and actively supports consensus within the team.

The final components of establishing common working approaches are the discussion of and agreement on what team members expect of one another. Identifying and articulating behavioral expectations are key steps in early team formation for several reasons. These expectations lay the foundation for development of trust within the team. In addition, being clear about the expectations one holds of others is instrumental in preventing unnecessary conflicts. Too often, people do not meet others' expectations because they did not know the expectations even existed. The group discusses what they expect or need from one another in order to do a good job. This often includes expectations for appropriate meeting participation, communication techniques, and acceptable team behavior. The following examples from real teams demonstrate expectations related to these areas.

We expect team members to

- Be on time and prepared for meetings and to fully participate as evidenced by an attentive attitude, asking clarifying questions, and remaining open-minded about the contributions of other team members
- Communicate openly, honestly, and directly with each other, especially if we fail to meet each other's expectations
- Work toward the goals of the team and support the success of the team first and individual work second
- Stay focused on our goals, and complete tasks and projects within agreed-upon time frames (communicating any unavoidable delays to other team members as soon as possible)

### Step 5: Specify Performance Goals

Closely related to the team mission are the team's performance goals. Larson and LaFasta (1989) examined high-performing teams and found, without exception, that these were teams with clearly identified performance objectives and goals. These can also serve as a measurement of the team's outcomes which gives a team the ability to hold itself accountable.

Team goals are distinguished from system, organizational, or department goals. "Teams take broad objectives or directives from the organization's management and shape them into specific, measurable goals for the team. Specific goals are stated in concrete terms so that it is unequivocally possible to tell whether or not they have been met" (Manion, Lorimer, and Leander 1996, 63). The most powerful goals provide for "small wins" along the way, and these intermediate victories serve to motivate and reinforce the team's direction along its chosen path.

Motivating goals are often those with "stretch," forcing the team to extend itself and reach beyond what was previously dreamed of. These ambitious goals produce momentum, growth, and commitment within the team. "Teams that face a significant challenge, or that develop their own ambitious goals, have a greater sense of urgency that forces them to focus their efforts in a unified direction. . . . The true strength of a team is realized when it faces and overcomes seemingly unbreachable obstacles to attain a worthy goal" (Manion, Lorimer, and Leander 1996, 63).

## Step 6: Hold the Team Accountable

A final and essential step is to hold the team accountable for its outcomes. This is a constant process of reviewing outcomes and determining whether established standards have been met. If desired outcomes have not been attained, the team evaluates its process and its work to determine what went wrong and then takes corrective action.

"Mutual accountability differentiates a real team from a working group. In both teams and working groups, individuals hold themselves accountable for the outcomes of their assignments. A team, however, takes the next step—members hold themselves mutually accountable for the team's outcomes or results. They continuously measure themselves against their established goals and objectives" (Manion, Lorimer, and Leander 1996, 77). The team reviews its decisions for their effectiveness and its processes for beneficial outcomes. All team members are equally accountable for the outcomes of the team.

*Pitfalls of Creating Teams*    There are many potential pitfalls along the journey in the development of teams. The most frequently observed are included here.

Often when a team is in trouble, the solution implemented includes the leader giving a pep talk or bringing in a dynamic, charismatic speaker who generates enthusiasm and excitement within the team.

This is a quick fix in that the results never seem to last long enough to get the team through the next crisis. More effective in turning the team around is a challenge that creates a sense of urgency. Giving the team a stiff work assignment that they see as important does more to mobilize stagnated energy and turn it into a productive force than any motivational speech could possibly do.

Not recognizing the special needs and unique challenges based on the type of team is a second common error. Each of the three major types of teams has unique challenges, and to assume they are all similar is to underestimate the difficulty a particular team may have. For instance, most leadership teams find defining their work and purpose to be problematic. This may seem contradictory because this type of team is composed of leaders who as individuals are usually self-directed and focused clearly on their work. However, most leadership teams confuse their work as a team with the work of the organization as a whole—for example, ensuring the delivery of safe, quality patient care to members of the community versus leading others and creating an empowering environment in which employees deliver safe, high-quality patient care to members of the community.

An ad hoc team formed to lead a change initiative often has difficulty in handing off the project to those who will actually implement it (usually managers) because they feel a large degree of ownership. This is a basic principle of innovation: The people who implement a change are not as attached to the change as those who create it. In early work-redesign projects in health care, this was a common experience, as described below.

Several major organizations assembled specific project or design teams composed of employees who then led the restructuring initiative. These employees became highly skilled at the principles of work redesign and reengineering and were seen as "the experts" in the organization. Although one team member usually functioned as a transition facilitator to assist managers with implementation of the project, implementation became the manager's responsibility. In almost every case, the involved manager did not have the same level of understanding or commitment to the design as the team member. This was true even though many managers had served as ad hoc members to the team.

Understanding the unique challenges of each type of team alerts the leader to potential problems. A more complete discussion of these types of teams can be found in *Team-Based Health Care Organizations: Blueprint for Success* (1996) by Manion, Lorimer, and Leander.

Ignoring any one of the key elements in creating teams is another major pitfall but one that is relatively easy to correct. For example, a team that had frequent and recurring problems finally called in an external consultant to help. During this work, the consultant discovered that the team had never established their expectations of one another or agreed-upon common working approaches. Simply doing these two things cleared up about 90 percent of the conflicts.

Minimizing the development time to grow a team is common. Too many managers and leaders today believe if they simply call a group a team, it somehow becomes one. Not taking the time to apply the proper steps of team development often creates a situation in which the group struggles needlessly, trying their best but unable to determine why it's just not working. Unless team members come together to accomplish their work collectively, they do not become a team.

Being able to create high-performing teams is one of the most critical challenges facing leaders today. Virtually every future organizational structure (adhocracy, network, or clustered organization) is based on the premise that teams are to be a prevalent structure. Leaders must have the ability to tap into and release the potential of a team.

## MANAGING CHANGE AND TRANSITION

The final two key processes explored here are the interrelated processes of change transition. These create significant challenges for today's leaders. Change today is different. Its pace is faster than ever and promises to continue accelerating well into the new millennium. The very nature of work has been altered by the continual onslaught of technological improvements. Where services are delivered is rapidly shifting from acute hospital care to ambulatory and home care. Fewer and fewer stand-alone organizations exist. Solutions are shorter lived. The very changes instituted to solve problems today may actually become tomorrow's problems. Any major change in an organization today must be realistically viewed as only a stepping-stone to the next change; and these stepping-stones are getting closer and closer together.

### Change versus Transition

Leaders today are challenged by these tumultuous times, and without an understanding of the underlying processes of change and transition, the situation could indeed appear hopeless. The first step for any leader is to clearly differentiate between change—an external event that causes an alteration or modification in what has previously existed—and transition, the internal process experienced by an individual during which he or she psychologically adapts to the change (Bridges 1991). Transitions take longer than change, and because they are internal may not be evident to others. Change is complex, being both a process and an outcome. Leaders effectively manage both.

## The Change Process

Understanding change as a developmental process aids the leader in recognizing important sequential steps (Manion 1993; Manion, Lorimer, and Leander 1996). Five phases can be differentiated, based on an energy model adapted for organizations by Nancy Post, an organization development consultant (1989). The five phases, illustrated in figure 5-5, include

1. Preparation
2. Movement
3. Creation
4. New reality
5. Integration

Each of these five phases involve several key issues or concerns. Imbalance is created when a key issue is ignored or passed over, or if there is overemphasis of one issue, overshadowing the others. Not following the process sequentially results in a prolonged and less effective change process. When a leader understands these five phases and ade-

**FIGURE 5-5.    A Five-Phase Change Model**

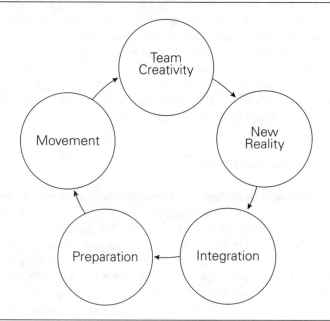

Reprinted with permission from "Chaos or Transformation," *Journal of Nursing Administration* 23 (no. 5), © 1993 by J. B. Lippincott Co.

quately addresses the key issues within each phase, it takes less energy to implement change.

*Phase 1: Preparation*    The two major issues in this phase include setting the direction and allocating resources. Addressing both of these issues during initiation of a change will lay the foundation for a successful effort. In their enthusiasm to begin immediately, many initiators of change pay only scant attention to this stage, or once the direction is shared, they forget to review available resources and obtain those necessary for implementation. All issues are equally important.

The purpose of the change must be examined. Why is this change needed or appropriate? How will it impact patients, key customers, employees, or the long-term viability of the organization? Will this change help the organization to meet its basic mission? By clearly defining and articulating the purpose of this change, the leader sets the direction for those who will implement it.

Once the purpose is identified, the leader considers resources required to implement this change. Although money and financial support are key resources, the lack of other critical resources can be devastating to a change initiative. These other important resources include adequate time; availability of coaches, mentors, and other support people; skills of employees and managers; and interest from those who must implement the change.

*Phase 2: Movement*    During this phase, the two primary issues are developing a vision and implementation plan, and providing a decision-making structure that enables the project to move forward.

Vision, as described in chapter 3, is a compelling picture of what the situation will be in the future. A leader's ability to envision a different future, one that is energizing and desirable, makes it possible to create a new reality. The most powerful visions are those of a preferred, rather than predicted, future. The envisioned future is a stretch and a challenge. Equally important is the plan developed that will create this new reality—a specific, concrete, step-by-step plan with time frames and a structure that will move the vision from dream to reality.

A decision-making structure is also determined at this phase. What is needed to move from idea to concrete change? Is a project team or committee useful? What should the decision-making authority of the people involved be? How does the change impact the present organization or department structure? What will measure success?

*Phase 3: Creation*    This phase is the most dynamic of the five and marks the beginning of actually making the change. Prior to this point, most of the work is preparatory and sometimes considered tedious by enthusiastic and eager leaders. Without the work in the first two phases, however, this phase would not result in lasting change. The four major issues for this phase include coordination and cooperation, setting priorities, communication, and climate.

Change initiatives fail under the burden of poor coordination and lack of cooperation from participants. If coordination is weak, participants may come to believe that the left hand doesn't know what the right hand is doing, which erodes trust and confidence in leadership. During extensive change, those affected are likely to become more egocentric and focused on themselves. Unless leaders are prepared for this phenomenon, they can easily feel anger toward normally cooperative employees and departments that suddenly become obstructive and resistant.

Clearly identifying priorities encourages both leaders and participants to stay focused on the change effort. It is a leadership function to continually evaluate pressing priorities and restate them as often as necessary to help others remain focused on the change. Congruency between leader behavior and stated beliefs is of utmost importance at this time. Because change is difficult and demanding, people implementing a change continually read "the signs" to ensure their effort is worthwhile. Leaders must avoid becoming distracted by a new project or the next change, which could cause participants to conclude that the change they are working on is no longer a priority.

Communication is important during all phases of a change initiative, but at this point it becomes critical. A defined communication plan must be conscientiously implemented, including strategies for keeping key stakeholders abreast of changes. Chapter 4 includes a more extensive discussion on all types and methods of communication.

Creating a corporate culture, or climate, supportive of the change is essential. If the change requires people to behave in a manner incongruent with the culture, it is unlikely that the change will be successful.

***Phase 4: The New Reality*** Once the change has been made and the situation is altered, the true impact begins to sink in. Stabilizing the change at this point so that it is anchored for the future and achieving the desired results from the change are the major issues of this phase.

Stabilizing the change is of paramount importance. The leader must execute specific measures to anchor the change into the current reality because without constant pressure, people will revert back to their previous behaviors. Methods for this "include formalizing structures or processes that were used during a trial period, establishing new routines, or formally communicating the new processes to key stakeholders" (Manion, Lorimer, and Leander 1996, 202). An even more powerful method of anchoring the change is to modify the reward system within the organization to ensure that new behaviors are reinforced. Reward systems include recognition and compensation mechanisms.

The second key issue in phase 4 is achieving desired results so that acceptable productivity levels are regained. Few plans unfold as they were designed. In actually executing a change, some planned approaches work and some do not. Sorting through to find the successful strategies and to eliminate those that are unsuccessful is part of the work of this phase. Leaders must be patient with declining productivity during this trial period.

*Phase 5: Integration*    Integration is the final phase of the change process, involving review of quality measures, evaluation of results, and managing closure. Unfortunately, this stage is often undervalued or simply overlooked.

The quality measures identified in phase 2, the movement phase, should now be reviewed. Results obtained are then evaluated using these measures to determine the success of the initiative. Were desired results achieved? Did any intolerable, undesirable consequences occur? What was the impact on the system, organization, or department? Has quality of service improved? In addition to reviewing quality indicators, the actual change process should be evaluated. What organizational learning occurred as a result of this process? How resilient were employees? What leadership skills emerged? How were emotional reactions handled?

The skill with which the leader deals with closure is instrumental in positioning people and the organization well for the next change. "Closure is often the least understood and most often overlooked issue of the entire developmental cycle" (Manion, Lorimer, and Leander 1996, 205). Celebrations are appropriate and help mark the transition occurring. However, closure often includes grief, which can be difficult to manage. Allowing and supporting any feelings of grief promotes respect for the natural progression of any change and models healthy adaptive behavior.

## The Change Process: Five Steps for Success

This five-phase process for implementing change is applicable to change projects of any size. It has guided mergers of hospitals, as well as closures, and been used to implement change in a single department. Understanding all the key issues of each phase helps leaders determine progress and prevents common missteps. Following the phases sequentially reduces the amount of effort and energy it takes to make a change. A more thorough explanation of each phase can be found in chapter 8, Chaos to Creativity: Leading Change and Transition, in *Team-Based Health Care Organizations* (1996) by Manion, Lorimer, and Leander, and "Managing Change: The Leadership Challenge of the 1990s" in *Seminars for Nurse Managers* (Manion 1994).

Too often, key issues are not considered, creating major problems later in the process. How many times are changes embarked upon without enough resources to follow through or without even considering key but less obvious resources such as leadership skill and coaching abilities? Or a dynamic, charismatic leader is excited and enthusiastic about a change, exhorts followers to embark upon the change although little or no preparatory work has been done? Or everyone was excited about the change, but it did not unfold as planned, nothing was put into place to anchor the change, and as a result, it becomes one more thing not followed through on.

## The Transition Process

Change alters the way something is done, while transition is the psychological adaptation to change. There are three stages to transition, as identified by Bridges (1992). These are depicted in figure 5-6 and include

1. The ending
2. The neutral zone
3. New beginnings

**Stage 1: The Ending**    Bridges (1988, 1992) has studied people's reactions to transition for years. He points out that once a leader understands the dynamics of transition, he or she begins to see the need for endings almost everywhere.

Every change in leadership terminates relationships and plans that had been central to people's lives. Every merger takes away power and status that people had built their worlds upon. Every change in product lines or services brings to an end the functions and competencies that

**FIGURE 5-6.   Stages of Transition**

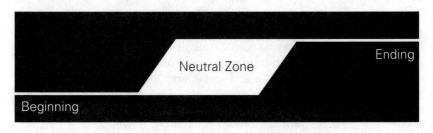

Reprinted with permission from *Participant's Guide—Managing Organization Transition*, published by William Bridges & Associates © 1992.

made people feel valuable and the groupings that made them feel at home. Even promotions cause people to leave behind their familiar worlds. In short, every change causes loss, whether the change is large or small (Bridges 1988, 37).

This first stage of transition is painful because it entails saying good-bye to the world once known. Valued relationships may end with this change, and comfort with the way things were done is lost. This stage begins with an awareness that change has forced a closure, a destruction of the known world. This is unsettling—even frightening—to most people.

People in this stage of transition are difficult to work with because they are experiencing the emotions of grief. Anger, irritability, depression, negativism, resistance, and resentment are common during the lowest emotional periods (Manion 1995). Employees and leaders alike feel vulnerable and out of control. Indeed, in many workplaces it is not safe to express anger because of potential retaliation. When employees are angry with the person to whom they report, this increases their fear.

*Stage 2: The Neutral Zone*    Once the ending phase is complete, the next stage is the neutral zone. At first glance, this stage seems anything but neutral. It is characterized by disruption, confusion, and fear. "The neutral zone is the psychological in-between time, when it isn't the old way anymore, but it isn't the new way yet either. The old identity is gone but the new identity isn't clear. The old procedures and systems, the old values and norms, the old expectations and priorities are no longer operative or valid, but the new ones haven't taken shape yet" (Bridges 1992, 45).

For most adults, the neutral zone is the most uncomfortable of all transition stages. It can cause tremendous frustration and anxiety because it exists between two worlds, the comfortable known and the frightening unknown. Even if the past was undesirable and fraught with unhappiness, at this point it might be romanticized and remembered for only its good elements. Because it is being compared with the  unknown quantity of the future, the past can look pretty rosy in retrospect. The change is in place and the situation has altered, so many people assume that internal adaptation will follow at the same pace. Nothing could be further from the truth. Internal adjustment always takes longer.

There is a tremendous urgency in organizations going through change to push people through these first two stages because the characteristic emotions and behaviors are so discouraging. However, without fully experiencing these two stages, transition is not complete; the negative feelings are just suppressed. The more repression that occurs, the less likely the positive, creative side of transition will be achieved.

Oddly, the second predominant characteristic of the neutral zone is creativity. Because everything is up in the air and uncertain, there is tremendous potential for transforming the way things are done. Chaos and confusion abound, from which creative and innovative ideas arise. "During any period of significant change, one of the leader's most important tasks is to use the change as a challenge to all the assumptions and practices that got the organization to where it is" (Bridges 1992, 51). In times of profound crisis this challenge reaches to the very core of the organization. What is its mission? How does the organization identify itself? In the face of less significant change, it may simply be an opportunity to ask, "Is there a better way to do the things we do?"

***Stage 3: The New Beginning***    Bridges (1992) differentiates between the start of something (the change itself) and the new beginning. The beginning implies that people are comfortable with the change and their new identities and that their world has been rebuilt. With a new beginning, comfort and ease have returned; people feel at home again. This is the easiest stage of transition to manage, although it must not be overlooked. At this time, anchoring and stabilizing the change are important.

***Pitfalls: Managing Change and Transition***    Not recognizing the difference between change and transition often leads to one or the other being ignored. Although these two processes are highly interdependent, the value of separating them is to ensure that specific interventions are used to manage each. Change can be made, but when people do not successfully make their transitions and adapt to the change, the change is compromised. People who never adapt to the change have the potential of undermining and destabilizing the change, whether intentionally or inadvertently. In the same way, mismanaged change affects people's ability to successfully adapt to an altered situation.

Examples of this pitfall abound in health care today. Hospitals merge, organizations convert to a team-based structure, or an integrated system is developed—all representing the merging or changing of internal organizational culture. But when shaping a new culture and managing people's transition to this new reality are poorly handled or ignored by leaders, the results of the initiative are underrealized. Is it any surprise that the full promise of vertical integration within health care systems has yet to be realized?

The most common mistakes in managing change and transition are ignoring the process and rushing people through the stages. Because certain stages result in unpleasant emotions and potentially strained interpersonal relationships, there is a natural desire to pass quickly through these stages or bypass them completely. Although this seems effective in the short term, it only slows the process later.

Less effective managers and leaders mistakenly believe that managing transition, the people side of change, is a luxury and something too expensive to do. In one organization, managers were upset and concerned about the multitude of changes occurring. They believed that their executives were discounting the managers' observations and feelings. When the group of managers attempted to talk with their executive leaders about their concerns, they were told in no uncertain terms that the change was a speed bump and they should just get over it! The group of managers felt chastised, belittled, and devalued. One would have to question the effectiveness of these executive leaders, since it is the management staff who usually leads the rest of the organization through change. One wonders how the executives were planning to gain support for the widespread changes after totally and completely alienating this group of people.

For the "just get it done," non-process-oriented leaders, accepting the emotional issues of transition is just not in their consciousness. They often ignore the presence of messy emotions and decide they won't let them affect the implementation of change. In the words of one CEO, "I don't want my people being told about these emotions—it's just too negative." Unfortunately, not teaching people what to expect does not prevent the feelings or make the emotions go away.

During times of change and transition, people are often exhorted to be more creative, to come up with ideas for dealing with a difficult reality. This can create a no-win situation if the leader is not aware of where employees are in the stage of transition. If employees are trying to cope with closure and are experiencing the emotions of grief, asking them to be creative often results in a demoralizing and self-defeating situation.

Some leaders mistakenly expect these processes to be predictable. Although there is a predictable sequence, no one can accurately forecast the full effects of a change on another person. The change that triggers the emotions of transition may be different for different people. While one individual may experience a title change as a significant loss, another barely notices. Moving a work space may upset an individual tremendously, and for another, it is changes in relationships that are far more significant.

## CONCLUSION

Exemplary leaders are highly skilled at managing processes. They recognize and understand the operative process and are able to guide it in a way that ensures relevant, synergistic outcomes. When process bogs down, they are able to assess the problem, intervene, and redirect the process. Good leaders respect the sequential nature of process and allow it to unfold within its natural time frame. They have the judgment to determine when a process needs a little extra nudge or redirection. Tomorrow's highly effective leader is a master at empowering others, resolving conflict, leading problem-solving groups, decision making, building teams, and managing change and transition.

# 6

## Developing Others

"Managers who see themselves as coaches will also tend to see their employees as individuals of innate talent and worth."

—*Ron Zemke*

L eadership is the art of influence, the capacity to move or impel others to a certain course of action. Each competency explored in this book increases the leader's ability to influence others. A healthy, vibrant relationship with followers is the foundation for exemplary leadership, which is fully explored in chapter 2. Shared values, a strong sense of purpose, and clarity of vision build commitment to a common direction. Free-flowing, consistent, and accurate communication between leaders and followers directly affects leaders' influential abilities. Skill at leading processes is another instrumental competency, as discussed in chapter 5. A final manner in which leaders influence is through participation in the development of the skills and abilities in followers.

### THE LEADER'S ROLE

Developing others is the final leadership competency addressed in this book. It could be argued that an effective leader, accomplished in the other skills already presented, spontaneously and involuntarily develops others. People observe the leader's behavior and are simply influenced by it. Most leaders, however, are not content with a passive role in developing others and instead choose an intentional path that actively focuses on supporting the evolution of followers into leaders. The intentional development of others is the focus of this chapter.

Coaching for performance improvement, providing opportunities, and teaching are methods for developing others that are explored thoroughly in this chapter. Approaches that increase the leader's effectiveness are identified, and a specific coaching process is delineated. All are based on the premise that the leader's influence on others increases if the leader engages actively in the process of developing followers.

## Coaching

Today's leadership rhetoric is filled with references to coaching. Leaders and managers are exhorted to become coaches, articles and books on coaching in the workplace appear with regularity, and seminars on the topic are selling out. With this insistent and repetitive urging to become a coach, why aren't more leaders excellent coaches? In moving beyond the rhetoric to explore the reasons leaders in health care continue to grapple with the coaching role, there is both good and bad news.

The good news is that through years of experience and learning, some leaders and managers do develop excellent coaching skills. However, they may not have a concrete framework that is easy to pass along to others because they learned their skill over years of practice, trial and error, and careful scrutiny of what worked and what did not. Excellent coaches with years of experience acquire intuition, a sense of knowing something without understanding how one knows it. Coaching becomes a consistent and vital part of their leadership practice because they have directly observed and received its many benefits. These health care leaders continually seek to further refine and define their coaching role. What exactly does it mean? What do I do as a coach for my followers?

Now the bad news: Many health care managers and leaders engage in a passive form of coaching, characterized predominantly by inconsistent and sporadic coaching. On one project, they take an active coaching role only to be accused by followers of micromanaging, and on another project, they offer little or no guidance or advice because they are too busy. Perhaps the only consistent behaviors are the annual performance appraisals and disciplinary processes meant to address and correct performance problems. This is a reactive, rather than a proactive, process—often something to be dreaded rather than seen as an integral part of their role.

Unfortunately, the bad-news description is more commonly found in today's workplace, as examined by Ron Zemke in *The Corporate Coach:* "Given the growing popularity of the coaching metaphor and the facility with which it slips from the lips of consultants and managers alike, you might expect by now that most managers would excel at listening, setting a positive example, giving praise, pointing out areas of improvement, and encouraging employees to stretch and grow—the skills of coaching. Naturally you'd be wrong." He goes on to report on recent studies, all of which conclude that "on a wide range of skills, managers were rated lowest in their ability to give employees useful feedback on job performance" (Zemke 1996, 26, 27).

## Why Leaders Don't Coach

If coaching is so important and popular today, why is it so rare? Why is it inconsistently practiced? Why is there aversion to functioning as a coach? There are many possible reasons.

*Lack of Understanding*   Leaders know that coaching followers for performance improvement is important; after all, isn't everyone telling them so? Some leaders are ineffective coaches because they do not understand the principles involved; they may never have been coached themselves and so have no role models in their past from whom they could learn. When leaders are managers and part of the organizational hierarchy, managerial responsibilities further cloud the issue. Some believe completing performance appraisals on time means their coaching responsibilities are over for the year. There is confusion over the difference between counseling and coaching. Counseling, as defined by Minor, is "a supportive process by a manager to help an employee define and work through personal problems that affect job performance" (1989, 2).

*Lack of Time*   Recent years of downsizing and restructuring in health care organizations have taken their toll in terms of formal leadership positions. Leaders with hierarchical positions have more responsibility and broader spans of control than ever. The rapidly accelerating pace of change places many additional time demands on today's leaders and can easily result in physical and mental exhaustion. Unfortunately, coaching is a leadership function that is easily put off. Finding time to coach just does not feel like a priority when facing a full and frenetically busy day. Good leaders understand that coaching is an investment for the future. It takes time in the present but returns huge dividends in the future.

*Fear of Confrontation*   Addressing performance gaps sometimes feels like confrontation, especially if it is received less than graciously by the performer. Reluctance to correct or suggest alternative approaches creates a downward spiral. Afraid of offending the person or precipitating an emotionally negative response, the leader delays giving the person much-needed performance feedback. The leader becomes increasingly conscious of the performance gap and with every occurrence comes to believe more and more strongly that this must be addressed. Reluctance fuels procrastination, and when the issue is finally discussed, the simple performance gap has become a major issue. When the leader and follower both clearly understand the purpose of coaching, and issues are addressed immediately, performance feedback does not assume horrific proportions.

***Lack of Confidence***   Coaching skills are learnable, but trial-and-error experience can be painful. Classroom time on coaching rarely goes beyond theory. Although being coached is one of the best ways to learn coaching, in the absence of it, some leaders feel they are fumbling through the process. And they may even be coaching followers who are more highly competent in a particular area than they are, so it is no surprise that confidence may waver and weaken.

***Lack of Incentive***   Little in today's organization incites leaders to develop others. One department manager noted that when he worked hard to develop people within his department, they were promoted to positions elsewhere in the organization. Initially he was pleased and satisfied by this as he believed this was his role as a leader. Over time, he realized that an employee's promotion left him with a major deficit in his department and the need to start the process all over again—finding the right employee and pouring time and effort into guiding the new employee's development. As a fully mature manager-leader, he continues to engage actively in this process, though he admits he is tired after several decades of this cycle. How different he would feel, he has mused, if the organization would give him a $10,000 bonus for every employee promoted outside of his department! It often costs more than that to successfully recruit an external applicant for a position, so both he and the organization would conceivably come out ahead.

These reasons all offer some explanation for the lack of active coaching present in today's health care organizations. Admittedly, the good news–bad news scenario is more likely a continuum with each at opposite ends. More leaders and managers are likely to fit somewhere in the middle than in the extremes at either end. This chapter section defines coaching and proposes a concrete process that creates a structure to help make the coaching process easier to engage and apply in day-to-day work.

## Coaching Defined

Coaching has become a buzzword in health care leadership circles. Buzzword status is dangerous because the term becomes so commonly used in a superficial manner that it often becomes meaningless. Instead of frequent use increasing understanding, the opposite occurs. Examples of recent buzzwords include *empowerment*, *paradigms*, and *teams*.

*Webster's* describes *coaching* as a verb meaning "to give instruction or advice." *Coach* is further defined in terms of sports and the arts, but no mention is made of the coach in the business or work world. For purposes of this chapter, *coaching* is defined as a process of facilitating an individual's development through giving advice and instruction; encouraging discovery through guided discussions and hands-on experiences; observing performance; and giving honest, direct, and immediate feedback. The goal of coaching is to improve the individual's skills and abilities. Don Shula, longtime coach of the Miami Dolphins, says, "A good coach provides the direction and concentration for performers' energies, helping channel all their efforts toward a single desired outcome. Without that critical influence, the best achievements of the most talented performers can lack the momentum and drive that make a group of individuals into champions" (Shula and Blanchard 1995, 28).

It is helpful to distinguish between the process of coaching and the role of coach. As a process, coaching refers to the way outcomes are achieved. It includes the procedure or structure applied in order to obtain desired results. In the definition, for instance, giving advice and instruction is one way that the desired outcome—facilitating the individual's development—is realized. In this instance, coaching is an action, an active verb.

*Coach* is also a term used to describe a position or role taken on by a person. The coach is an individual who applies a process of coaching. This implies some level of formal structure, for within every position or role there are responsibilities. The level of formality in the relationship can range from contractual (a legal agreement defining the role and relationship of coach to the individual receiving the coaching), where everything is clearly spelled out, to a loose, implied-only agreement by the involved participants.

In today's workplace, the structure tends to be on the loose to nonexistent side. A leader or manager may intellectually know, and even accept, that coaching is an important function of his or her role, yet engage in the process only sporadically and reactively, with actual coaching occurring when new tasks and responsibilities are delegated or performance shortfalls are apparent. Formalizing the coaching relationship to some degree may provide a structure that converts an inconsistent and reactive process to one that is consistent and proactive.

## THE COACHING ROLE

Comparing the coaching roles of health care leaders to athletic coaches sheds light on the concept. There are many similarities, although there are also some striking differences, such as this major one: Most individuals are on a sports team because they are highly motivated to be there—not always the case in the workplace. Some similarities, however, are striking: The coach recruits and selects players, determines the game plan, works with the team to improve performance by giving feedback, continually evaluates the team's performance, and motivates and encourages the team.

In health care organizations, as in sports, the coach does not have to be a star player—not always the best criterion for a good coach. The coach is highly skilled at helping others do better. Without the objective viewpoint of a coach, a performer may repeat the same mistake over and over again. In sports, the coach would not dream of missing a game or not being present when the team practices. Yet many leaders in health care are so inundated with paperwork and meetings, their coaching is primarily by voice and electronic mail, with little time spent actually observing performers at work. "Coaching is an intensely personal business. You can't coach people from a distance, with aloofness. People need to see that you are at least as interested as they are in what's going on" (Shula and Blanchard 1995, 125).

Sports analogies may induce visions of competition, one team winning over another. In this regard, the health care leader-coach may be more like a theater or movie director, a symphony conductor, or a dance coach. These coaches function in much the same way as a sports coach but the desired outcome is one that is mutually beneficial for all rather than victory in a win-lose competition.

Before presenting a process for effective coaching, there are at least two general principles or concepts to address that provide a grounding in the basic theory. The first relates to the formation of a relationship between coach and performer, and the second is application of the principles of motivation.

### Building the Relationship

A prerequisite to effective application of a coaching process is the establishment of a relationship between coach and performer, or player. Coaching, much like leadership, simply cannot exist in the absence of a relationship. Its very essence is interaction between people. And without a sound relationship, the performer is simply unwilling to act on the advice and counsel shared, as established by principles presented in chapter 2. The presence of a relationship characterized by trust, mutual respect, and open communication (discussed at length in chapters 2 and 4) greatly influences the quality of a coaching relationship.

*Trust*    Trust, the foundation, comprises the three elements of competence, congruity, and constancy. A coach who knows the rules of the game and has established his or her own competency can be an excellent coach without ever having reached star status from their own performance. In fact, some star players who have gone on to be coaches have failed dismally because good coaching takes far more than expert performance skills. More important are adequate knowledge of the game and expert coaching skills.

The second element of trust—congruity—enhances faith and is heightened when the coach behaves in a manner that matches the message that the coach is sending the performer. Successful sports coaches understand this concept. Don Shula is the winningest coach in National Football League history. In discussing reasons for the phenomenal success of his teams, he says:

> A lot of leaders want to tell people what to do, but they don't provide the example. "Do as I say, not as I do," doesn't cut it. Of course, I'm not about to show players how to run or pass or block or tackle by doing these things myself. My example is in things like my high standards of performance, my attention to detail, and, above all, how hard I work. In these respects, I never ask my players to do more than I am willing to do. My own preparation for every game has to be exemplary. I am dedicated to success and will do whatever it takes to achieve it. I am generally the last one off the practice field. (Shula and Blanchard 1995, 56)

The final element of trust—constancy—exists when the performer knows the coach can be counted on—that the coach is at practice sessions with the team and stays until the end of the game even though it is a discouraging and dismal loss. The coach does not bow out and head for the locker room early just because the team is behind. Observation of team and individual performance is not possible if the coach is not at the game. Videotaping is a wonderful way of replaying performance, but it is not the same as being there. No sports coach worth his or her salt waits until after the game to review performance and give corrective feedback.

*Mutual Respect*    Mutual respect is needed in a good relationship. The coach's job is to push players toward their peak performance. Players need to believe that the coach has something to offer and is focused on helping them improve. When the motivation of the coach is to help the team members be their very best, players may not like what they are asked to do, but they respect it. "Lots of leaders want to be popular, but I've never cared about that. I want to be respected. Respect is different from popularity. You can't make it happen or demand it from people, although some leaders try that. The only way you can get respect is to earn it" (Shula and Blanchard 1995, 50).

Being pushed to satisfy the coach's ego is not highly valued by players. A women's collegiate volleyball team provides a good example of this. The coach was recently graduated and this was her first coaching job. She drove the team mercilessly because she wanted a championship team in her first year out of school. Her relentless pursuit of this goal in spite of the fact that the team just did not have the experience or ability necessary led to her complete ineffectiveness as a coach. By the end of the year, there were not enough players left to take the court as a team. The players knew she was not interested in helping them improve their performance for any reason other than her ego's needs.

*Communication*     Communication is the final requirement for a healthy relationship between a coach and performer. Issues and principles of communication discussed fully in chapter 4 can be reviewed for their applicability to coaching. Without the ability to articulate direction, vision, and goals and to give feedback, the coaching process simply does not work. Good communication skills are the vehicle through which the coaching process is carried out.

Perhaps as important as the quality of the relationship between the coach and performer is the definition, or structure, of the relationship. Role definition and agreement are essential, especially in the workplace where nebulous coaching relationships exist. Establishing the specifics of the coaching role, what it entails, areas included, and approaches to be used adds clarity to an otherwise vague process. The coach and performer work out the coaching agreement together to ensure mutual understanding of the various roles. A structured coaching relationship elevates what is often a casual and sporadic process to a consistent, development-focused process.

## Motivation

Understanding and applying the principles of motivation are inherent elements of the coaching role of an effective leader. Influencing others requires comprehension of the reasons people act in certain ways. *Motivation* is that which causes a person to act in a particular manner. There are a multitude of theories related to motivation, and all have relevance for the leader seeking to better understand a follower's nature. These theories include need-fulfillment (Maslow's hierarchy of needs), Herzberg's two-factor theory (what satisfies does not necessarily motivate), expectancy theory (a person behaves in a certain way if he or she believes their effort will yield a reward), and equity theory (expected outcomes are determined by comparing one's work and rewards to others doing a similar job). Rather than reviewing these theories, which can be found in almost any text on organizational behavior and development, this section briefly reviews some common misconceptions about motivation and discusses two major principles of motivation applicable in a coaching situation. The first is the principle of expecting the best, and the second is knowing what outcome is desired and then reinforcing it by reward.

*Misconceptions about Motivation*    Anyone seeking to influence another person needs to be skilled at motivating. There are many common misconceptions about motivation, several of which are described by McGinnis (1985), who also offers examples to refute them.

*All motivation is intrinsic:* Perhaps the most common misconception is that no one can motivate another person and that all motivation comes from within. For years, managers have been told: "You cannot motivate another person; all you can do is create an environment that is motivating." Although intrinsic motivation is very powerful, it is not the only source of motivation. Everyone remembers an instance where the presence of someone else—an inspiring teacher, a dynamic and encouraging coach, or simply the presence of loved ones—led to increased performance, even performance beyond expectation. McGinnis (1985) cites several historical examples, such as Wellington reportedly saying that when Napoleon was on the field, it was like fighting an additional 40,000 men. Winston Churchill's leadership breathed hope into a dispirited and frightened England during the last seven months of 1940 and changed the future of the modern world.

*Some people just are not motivated:* Another misconception is that some people are just not motivated. But everyone is motivated, though it may be by and for different things. The team member who is usually late and takes an extra half hour to get rolling in the morning may be the first one out the door in the afternoon, full of enthusiasm! The 15-year-old who requires continual nagging to get out of bed on a school morning can get himself up and out of the house at 4 A.M. on Saturday for a fishing trip with friends. These two have plenty of motivation—it is just inspired by particular things. The challenge for the leader is to channel that already-existing energy into endeavors good for the team or organization.

When first introduced to the idea of self-directed or self-managed work teams, many managers and supervisors react with skepticism. From their years of observing employee behavior, these leaders simply cannot conceive of these people accepting more responsibility willingly, such as participating in peer review, self-scheduling, managing inventory and supplies, or jointly interviewing applicants for an open position on the team. Yet most employees in a bureaucracy learned long ago that it simply does not pay to get involved beyond the minimum required in a day's work. When they realize that they really can, and are allowed to, make decisions that directly impact their work life, their enthusiasm returns. Most people prefer having control over their lives.

*Motivation is manipulation:* A third misunderstanding is that motivation is manipulation. In its negative connotation, manipulation is when a person tries to persuade another to a certain course of action that is not to the individual's benefit but to the motivator's benefit. Genuine motivation is finding mutually beneficial goals that are good for both individuals and then forming a satisfying partnership to achieve these goals.

*Motivational people are born, not made:* Contrary to this final misconception that motivational people are born, not developed, anyone can become an effective motivator. It simply takes an understanding of the theories and basic principles. This is good news for leaders wanting to further develop their effectiveness. Applying the principles of motivation increases the leader's ability to influence others. Two primary principles are identified and explained below.

**Expect the Best**    In coaching, attitude is everything. To put it simply, coaches who like people and who believe that people have the best of intentions often get the best performance. It is a well-documented fact that people live up to the expectations they and others have of them. Henry Ford said it best: "Whether you think you can or you think you can't, you're right!" If the coach expects the best from his or her performers, that is what the coach gets. Good coaches do not waste time looking for and exposing the faults of their performers. Instead they look for strengths and abilities that others have overlooked, and they find ways to encourage these special talents. If the coach is constantly on the watch for the person's worst side, performers become defensive and self-protective, and the door to an effective coaching relationship closes.

The coach can quickly turn a person or team into what he or she expects of them. Take for example the manager-coach in this particular situation. Over the past several months, Jim's department has been converted to work teams, and these teams have been assuming more responsibility. Jim does not really believe that employees can effectively make decisions that he spent years learning to make, but he feels he has no choice because the entire organization is converting to teams. Jim had a short vacation planned but was concerned about what might happen in his absence. Sure enough, on his return he learns that one of the teams has made a poor decision with significant negative ramifications for the department.

Jim's reaction greatly influences the team's future behavior. On the one hand, Jim could say, exasperatedly (even if only to himself): "I should have known better than to take any time off. You just can't give these people any responsibility. They don't have the knowledge or information managers have. I didn't think they were ready, but I didn't have any choice." To further reinforce this reaction, every time the team asks for more responsibility, he reminds them of the fiasco the last time they were left alone. And when he is gone for a day or longer, he makes it a point to call in and check up regularly to see what's going on. Or he asks a fellow manager or a supervisor to check a couple of times throughout the day just to be certain things are OK. What's the message to the team? What happens the next time the team is faced with a situation in which they need to make a decision? How does the team feel about itself?

On the other hand, Jim's reaction to the situation could be based on the belief that the team can accept responsibility and make good decisions. His reaction might then have been more like this: "Team, this decision was a mistake. It isn't like you. Let's take a look at what was happening and how you can clear this up. We won't make a big deal out of this, but I want to help you figure out what you might do differently next time. We all learn from doing, and if you're not making any mistakes, you're probably not making any decisions. And I want you to make decisions, because I know you have good judgment and can make good choices."

The leader's belief about people influences how he or she approaches these coaching situations. And these beliefs create a self-fulfilling prophecy, which begins with an assumption that is not necessarily true. But believing it true, the leader acts as if it is and creates a cycle of behavior that results in the very behavior initially believed (see figure 6-1). This concept explains how the principle of "expect the best" works. Research has documented the validity of this concept and has further discovered that people prefer others to behave as they expect them to. If a coach has a belief about an individual, and the individual does not behave in a manner to support this belief, the coach becomes uncomfortable. For example, if an individual succeeds where a coach thought the individual would fail, this creates dissonant feelings in the coach.

The self-fulfilling prophecy concept is critical for workplace coaches because they have all kinds of expectations about the people they work with and some of these expectations are damaging. For example, executive leaders who believe that employees do not want additional responsibility or involvement in decision making are less willing to share responsibility. A manager's belief that employees without a professional education cannot manage themselves, or are not as creative as those employees with more education, directly affects the degree of delegation that occurs. These are common beliefs operating in today's workplace, and they limit the potential of individuals' and teams' achievements. Effective leaders continually seek to understand their own behavior to determine the presence of unrecognized negative assumptions.

***Reward the Desired Behavior***   To effectively influence others, the coach must be crystal clear about the behavior he or she is seeking and then reward that behavior. If the desired behavior is not rewarded or recognized in some manner, it is gradually extinguished. Or, worse, if contradictory behaviors are rewarded and reinforced, this results in poor outcomes, leaving leaders scratching their heads and wondering: "How did this happen?"

**FIGURE 6-1.  The Self-Fulfilling Prophecy**

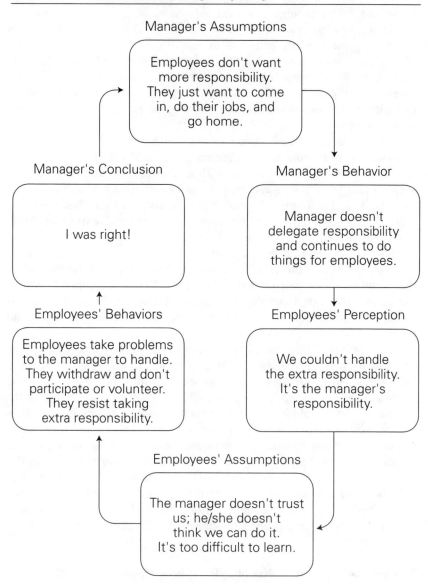

The concept of reward is broader in scope than simply monetary rewards. In the workplace when reward is discussed, it is automatically assumed money is that reward. What is really needed is a variety of rewards. Money is certainly an important one, but it is often tied directly to the annual performance appraisal system. In too many organizations today, this system is more deflating than motivating. A large system in the Midwest implemented a new rating scheme for the annual performance appraisals. Department managers were told that roughly only one employee for every twenty should receive the highest rating. In one small department, the manager was directly advised that only one of her employees could be given this high rating.

The manager was in a dilemma because she had several exemplary performers and she had to make a tough choice about who would receive the highest rating. One employee, Jane, had led a major housewide change initiative, coauthored an article for publication in a professional journal, and given a presentation at a national conference in addition to carrying her normal workload. Jane was devastated when she was given a rating of average after a year of exceptional performance. Is it any wonder that employees disengage and remove themselves psychologically from their workplace? In this instance, the difference in money was negligible, but in terms of recognition for achievement it was felt as a slap in the face. The organization unwittingly lost the commitment of one of its best members.

Good leaders use a variety of rewards, such as increased opportunity, going to lunch together, more individual time with the coach, increased flexibility in scheduling, visibility, praise, greater freedom, and even increased responsibility. These rewards are more likely to leave an individual with something to remember. Rewards are most effective when they are awarded closely following the behavior or accomplishment being acknowledged and when specific behaviors are identified. The rewards must also be offered sincerely.

Wells Fargo has developed innovative ways of rewarding people. At the year-end holidays, employees are given a $50 bill. However, the stipulation is that each employee would give their $50 to a coworker, someone who had been the most helpful during the past year! What a wonderful way to reinforce cooperation and teamwork among coworkers. Employees who received the most $50 bills were also given a choice of another holiday gift from the company. The list included items such as two pounds of Mrs. Field's cookies every month for a year, a two-hour body massage on April 15th, a new puppy, or a menu item named in your honor in the Wells Fargo cafeteria! These gifts made a tremendous impact and were not soon forgotten.

A good coach is very careful to avoid rewarding behaviors contradictory to those desired. If, for instance, increased responsibilities are always given to two or three members of the staff because they are especially willing and competent, after a time, these staff members may feel like they are pulling the weight for the whole team. If raising issues and offering different viewpoints are considered positive team behavior, then that behavior is recognized and remarked upon, rather than the compliant behavior of simply going along with everyone else. An executive in one organization was known for belittling and chastising people who offered opinions differing from his, yet he constantly verbalized the importance of speaking up and being honest.

In a local newspaper some years ago, there was a classic example of a punitive reward for good behavior. The nationally syndicated columnist Sandra Pesmen (1990) received the following question: "I called my top commission salesman in another city last week and couldn't find him in the office or at any customer's offices. So I called his house at 1 P.M. and he answered the phone. When I asked what he was doing there, he answered that he'd filled his quota for the month, and if he worked any harder and made more sales, he'd just have to pay more to Uncle Sam. I'm furious but wonder what to do. He is a good rep, works well with our customers there and knows our line."

Pesman's answer is insightful and representative of the mentality prevalent in some sectors of society. She responded: "Try and remember you're the boss. Cut his commission so he'll have to work harder to make the same personal profits. While he's doing that, he'll be increasing the company profits, which is the main goal. If he gets angry over that and quits, remember no one is indispensable." So, the bottom line here is that every time this salesman increases his sales, he gets less, not more. What is this company rewarding? And why would anyone in their right mind continue working hard for them?

These two basic concepts—building a foundational relationship and applying the principles of motivation—increase effectiveness of the leader involved in developing the skills and abilities of followers. Some leaders understand these concepts inherently, but for others, this review may be used as a reminder of their importance.

## THE COACHING PROCESS

The most effective coaching process is based on a partnership relationship between coach and performer. The essence of the relationship is one of mutual benefit, an exchange of equal contribution between the two parties. Zemke (1996) notes: "Managers who see themselves as coaches will also tend to see their employees as individuals of innate talent and worth. Managers who see themselves as coaches will strive to act as trusted advisers to help people develop those talents and use them in concert with others toward the achievement of a common and shared goal. Managers who see themselves as coaches tend not to think of their employees as vassals" (27).

Indeed, active coach-leaders and coach-managers see themselves in partnership with performers. The coaching process includes six steps, as illustrated in figure 6-2.

1. Establishing the purpose or goals
2. Assessing the performer's needs
3. Reaching an agreement on expectations and parameters
4. Teaching or training
5. Observing performance
6. Giving feedback

### Establish the Purpose or Goals

The first step of the process is to determine the purpose of the coaching. Why is the leader coaching the individual? Is there a performance gap issue? Does the individual need to improve performance simply to meet the expectations of the role or job? Is the leader trying to develop advanced skills in the performer? Is the leader evaluating the individual's strengths and capabilities to determine future promotion opportunities?

**FIGURE 6-2.  The Coaching Process**

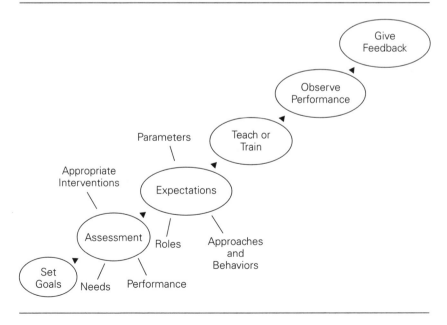

Is the coaching part of a successive planning strategy? The strongest goals are those developed mutually by coach and performer.

Without a specific goal in mind, coaching is less likely to be intentional and proactive, as discussed previously. In some instances the coaching plan is specific and concrete enough that goals are actually written and agreed upon. For instance, the CEO coaches several members of the executive team so that they are able to attend and function effectively at key committee meetings. A manager focuses on developing a staff member to lead a staff action committee for problem solving of special department concerns. Department leaders converting to a team-based structure often use a unique, explicit coaching plan for each team leader and each team.

In other instances, the purpose of the coaching is more general and nonspecific: It is simply a desire to intentionally focus on development needs of others. It is comparable to the reactive form of coaching mentioned earlier. A situation arises spontaneously and it is natural for the coach to teach, train, or give feedback on observation of performance.

Once the purpose or desired direction is clear, then the precise needs of the performer are determined by completing an assessment, as described below. Although assessment of the performer's needs is the second step of the coaching process, assessment is also inherent within each step. For instance, some level of assessment occurs before the purpose or goal is determined. Prior to teaching or training, assessment of appropriate interventions is necessary. And observing performance, the fifth step, entails assessing or appraising the results of the coaching to determine whether it was effective or not.

## Assess the Performer's Needs

The second step of an effective coaching process is assessment. It may be completed by the performer, the coach, or both. First, the desired skill or competency is identified. In some instances, the performer becomes aware of a need for coaching in a specific area. It may be a new skill or job responsibility with which the individual has little or no experience, or circumstances may have changed significantly since the last time this responsibility was accepted. In other instances, the coach may have been alerted to the need for coaching by observing a gap between actual performance and acceptable or exceptional completion of the responsibility.

However the need for coaching is identified, the focus of assessment includes appraising the performer's level of development or accomplishment of the task or responsibility. In their situational leadership model, Hersey and Blanchard (1993) have categorized four development levels that assist both coach and performer in assessing the individual or team and determining the most effective coaching intervention. Each level is based on two aspects: the performer's competence and commitment. Competence refers to the performer's knowledge, skill, and experience. Commitment includes willingness to perform or interest in accepting the responsibility or task, confidence, and level of the performer's motivation. The four development levels are described in the following sections along with the coaching interventions, to help the individual realize what he or she may need.

***Development Level 1: Novice***   This is a new responsibility for the individual. The person may have had education and theory but no actual experience or practice with the responsibility. Performers at this level are usually excited and enthusiastic about trying a new skill. Thus, competence level is low but commitment is high.

*Development level 1: Coaching interventions:*  Coaching interventions include sharing any information needed by the performer. This includes telling the performer what to do, and how, where, and when to do it. It can include making educational opportunities available to the individual, suggesting reading resources, or even recommending practice with a specialized coach. However it is accomplished, the coaching intervention is to provide the competence that the performer lacks. Commitment and enthusiasm are high, so little encouragement is needed.

Any information provided is very structured and detailed, with the situation closely controlled and monitored by the coach because the performer does not yet have the necessary skills. In fact, too many explanations and examples can cause confusion because the performer needs only the basics at this stage.

***Development Level 2: Advanced Beginner***   This is a higher development level because the performer has had some experience using this skill or taking on this responsibility but is not accomplished at this point. Perhaps the individual is a novice in the situation in which the task must be applied. Commitment is variable because after trying something and not having things proceed as well as expected, the results are often discouragement and frustration because the task is not as easy as first believed. As a result, the performer lacks self-confidence and may even resist the idea of trying again.

*Development level 2: Coaching interventions:*  At this level, the performer has some competence but low commitment. The coach's role is to furnish the additional technical competence needed and plenty of enthusiasm and support. In addition to the "how-tos" of level 1, the coach adds personal examples and perhaps discloses his or her own early difficulties in gaining the particular skill. The coach asks questions about the performer's experiences and previous successes and listens carefully to the answers. This provides an opportunity to redirect or reinforce behavior.

Guided discussions are very appropriate at this stage because the performer may be making progress without realizing it and may simply need an individual with an objective viewpoint to recognize that and point it out. This is heartening, and when used with praise and positive reinforcement, it can provide the encouragement the performer needs.

**Development Level 3: Competent**    At the competency level, the performer is experienced in applying the skill or has the competency required to assume the responsibility but has variable commitment. The individual may have high competence in this skill but in a completely different setting and may lack confidence in that ability because he or she does not recognize its transferability. Or the people involved may be new to the performer. This performer is high on competence but variable on commitment.

*Development level 3: Coaching interventions:*    At this level, the performer is competent, and any information or knowledge provided by the coach is minimal, often limited to key parameters and expectations that apply. For example, the only structure given by the coach may be to share the final date by which the task is to be completed or identify key constraints, such as budget limitations or expected stakeholder involvement. The performer is fairly experienced with this responsibility and just needs a coach available to talk through ideas and possible solutions.

However, commitment is variable at this point. The performer has wavering self-confidence in his or her ability to achieve the desired outcomes. The current situation may be significantly different from any in his or her experience base or simply more complex or difficult than usual. Whatever the case may be, at this point the coach provides the much-needed encouragement and support through guided discussions, asking questions and listening carefully to answers, and reminding the performer of previous successes and lessons learned in the past. With a highly competent performer, the focus is that little extra push of encouragement and confidence that a trusted coach can give.

**Development Level 4: Expert**    This is the highest level of development achieved by a performer. Experience in the performance area is broad enough that the individual has not only the technical competency but a high level of judgment in applying the skills. Additionally, commitment is high. The performer is motivated, confident, and enthusiastic about the responsibility.

*Development level 4: Coaching interventions:* For the highly competent and committed performer, the coach really does not need to provide much of anything. There may be a need to provide the barest of structure in the same manner that performers at level 3 need—such as clarification of a time frame, or key parameters and constraints. These are often negotiated between the coach and performer, as would be expected in an equal partnership.

Although recognition and rewards are always important, they are less important to the performer at this level of development. Much of the commitment and enthusiasm is generated from profound intrinsic motivation. As in development level 1, the performer has plenty of zeal and is excited about what needs to be accomplished.

**Completing the Assessment**    Ways in which a performer's development level is assessed include observing actual performance, self-reporting by the performer, and information coming from third-party sources. Yet another source of information may be knowledge of the logical process. For example, if an individual has performed well as a leader of a department, the next step in his or her development might include leadership opportunities of cross-department or cross-divisional projects or problem-solving groups. If an executive leader has performed well and mastered his or her responsibilities within the organization, the next step may be opportunities that are systemwide.

Accurate assessment is crucial because the individual's development level determines the coaching intervention required. If the assessment is inaccurate, the resulting intervention may range from ineffective to downright harmful. For instance, if the performer is at development level 1 and is low on competence, the coach's role is to provide access to needed knowledge and information. If the individual was erroneously assessed at development level 3 with a high level of skill and the coach determines that encouragement and support are needed, the coach falls short. The performer then becomes frustrated and demoralized by not performing at the expected level.

A good example of this was observed in an organization undergoing massive change. A special project team of employees was identified and assigned to the project for a two-year period. The team's purpose was to lead the major change initiatives in the organization. Tom was appointed team leader. Having received his master's degree in hospital administration, Tom had recently completed his administrative residency at the hospital. A tall, imposing figure of a man who emulated the corporate dress-for-success code, Tom exuded confidence and capability without being arrogant. He was a relatively young man, however, having completed his master's work immediately following his undergraduate program; and he had no management experience. It was erroneously believed that he was at development level 3 in terms of managing the team because he had significant leadership experience and he certainly looked the part. Unfortunately, this promising young man was overevaluated repeatedly. Not only did he not receive the specific, basic managerial skill development and direction he needed, but when he did not meet people's expectations (which were unrealistic), he was faced with their extreme disappointment and negative reactions. Tom was in a no-win position.

The same can happen with children. In one family, both the father and mother were very tall. Their young son grew rapidly, and at six years, he towered over all of his friends, his appearance easily that of a child twice his age. The mother reported being embarrassed and concerned by the judgmental comments and behaviors of other people who assumed that this six-year-old behavior was coming from a twelve-year-old! Her son's behavior was very appropriate for his age but unacceptable to others who had assessed him and come to very inaccurate conclusions.

Inaccuracies in assessment also occur in the opposite direction. When the individual or team has a higher level of competency than the leader believes and the leader provides more detail and direction than is needed, the performer is irritated and concludes that the leader is micromanaging or afraid to relinquish control. When teams or individuals are at a level 3 or 4, they are highly competent. If the leader closely monitors and supervises their work (appropriate behavior for level 1 and 2), resentment and anger often result.

## Agreement on Expectations and Parameters

Once the goals and direction are clearly established and an appraisal of the performer's needs is completed, the next step is to identify and agree on expectations and applicable parameters. Clarifying the operant expectations helps prevent misunderstandings. Expectations between coach and performer may include the role of each person as well as the most helpful desired approaches and behaviors. Parameters must be clearly identified and understood by the performer. Each of these issues is examined with examples to illustrate their relevance within a coaching situation.

***Expectations: Roles and Responsibilities***    Early discussions about the roles and responsibilities of each party in a coaching relationship are essential. When the coaching relationship is a legal agreement between parties, roles are made particularly clear. The conductor of a symphony orchestra regularly practices with the musicians and is responsible for procuring the best possible performance from them. The athletic coach is employed for the same reason: to develop individual team members to work as a team that will achieve peak performance. In the workplace, relationships are less clearly defined. Some coaches are very effective in developing performers yet are not in management positions. And many managers today see their coaching role as additional to their other responsibilities, something done haphazardly, if at all.

Thus, in today's workplace there is an increasingly greater number of performers who are unclear about the coaching role and may actually resent someone else observing their performance. In fact, their experience with the manager as a coach is limited to the annual performance appraisal or the less frequent disciplinary action. And these processes are often unsatisfactorily handled.

A conversation about the respective roles and responsibilities of each party formalizes the relationship and moves it from incidental and accidental to one of intention. This objective consideration of who does what reduces the likelihood of emotions hampering the process. A coach's role is to facilitate or support the development of skills in the performers by observing performance and providing honest, direct feedback; by giving advice and instruction; and by encouraging discovery through guided discussions and hands-on experiences. The performer's role is to practice, perform, and use the coach's feedback, guidance, and instruction to further improve performance.

*Expectations: Desired Approaches and Behaviors*    Expectations concerning desired approaches and behaviors include such elements as the type of coaching required and the ways in which performance is observed or feedback is delivered. In discussions between coach and performer, expectations and needs related to specific behavior can be clarified. This actually forms an operating agreement. For example, the coach gives the individual immediate feedback after observing performance. But what is immediate feedback? Within a few minutes, a few hours, or several days? Is it important that the feedback be delivered privately? Are voice-mail and E-mail messages acceptable? Is feedback to be confidential? Will there be time to discuss the feedback and ask questions? What does the coach expect of the performer who is receiving feedback? Are the suggestions and corrections to be incorporated in the next "performance"? Is the feedback to be received with an open mind and a willingness to try alternatives?

Expectations and agreement on coaching interventions are determined by the needs of the performer and are an important point to discuss. Ideally, in a healthy coach-performer relationship, results of any assessment are discussed and an agreement is reached on specific coaching interventions to be provided. Even the most highly skilled performer has a need, at times, for direction and instruction. If the current situation is new to the performer, ways to increase knowledge and competence are the focus of the coaching. No matter how capable a performer, today's workplace is continually presenting new challenges for which competency must be developed. It may be gained if there are many similarities between the  performer's present and previous experiences, but the need for direct instruction and advice are paramount in the rapidly changing health care environment today.

One situation in a midwestern health care system is a classic example. Rose, CEO of the system, knew that as the system expanded to integrate a freestanding rehabilitation facility, a large home health facility, and a physician practice clinic, she could prepare for her own role changes by selecting a chief operating officer whose focus would be primarily on hospital operations. Her final candidate came from within the current ranks of her executive staff. Don, a young man, had the necessary educational qualifications and demonstrated leadership abilities. His current responsibilities included the marketing function and physician relations in the organization. When Rose made the appointment, she was well aware that his downside was lack of experience and knowledge of hospital operations. In making her decision, she was clear about her coaching role with Don. He would need directive interventions and learning opportunities to assist him in the development of these competencies.

When competence and skill are what will be provided by the coach, there can be emotional elements—both negative and positive—to consider. Don was excited and pleased about his promotion because of the trust and confidence in his abilities expressed by Rose. If Rose and Don had not talked about his learning needs and the appropriate coaching interventions, he might have felt uncomfortable with the high level of direction provided by Rose. There is added pressure from Don's wanting to perform well after receiving such a big promotion. This was a time of increased vulnerability for Don, with others watching to judge the appropriateness of the promotion. He felt a strong need to perform capably and competently to show worthiness of the trust extended.

In any system converting to a team-based structure, there are a multitude of examples illustrating the importance of discussing together appropriate coaching interventions. When the structure in an organization is converted from a department form to designed work teams within departments, the coaching needs of the new teams are often underestimated. Many managers and leaders make erroneous assumptions about the team's level of development. If individual department employees were at a high development level, it may be assumed that their team's development level is also high. But although team members' skills and competencies certainly influence the team's ability, the two are not the same.

This false assumption is often reinforced by highly skilled and capable team members from whom may be heard comments such as "We're already a team; we've been working in this department together for years," "I've been making these decisions myself for years and you've never complained," or "I am a self-directed individual, so that makes this a self-directed work team." In early stages of team development, the team needs a manager-leader who provides the competence that the team lacks: how to work as a team. Yet unless the role of the coach and his or her assessment are discussed together, too often the team feels that the manager is giving a mixed message: "You said we're a self-directed work team, so why are you telling us what to do?" Everyone involved feels they have failed and been failed because their expectations were not met.

Sometimes these issues and the need to talk through and agree upon expectations become clear during the process of working together. In the beginning, many of these behaviors are assumed; but the danger of not talking through expectations is that they are much more difficult to discuss once they have been violated. The performer may have assumed that negative or corrective feedback would be given privately, only to discover that the coach is giving feedback of a critical nature in the middle of a staff meeting. It is better to have a discussion prior to the occurrence of problems to prevent emotional reactions that can make effective resolution more difficult.

*Relevant Parameters*    Any constraints, limitations, deadlines, or other parameters are identified for the performer. If the coach does not think these through and share them with the performer, outcomes can be adversely affected, and enthusiasm and commitment may spiral downward, making the performer feel as though he or she has failed. Some individuals perform acceptably without this clarification, but this is not a chance worth taking—unless, of course, the coach is trying to assess the performer's ability to sort out and determine these important boundaries (which in itself can be considered a useful skill).

In a major system on the eastern seaboard growing in both size and scope, the CEO began delegating more and more responsibility to the COO. A major project taken on by the COO was a restructuring and work-redesign initiative for the acute-care hospital facility. This initiative was the CEO's favored and important project. Instead of the CEO actively coaching the COO, it was a sink-or-swim affair. Key constraints and expectations were covered only loosely or assumed to be understood. The COO misread and reversed the importance of many of these key parameters and forced the project through in an unrealistic time frame without adequate resources. The resulting negative impact on physician and customer satisfaction—the parameters most important to the CEO and board of trustees—eventually cost the COO his job.

Clarifying expectations and parameters at the beginning of the coaching process can avoid this kind of scenario. In one changing organization the chief nurse executive was asked to become executive sponsor for a massive reengineering project. This was her most important large-scope project since she had assumed her role 18 months before. She was told by her coach that the most critical parameter was that there must be no negative impact on patient satisfaction ratings during the evolution to a restructured, team-based environment. Based on everything she knew about change and the limits to resources in the organization to mitigate the ordinary disruption of major change, this was an unrealistic expectation. As she accepted the responsibility, this expectation was a major discussion point. She negotiated much more realistic expectations, including an acceptable depth of decline in patient satisfaction scores and a reasonable length of time over which these would be explainable by the change.

The specificity of parameters is related to the development level of the performer. At level 1, more detailed information is needed. As the performer gains in experience and skill level, parameters become fewer or less concrete. For instance, when the performer is at level 3, the structure given may be only a time deadline or budget constraint.

An employee team leading the work-redesign implementation process in one care center decided to purchase beautiful color-coordinated linens for the patients—bedspreads, curtains, draperies, and bed linens. To the dismay of everyone, it was discovered that the particular fabric blend they had chosen could not be processed in the organization's laundry equipment. So these wonderful decorator linens sat in a warehouse, unused. It became an organizational example of why empowerment does not work and why employees cannot make decisions such as these. Granted, someone on the team could have suggested getting input from the experts in linen services, but a thorough coach would have identified the important parameter that the linens must be able to be processed in the organization's laundry equipment! Or a parameter identified by the coach might have been that the team involve an expert from the linen service department before making a final decision.

A major difficulty with expectations and parameters is that they are frequently implied rather than stated, and it is assumed that those involved understand and agree on the important expectations. This increases the likelihood that one or the other party involved in the coaching agreement fails to meet the unstated expectations of the other. No matter how highly intuitive the participating individuals, they probably cannot read someone else's mind! Expectations, needs, and parameters must be clearly articulated and agreed upon by the various people involved.

### Teach or Train for the Desired Skills

The fourth step of the coaching process is to teach or train for desired skills. Teaching others is also a specific manner in which a coach develops others and as such is discussed more fully under its own heading in this chapter. But because it is also a step in the coaching process, it is discussed here briefly.

Once the purpose of coaching is determined and the assessment is complete, it becomes clear what specific skill development is being sought, which may be individual competencies or group and team skills. A good coach requires both individual and team practice. Individual practice focuses on increasing proficiency of the individual's performance. Group, or team, practice is preparation aimed at the collective functioning of the group and its ability to orchestrate individual talents among them in order to deliver a fine performance.

The coach determines what needs to be taught and when and how to best teach it. The "what" encompasses both technical or professional and supportive skills. Technical or professional skills pertain to the elements of an individual's job or work, such as completing a budget analysis or preparation, doing a counseling session with an employee, or preparing a collaborative strategic plan. Supportive skills are more general in nature, such as communication and coaching skills.

Selecting a teaching approach is paramount. Too often, didactic classroom-style teaching and formal academic programs are the methods used. Although these are valuable, other possibilities are often overlooked. Tape-recording and videotaping are powerful methods of instruction that can provide immediate, objective feedback on performance. Videotaping a meeting and replaying it to critique participants' performances provide powerful lessons in group process. In one hospital's information services department, the clinical support team decided to tape-record conversations with customers (with the customers' permission) to evaluate the team's effectiveness in handling complaints and support on their help line.

In considering how to teach or train a performer, an effective coach capitalizes on every teachable moment. It is as much an attitude as a technique. Using the day-to-day environment and continually seeking opportunities to demonstrate a point or teach a technique drives home the expectation that learning is an integral part of the workplace, not just something that happens in a classroom. Staff and team meetings are planned to include some teaching at each meeting. And teaching is not limited to that provided by the coach. Exemplary performers also teach others, both formally and informally; and team members are therefore expected to coach and teach one another.

When to teach is more of an issue with regard to training through a formal learning setting such as a classroom. The most effective teaching and training are done at the time the skill or learning is needed, when it can be applied immediately and become anchored as a change in the learner's behavior. However, most situations are not ideal and the issue of when to provide training is fraught with difficulty. Training and teaching most often occur prior to when it is actually needed or too long after the fact. This reduces the usefulness and adversely impacts learning.

## Observe Performance

An active, involved coach spends a great deal of time simply watching people perform. If this necessary step of the process is dispensed with, the coach has no way of determining the success or effectiveness of the first four steps. Performers need to feel comfortable being observed. If the coach's role has been discussed, the need for direct observation is received as a gift rather than interpreted as micromanagement. It is the performer's opportunity to have an objective party provide feedback that will either reinforce good performance or correct faulty technique.

Direct observation is the best and preferred method for a coach to evaluate performance. Nevertheless, third-party reporting or self-reporting are acceptable. Third-party reporting may be negatively associated with "tattling," which is unfortunate. This association has developed because many people are uncomfortable sharing criticisms or negative comments directly with the person they have observed and will, instead, share these observations with others. To avoid this negative connotation, sharing of third-party reports should be kept to positive observations. Everyone enjoys and appreciates hearing positive comments about their performance and values the third party who takes time to give positive feedback to the coach. The coach who receives negative third-party reports should only use the information as an indication that there may be a need for personal observation and evaluation.

In the self-reporting process, the coach and performer talk through how a scenario played out, what was tried, what was effective, and what did not work. Techniques for questions that will draw out information in a comfortable, nonthreatening manner are important for this approach to work.

Another way the coach can evaluate performance is by evaluating actual outcomes against intended outcomes. Did the performer meet expectations? Were the outcomes acceptable or outstanding?

An advantage of observing performance directly is that the coach can evaluate the performer's ability. How long did it take the individual to learn the skill? What kind of teaching or training seemed to be most effective for this person? Did the performer demonstrate good judgment in asking for assistance during complex, difficult situations, or did he or she prefer to "go it alone"? Was the performer able to pace him- or herself appropriately? What workload level can this performer handle? Does this individual feel comfortable negotiating modifications of workload? By observing performance, the coach learns a tremendous amount about the performer and becomes a more effective coach for this individual.

## Give Feedback

This final step closes the loop and finalizes the entire process. Without feedback, the whole process is negated, as the performer has no way of determining the success or effectiveness of the first five steps. Having no feedback would be like playing a baseball game without innings or a scoreboard. A score of 2–1 in the bottom of the first inning is quite different from a score of 2–1 in the ninth inning. In the same way that the score of a baseball game lets the team members know how they are doing, feedback lets performers know how they are doing.

The coach is, admittedly, only one source of feedback for good performers who are continual learners. They seek feedback from a variety of sources and are always evaluating their own performance. However, none of this other feedback can equal the value of honest, direct feedback from a trusted coach whose only interest is in helping the performer to improve.

Expert coaches study the people they coach; they know them and look for strengths that others have overlooked. When small successes occur, they know how to transform them into larger successes. The exemplary coach uses positive feedback, praise, and compliments, as well as redirection when necessary.

Nearly everyone wants to be appreciated and recognized for their particular performance. However, most positive feedback is general rather than intentionally specific about the behavior that should be reinforced by it. Effective praise will reinforce that specific behavior. It is the difference between saying "Thanks, you did a great job" and "Thanks, your persistence in getting the team to explore their differences has resulted in achieving consensus on this decision."

In his book *How to Motivate People*, Fran Tarkenton (1986) says that positive reinforcement for both normal behavior and exceptional performance is critical. He points out that people do a good job about four times as frequently as they do lousy work. It makes sense, then, for anyone wanting improved results to recognize that performers do a good job at least 80 percent of the time. Tarkenton says negative feedback should be given in the same proportion. So an individual should be praised at least four times as often as criticized. He notes that almost the opposite is true. Eighty percent of the typical feedback is based on the 20 percent that is poor performance.

Exemplary coaches are always seeking opportunities to give feedback; and in order to give praise, the coach must observe and catch the performer doing something right. Blanchard and Johnson (1981) are strong proponents of this philosophy. McGinnis (1985) offers several guidelines for giving praise:

- Hand out commendations in public.
- Use every success as an excuse for celebration.
- Use some gesture to give weight to the commendation.
- Put compliments in writing.
- Be very specific in praise.

One problem with praise is that it can be overdone. If a person has established good, consistent performance and continues to be praised for the same thing, it soon becomes meaningless. The coach needs to find new behaviors about which to offer praise. A second challenge is that, if the first five steps of the coaching process have been accomplished and the performer shows signs of positive change, the coach must reinforce this new or changed behavior. It is terribly demoralizing to go to a great deal of effort to improve a skill or change a behavior and then realize that the coach doesn't even notice.

This last principle can be tricky when the behavior is in the right direction but the outcomes are not acceptable. One manager-coach was strongly urging a team to begin to take responsibility for solving problems and making decisions on their own initiative. The first decision they made was poor, mostly because it was limited in scope. The team had not considered the impact of their decision on other teams in the organization. The manager praised the fact that the team made a decision, but then coached them through an evaluation of the outcome to help them see what key factors they had missed.

Giving negative feedback is often more difficult for coaches. In some instances, the performer tries a skill or attempts a technique that does not work. The observant coach immediately redirects the individual by giving feedback or "scold instruction." The coach would say something like: "Don't do it that way; do it this way."

Sometimes a redirection or correction is needed that is more negative. Blanchard and Johnson (1981) advocate giving one-minute reprimands. Their point is that the redirection occurs quickly and honestly. Keep in mind the following steps in giving a redirection:

1. Do it immediately in order to correct the behavior as soon after it occurs as possible.
2. Confirm the facts with the individual before going further to ensure the information is accurate.
3. Be very specific and direct in saying what is wrong, focusing criticism on behavior rather than the person.

4.  Show honest feelings so the individual knows the coach is frustrated, angry, disappointed, or whatever.

It is impossible to be effective if a coach is afraid to correct the performer's mistakes. When asked how he felt about negative feedback, one performer said, "I feel good when the feedback is positive, but I can change my behavior and improve my performance when it is negative. Hearing negative feedback may not be pleasant, but the results are more satisfying to me because it helps me move in the long run."

Coaching, then, is the primary means through which a leader can develop others. Intentional, proactive coaching involves performers using a specific process, including establishing the purpose, assessment, agreeing on expectations and parameters, teaching and training, observing performance, and giving feedback.

## PROVIDING OPPORTUNITIES

Potentially the most powerful method of developing others is also one of the simplest: providing opportunities. An exemplary leader continually seeks opportunities to stretch and challenge followers, reveling in the accomplishments of others.

The extent to which a leader makes new opportunities available to followers demonstrates the importance the leader places on the development of new proficiencies. Furthermore, it delivers a high-impact message of trust and confidence in the follower's ability to perform well in a particular situation. Providing opportunities means seeking these occasions, presenting them to followers with enthusiasm and encouragement, removing barriers or obstacles, getting out of the way of the developing performer, and celebrating achievements.

Many high-performing leaders could undoubtedly look back over their own career paths and identify times when someone tapped them on the shoulder and asked them to take on a responsibility or charge that they had not heretofore considered. Looking for ways to share the responsibility of leadership is one source of opportunities for followers. Is there a way to delegate some of the leader's responsibility? Reciprocally, exemplary followers continually seek challenge. However, their path is smoother and faster if facilitated by an influential leader working on their behalf.

Removing barriers or obstacles for the follower is an important leadership responsibility, discussed briefly in chapter 5. In the context of follower development, it might mean an introduction to the right person or simply speaking highly of the follower to other leaders in the organization. Recommending a follower to serve as the chair of an influential task force or committee, positioning the individual to receive appointments to boards or groups within the community or state—even promotions outside of the current position—are all ways a leader can remove barriers and champion followers. Many established and highly visible leaders receive more opportunities for service than they could possibly handle. Sharing some of these opportunities with followers is an intentional way of supporting a follower's development.

If the leader is also the performer's manager, removing obstacles may mean something as rudimentary as providing time within the normal work week for the follower to engage in these other activities. Helping arrange for staff coverage, if necessary, and providing time away from the department to assume these new responsibilities say to the follower: "I am serious about your development needs. They are important to me as well as to the organization."

In some instances, simply providing the opportunity is adequate, but most leaders also become involved in coaching the follower to help develop the individual's skills. If the leader is not able to provide what the follower needs, a referral or recommendation to another available coach may be effective.

A good leader is delighted, rather than threatened, when a follower's skill level surpasses that leader's. Achievement of outcomes and improvement of the performer's skills are treated as occasions for celebration.

## TEACHING OTHERS

Outstanding leaders are often outstanding teachers. They understand principles of adult learning and apply them. Their teaching is intentional, and they engage in both spontaneous and deliberate teaching, obviously delighting in a follower's learning something new. This leader lives by the old adage: Give a man a fish and he eats for a day; teach a man to fish and he eats for a lifetime.

The principles of adult learning used by effective leaders are reviewed here to reinforce their application. Some people hear the word *teaching* and think of a formal academic model because it is familiar. But teaching is so much more than the traditional example of a teacher standing in front of a group and dispensing knowledge.

Most leaders today have been socialized and molded by an academic setting very different from what their children are experiencing. After years in an educational system with a relatively traditional approach, most adults expect to be listeners during the learning process, while the experts teach them, acting as information disseminators and advice givers. Ironically, it is not until the role of educator shifts from transmitter of information to facilitator and resource person for self-directed inquiry that the learner's needs are likely to be met.

Principles of adult learning conjure images of participants in a learning situation who are actively participating. So, what is expected is active exchange of ideas, questioning, and perhaps hands-on practice. Active participation, however, does not necessarily mean that a person is continually interacting and talking. Participation can be as simple as thoughtful, private inquiry in reaction to something the teacher has asked or presented. Taking generic principles or ideas shared by the teacher and applying them to one's own situation is also active participation. In some instances, a teacher's example may create a vivid picture in the mind of the learner that helps anchor the learning. So, activity does not necessarily mean flashy exercises and dynamic situations that need a skilled facilitator for guidance.

Malcolm Knowles was one of the earliest educators in this country to distinguish between methods used for teaching children in a formal academic approach and those used for teaching self-directed learners such as adults. He described adult learning as differing from childlike learning in at least four main respects. First, there is a difference in orientation to learning. Learning for children in school is often subject centered rather than problem oriented. The chief difference is in time perspectives. A child's perspective of formal education is one of postponed application while an adult usually wants to apply his or her learning immediately. Compare a child's interest in a geography lesson about a country far away to the adult who is planning a vacation to that same country in the next four months. This issue of timing is critical. How many young people drop out of school because they do not see their learning experience as applicable and useful in their lives?

Changes in a learner's self-concept is the second way childlike learning is differentiated from adult learning. An assumption of self-directed learning is that as a person grows and matures, his or her self-concept moves from one of dependency to one of increasing self-confidence. Children are dependent on others in their earliest years, but as they grow and mature, they expect to participate more actively in decisions affecting learning. In fact, Knowles suggests that when adults find themselves in a situation in which they are not allowed to be self-directed, they experience tension between the given situation and their self-concept, resulting in resentment and resistance. "Why is this person telling me what to do? Does he or she think I don't know?"

The third area differentiating the two types of learning is the role that experience plays in the learning. The assumption is that as an individual matures and accumulates experiences, these will serve as resources for learning and an ever-enlarging base to which to relate new learning. Teachers convey their respect for students by making use of students' past experiences as a resource for learning. The learner's readiness to learn is the last point of difference identified by Knowles. As individuals mature, their readiness to learn is more the product of what they need to know, because of a change in their environment or life situation, than what others believe they ought to know.

Knowles's observations are powerful for those seeking to improve their teaching skills. In the same way that individuals are at varying levels of development related to the skill they are trying to learn, each is also at varying levels of development in learning. In other words, learning is a skill that needs to be developed. If the assessment model for coaching provided earlier in the chapter is applied, the different levels of learning might look like this:

*Development level 1:* This level of learning could be likened to the learning of a young child. Enthusiasm and commitment abound. The learner lacks competence and knowledge, so the teacher provides structure by deciding the appropriate curriculum and learning experiences required. The teacher provides required information and knowledge, guides the learning process, and evaluates outcomes.

*Development level 2:* At this level the learner has some experience but variable commitment. Perhaps early attempts at learning revealed that it is not as easy as it seemed. This learner requires both strong direction and lots of support and encouragement. Direction is provided by the instructor determining what needs to be taught and how it will be taught. At this point, most teachers remain actively present and involved during learning situations, giving feedback and attention as well as praise and encouragement.

*Development level 3:* The learner at this stage has fairly wide experience with learning but perhaps lacks self-confidence in the subject area. The learner needs minimal structure from the teacher, requiring mostly encouragement and support. The teacher uses guided discussions and practice or live sessions to facilitate learning.

*Development level 4:* This level represents the epitome of the self-directed learner. The learner is responsible for defining his or her own educational needs, necessary resources, and appropriate time schedules. Evaluation of the learning process is also undertaken by the learner. At this level, the learner works in partnership with the teacher to appropriately define the learning outcomes expected and agree on an approach to learning. The self-directed learner has the ability to maturely evaluate educational materials and opportunities, and effectively manages his or her own time.

In the workplace, leaders are working with followers who are typically at levels 3 and 4. These learners are comfortable with learning and at level 3 may just need more coaching. These learners are the most likely to fall back into the more traditional modes of learning, such as didactic classroom presentations. Most leaders are blessed with at least some followers who are self-directed learners. These learners are open, curious, organized, motivated, and highly enthusiastic. They soak up learning opportunities like the earth soaks up rain following a lengthy dry spell. Anything the leader does to support their learning is deeply appreciated.

## Concepts of Learning

When the leader understands and applies the following concepts of learning, facilitation of learning increases significantly:

- *Learning is defined as a change in behavior.* Many people falsely believe that if the teacher opens his or her mouth and articulately shares information, learning has occurred. Learning only occurs when there is an actual change in behavior. Employees in an organization converting to a team-based structure can attend class after class of valuable information on how to make decisions and work as a team. If, however, their behavior does not change, and the information is not taken back and applied in the workplace, no learning has occurred.
- *Motivation of the learner is important.* Adult learners are motivated by understanding and accepting the purposes of the learning situation. If a learner sees a direct need for the new knowledge or skill, readiness to learn is greatly increased. When the learner perceives a personal usefulness for new learning and can readily identify the positive possible outcomes, learning is enhanced. In one organization, an employee attending basic interpersonal skills development classes in preparation for the conversion to work teams was heard to say: "If I had known this ten years ago, my marriage wouldn't have ended in divorce." This participant was highly motivated to practice these skills in her current relationship.

    Both learners and teachers are motivated by success. In planning early learning opportunities, there needs to be a fair certainty of success. For instance, if the leader is coaching a team leader of a primary work team on conflict resolution skills, the teacher should start small. Perhaps the first situation should be a role play followed by facilitating the resolution of an intrateam conflict. If the first conflict handled alone by the team leader is a major conflict between teams in different departments, or between the team and a major customer (such as a physician), the stakes are too high.

Teacher acceptance is also reinforcing and motivational. Learners do better when they believe the teacher accepts them unconditionally, in spite of the learner's need to gain competence in an area. One way this is demonstrated is by the leader-teacher's objective acceptance of mistakes and their sincere interest in helping the learner develop skills.

The extent of learning is determined almost completely by the learner's level of motivation. Adult learners make a choice about what they will learn. In many cases the motivation is intrinsic and may be as simple as the desire to know more, or intellectual curiosity.

- *Learning requires active participation on the part of the learner.* This increases the commitment of the individual and the level of ownership experienced. When the learner participates, information becomes knowledge. Internalized by the learner, the knowledge begets new experiences and successes.

- *Learning is deepened when the learning situation provides the opportunity to apply learning in as realistic a situation as feasible.* Using the skills and techniques in real-life situations greatly increases the learning because it is anchored in the individual's consciousness. Through use, the skills and techniques are also modified based on their usefulness, and the learner gradually evolves beyond the original teaching.

- *Learning is enhanced when learners accept responsibility for their own learning.* It is impossible to force someone to learn. The teacher's role is to make information and tools available, create the best learning situations possible, and provide the external motivation that encourages the learner during the process. Beyond this, it is the learner's responsibility to take the ball and run.

- *Learning occurs on successively deeper levels.* Sometimes highly expert teachers reduce their effectiveness because they try to give too much information at one time and move the learner too quickly. Of course, the higher the development level of the learner, the faster they go. In initial stages, information is delivered in chunks with opportunity to practice and apply the new learning. A learner can be quite good at a skill yet not have the judgment and appropriate decision-making ability to support the skill.

- *Effective learning depends on repetition and feedback.* Some adults are insulted when the teacher repeats a key piece of information, and they may feel impatient if they feel they have heard it before. In some of these instances, the learner probably never fully incorporated the message the first time! Conventional wisdom reports that it takes hearing something seven to eight times before it sinks in. The teacher's challenge is to find a multitude of ways to present the same information, changing and using new examples, and continually seeking ways to deliver the message through a variety of different channels.

Learners need the gift of feedback if they are to grow in their expertise. Feedback on performance gives the learner the opportunity to redirect and improve their dexterity with the knowledge. If the individual is not receiving clear, concise feedback on performance, he or she may think things are just fine when, in fact, there are problems.

- *Learning is stimulated by engaging a variety of senses.* Drawing a picture, using colors, or painting a graphic visual picture all increase learning. Most teachers rely heavily on auditory stimulation and forget kinesthetic learning (having the person move) and the olfactory sense (smell).
- *Learning is enhanced by an informal, friendly, and comfortable environment.* Atmosphere directly affects learning. If a room is too crowded, if ventilation is poor, lights are low, or the air-conditioning is too cold—all of these factors directly affect the learner's ability to listen and absorb information. Teachers who use embarrassment, humiliation, or shaming create a hostile environment where learning revolves around how to avoid these adverse reactions rather than the positive development of beneficial skills.

For adults to learn new skills, the ideal is a risk-taking environment where it is acceptable to make a mistake. Mistakes are viewed as learning opportunities that increase the knowledge base and the wisdom of those involved. An optimal learning environment is one in which there is a high amount of mutual trust and regard.

### Teaching by Example

Another key principle of teaching is to teach by example. This is a way to demonstrate a skill and show how something should be done. In addition, the leader's behavior demonstrates the expected leadership behaviors desired and rewarded in the organization. Leaders are continually modeling behavior, which can create a tremendous pressure for them. There is nothing a leader can do or say that escapes the notice of followers. Every behavior and response, even chance remarks give out some signals that will be picked up by a follower and passed on to others. Every action of the leader either validates or negates all the messages previously sent out. Followers can tell if a leader is sincere, honest, and congruent.

Some leaders are uncomfortable with this responsibility of influence and rail against the reality, claiming they don't want to be a role model, they don't want the pressure of followers watching their every move. The pressure to be a person of integrity, behaving consistently in accordance with their stated beliefs, feels overwhelming at times. Some leaders complain: "I'm only human. . . . I can't be perfect." Or they think: "What I do in my private life is my own business; no one needs to know." This is not to say that leaders do not need or have a right to privacy and time "offstage." Leaders not only have this right but need to have private time to rejuvenate, to relax, and to not feel like their every move is being monitored and evaluated. However, the reality of leadership is that there will be increased visibility and vulnerability. When an individual moves out in front of the pack and picks up the reins of leadership, corresponding responsibilities appear. A primary responsibility is modeling expected behavior.

The reality of leading by example can be especially difficult if the leader is somewhat shy or reserved. Instead of focusing on what has been lost (the privacy), perhaps this exposure can be considered a gift. Most people perform better with a small amount of competition. When others are watching and expecting a high level of performance, this can result in the motivation to do better, to reach new heights of performance, and to excel at what is being undertaken.

## CONCLUSION

Exemplary leaders actively and intentionally participate in and contribute to the development of skills in their followers. They coach for performance improvement by giving advice and instruction, encouraging discovery through guided discussions and actual experience, observing performance, and giving feedback. An involved leader positively influences followers by providing opportunities and engaging in teaching new skills. Followers grow and develop in their relationship with an exemplary leader.

# 7

## Conclusion: Leading in the Future

Health care has never been in greater need of exemplary leaders than in this period of tumultuous change that marks the close of the century. It now finds itself at a major crossroads, with system integrations, mergers and acquisitions, hospital closures, reengineering and restructuring, downsizing and "rightsizing," increased managed care penetration, new reimbursement models, and intensified human relations issues—all creating a tremendous demand for strong, skillful leaders. Even the leadership paradigm is shifting; the old command-and-control approach is simply no longer effective, and leaders at all levels need different skills for the future.

Some of these leadership skills or characteristics—integrity, a sense of mission, and vision—cannot be taught, except in life's classroom. The wisdom that comes from deep personal reflection and knowing what is most important brings a commitment to living by these values on a day-to-day basis, especially when difficult choices must be made that require courage and faith. Most exemplary leaders have a desire to serve, to act in the interest of future generations. And they believe they are in the right place at the right time. Fully engaged, with hearts committed, they clearly understand their purpose and envision a better future. A leader's vision creates the momentum that draws people to them and to their cause, to work together despite obstacles and challenges, to forge a new reality.

Although values, mission, and vision are not commonly taught through traditional methods, there are many leadership skills that are—the numerous interpersonal skills comprising the focus of this book. Without excellent interpersonal skills, tomorrow's leaders cannot be successful. Paramount to this success are communication skills and the ability to form positive relationships with followers and gain their commitment to and engagement in a common purpose, as well as being able to manage processes and develop others.

**197**

Relationships with followers greatly determine the degree of leaders' effectiveness. Trust, mutual respect, and open communication allow a leader's influence to flourish. Tomorrow's leaders collaborate and work with others in partnership. They thrive on interdependence and interconnections with other people.

Outstanding leaders recognize the distinction between compliance and commitment, and they want followers to fully engage with their hearts. These leaders are people who are not afraid to express their deeply held values and cherished beliefs, creating a collective sense of mission and a shared vision—a powerful force for transformation.

Exceptional leaders are master communicators. They constantly reflect on and evaluate their effectiveness, seeking to expand their verbal and nonverbal skills. They use anecdotes, analogies, and metaphors, and evoke powerful symbols to communicate the most important and deeply held values of the organization. They work diligently to overcome barriers to effective communication, becoming versatile in interpreting tribal language, gender, and style differences.

Exceptional leaders also understand and effectively manage process so that the processes engaged in are meaningful. They recognize and knowledgeably apply the sequential steps of a process, allowing it to unfold within its natural time frame, and they develop sound judgment that alerts them to the need to nudge a process along. As process facilitators, these leaders demonstrate by example how to empower others, resolve conflict, lead a problem-solving process, reach decisions, create teams, and manage change.

And, finally, extraordinary leaders constantly seek opportunities to develop others. They do this by intentional and proactive coaching, facilitating the development of followers' skills through the use of giving instruction and advice, and by encouraging discovery through guided discussions and hands-on experiences. They observe performance and provide honest, direct, and timely feedback. These leaders diligently seek to provide opportunities for followers and constantly teach and share their knowledge with them. Leaders themselves are continual learners, thriving among colleagues who are also continual learners.

Each of these competencies is essential, and without the complete package, influence is difficult to attain. None is easily developed, however, often requiring years of experience taking risks and making mistakes, and trying again and yet again.

Society cannot afford the cost and consequence of weak leadership in health care. Health care leaders today are stewards for the future, and healthier communities will be built only through full collaboration of the health care system, local government, and civic leaders.

Leadership development is an intensely personal, lifelong journey. Warren Bennis (1989) puts it particularly well:

No leader sets out to be a leader. People set out to live their lives, expressing themselves fully. When that expression is of value, they become leaders. So the point is not to become a leader. The point is to become yourself, to use yourself completely—all your skills, gifts and energies—in order to make your vision manifest. You must withhold nothing. You must, in sum, become the person you started out to be, and to enjoy the process of becoming. (112)

This journey is not an easy one, and it may help to reflect on this story of a bedridden gentleman. One day this man noticed a caterpillar crawling along the windowsill next to his bed. To his delight, it stopped in the corner and began spinning a cocoon. The man was excited because he knew eventually he would watch a beautiful butterfly emerge. Weeks later he noticed movement in the cocoon. Eager to behold the transformation to a new butterfly, he watched and waited. But the struggle continued. Growing impatient, the man decided to help speed the labor along. First he opened the window, and then he gently picked up the cocoon. Carefully opening it, he was enchanted to see the new butterfly emerge. It staggered a few steps and, to the man's dismay, fell over and died. What the man didn't realize is that it is in the efforts to emerge from the cocoon that a butterfly gains enough strength to fly away.

Like the difficulties for a butterfly emerging from a cocoon, leading's inherent struggles build the strength to lead and meet the challenges of today's health care organizations. Leadership is not glamorous; it is hard work. It takes courage to do the right thing even at high personal cost; and it takes a belief in something bigger than one's self. It takes the ability to dream about the wonderful possibilities, although dreaming is not enough. Perseverance and dedication are needed to implement the strategies that will transform present reality into that desired future.

# *References*

Abbasi, S., and K. Hollman. 1994. "Self-Managed Teams: The Productivity Breakthrough of the 1990s." *Journal of Managerial Psychology* 9 (7): 25–30.

Ackoff, R., E. Finnel, and J. Gharajedaghi. 1984. *A Guide to Controlling Your Corporation's Future*. New York: John Wiley & Sons.

Adams, D. C. 1995. "False Metaphors." *Hospitals & Health Networks* (November 5): 42–44.

Adams, J. L. 1986. *The Care and Feeding of Ideas: A Guide to Encouraging Creativity*. Reading, Mass.: Addison-Wesley.

Anderson, P. 1990. *Great Quotes from Great Leaders*. Lombard, Ill.: Celebrating Excellence Publishing.

Ankario, L. 1993. Quoted in "Know How to Lead." *Tampa Tribune* (March 3).

Annas, G. J. 1996. "Beyond the Military and Market Metaphors." *Healthcare Forum Journal* (May/June): 30–34.

Annison, M. 1994. "Leadership." *The Westrend Letter* (June): 1–4.

———. 1997. Keynote address at the Florida Hospital Association annual meeting, November 13.

Argyris, C. 1994. "Good Communication That Blocks Learning." *Harvard Business Review* (July/August): 77–85.

Baggs, J. G., and M. H. Schmitt. 1988. "Collaboration between Nurses and Physicians." *Image: Journal of Nursing Scholarship* 20 (3): 145–149.

Bandler, R., and J. Grinder. 1979. *From Frogs into Princes: Neuro-Linguistic Programming.* Moab, Utah: Real People Press.

Bardwick, J. M. 1991. *Danger in the Comfort Zone.* New York: American Management Association.

———. 1996. "Emotional Leaders." *Executive Excellence* (April): 13–14.

Barker, J. A. 1990. *The Power of Vision.* Videotape. Burnsville, MN: Charthouse Learning Corporation.

———. 1992. *Paradigms: The Business of Discovering the Future.* New York: HarperCollins Publishers.

Becker-Reems, E. D. 1994. *Self-Managed Work Teams in Health Care Organizations.* Chicago, Ill.: American Hospital Publishing, Inc.

Beckhard, R., and W. Pritchard. 1992. *Changing the Essence: The Art of Creating and Leading Fundamental Change in Organizations.* San Francisco: Jossey-Bass Publishers.

Belasco, J. A. 1990. *Teaching the Elephant to Dance: Empowering Change in Your Organization.* New York: Crown Publishers.

Belasco, J. A., and R. C. Stayer. 1993. *Flight of the Buffalo: Soaring to Excellence, Learning to Let Employees Lead.* New York: Warner Books.

Benner, P. 1984. *From Novice to Expert.* Menlo Park, Calif.: Addison-Wesley Publishing.

Bennis, W. 1989. *On Becoming a Leader.* Reading, Mass.: Addison-Wesley Publishing.

Bennis, W., and B. Nanus. 1985. *Leaders: The Strategies for Taking Charge.* New York: Harper & Row Publishers.

Berry, L. L. 1992. "Qualities of Leadership." *Retailing Issues Letter* 4 (1): 1–4. Center for Retailing Studies, Texas A&M University.

Blancett, S. S., and D. L. Flarey. 1995. *Reengineering Nursing and Health Care: The Handbook for Organizational Transformation.* Gaithersburg, Md.: Aspen Publishers.

Blanchard, K., and S. Bowles. 1993. *Raving Fans: A Revolutionary Approach to Customer Service.* New York: Morrow & Company.

Blanchard, K., and S. Johnson. 1981. *The One-Minute Manager.* New York: Berkley Books.

Blanchard, K., W. Oncken, and H. Burrows. 1989. *The One-Minute Manager Meets the Monkey.* New York: William Morrow & Company.

Block, P. 1988. *The Empowered Manager: Positive Political Skills at Work.* San Francisco: Jossey-Bass Publishers.

Blouin, A., and N. Brent. 1997. "Strategic Partnering: Clinical and Risk Management Concerns." *The Journal of Nursing Administration* 27 (no. 6, June): 10–13.

Bohan, G. P. 1990. "Building a High-Performance Team." *Health Care Supervisor* 8 (4): 15–21.

Bolman, L. G., and T. E. Deal. 1995. *Leading with Soul: An Uncommon Journey of Spirit.* San Francisco: Jossey-Bass Publishers.

Bridges, W. 1980. *Transitions: Making Sense of Life's Changes.* Reading, Mass.: Addison-Wesley.

———. 1988. *Surviving Corporate Transition.* Mill Valley, Calif.: William Bridges & Associates.

———. 1991. *Managing Transitions: Making the Most of Change.* Mill Valley, Calif.: William Bridges & Associates.

———. 1992. *Participant's Guide: Managing Organizational Transitions.* Mill Valley, Calif.: William Bridges & Associates.

———. 1994a. *Job Shift.* Mill Valley, Calif.: William Bridges & Associates.

———. 1994b. "The End of the Job." *Fortune* (September 19): 62–74.

———. 1995. "Leadership and the De-Jobbed Organization." *Organizations in Transition* 8 (no. 2, spring): 5.

Buggie, F. 1995. "Expert Innovation Teams: A New Way to Increase Productivity Dramatically." *Planning Review* 23 (4): 26–31.

Burns, B. M. 1978. *Leadership.* New York: Harper & Row.

Byham, W. C., with J. Cox. 1988. *Zapp! The Lightning of Empowerment: How to Improve Productivity, Quality, and Employee Satisfaction.* New York: Harmony Books.

Campbell, R., and R. Inguagiato. 1994. "The Power of Listening." *Physician Executive* 20 (9): 35–37.

Carr, C. 1992. "Planning Priorities for Empowered Teams." *Journal of Business Strategy* 13 (5): 43–47.

Chaleff, I. 1996. "Effective Leadership." *Executive Excellence* (April): 16–17.

————. 1997. "The Groupthink Challenge." *Team Management Briefings* (June): 4.

Chawla, S., and J. Renesch, eds. 1995. *Learning Organizations: Developing Cultures for Tomorrow's Workplace.* Portland, Ore.: Productivity Press.

Clark, M. 1996. "Metaphorically Speaking." *Healthcare Forum Journal* (May/June): 20–27.

Connor, D. 1993. *Managing at the Speed of Change: How Resilient Managers Succeed and Prosper Where Others Fail.* New York: Villard Books.

Covey, S. 1989. *The Seven Habits of Highly Effective People: Restoring the Character Ethic.* New York: Simon & Schuster.

————. 1990. *Principle-Centered Leadership.* New York: Simon & Schuster.

Covey, S., A. R. Merrill, and R. R. Merrill. 1994. *First Things First.* New York: Simon & Schuster.

Curtin, L. 1995. "The 'Gold Collar' Leader . . . ?" *Nursing Management* 26 (10): 7–8.

Dailey, R., F. Young, and C. Barr. 1991. "Empowering Middle Managers in Hospitals with Team-Based Problem-Solving." *Health Care Management Review* 16 (2): 55–63.

Delbecq, A. L., and A. H. VandeVen. 1971. "A Group Process Model for Problem Identification and Program Planning." *Journal of Applied Behavioral Science* 7: 466–494.

DePree, M. 1989. *Leadership Is an Art*. New York: Bantam, Doubleday Publishing.

———. 1992. *Leadership Jazz*. New York: Doubleday.

Dison, C. 1996. Interviewed by author, November 6.

Drucker, P. 1989. *The New Realities*. New York: Harper & Row.

———. 1992. *Managing for the Future: The 1990s and Beyond*. New York: Penguin Books.

Dubnicki, C. 1991. "Building High-Performance Management Teams: The Shape of Things to Come." *Healthcare Forum Journal* 34 (5): 10–11.

Dubnicki, C., and W. Limburg. 1991. "How Do Healthcare Teams Measure Up?" *Healthcare Forum Journal* 34 (5): 10–11.

Dumaine, B. 1994. "The Trouble with Teams." *Fortune* (September): 86–92.

Dychtwald, K., with J. Flower. 1990. *Age Wave: How the Most Important Trend of Our Time Will Change Your Future*. New York: Bantam Books.

Fagiano, D. 1994. "Designating a Leader." *Management Review* (March): 4.

Fielden, J. 1981. "What Do You Mean I Can't Write?" *The Journal of Nursing Administration* 11 (no. 3, March): 42–47.

Filson, B. 1994. "The New Leadership." *Hospital & Health Networks* (September 5): 76.

Fisher, K. 1993. *Leading Self-Directed Work Teams: A Guide to Developing New Team Leadership Skills*. New York: McGraw-Hill.

Flower, J. 1990. "The Chasm between Management and Leadership." Interview of W. Bennis. *Healthcare Forum Journal* 33 (4): 59–62.

———. 1991. "Being Effective." *Healthcare Forum Journal* 34 (3): 52–57.

———. 1997. "Job Shift." *Healthcare Forum Journal* 40 (1): 14–21.

Frick, D., and L. Spears, eds. 1996. *On Becoming a Servant-Leader: The Private Writings of Robert K. Greenleaf.* San Francisco: Jossey-Bass Publishers.

Garber, P. R. 1993. *Coaching Self-Directed Work Teams: Building Winning Teams in Today's Changing Workplace.* King of Prussia, Pa: Organization Design and Development, Inc.

Geber, B. 1992. "From Manager into Coach." *Training* 29 (2): 25–31.

Gibson, C. 1991. "A Concept Analysis of Empowerment." *Journal of Advanced Nursing* 16: 354–361.

Gilligan, C. 1982. *In a Different Voice: Psychological Theory of Woman's Development.* Cambridge, Mass.: Harvard University Press.

Glaser, R. 1990. *Moving Your Team toward Self-Management.* King of Prussia, Pa.: Organization Design and Development, Inc.

———. 1991a. *Facilitating Self-Managing Teams.* King of Prussia, Pa.: Organization Design and Development, Inc.

———. 1991b. *Learning to Be a Self-Managing Team.* King of Prussia, Pa.: Organization Design and Development, Inc.

———. 1992. *Classic Readings in Self-Managing Teamwork.* King of Prussia, Pa.: Organization Design and Development, Inc.

Glines, D. 1994. "Do You Work in a Zoo?" *Executive Excellence* (October): 12–13.

Goldberg, B. 1995. "Team Rewards and Team Benefits." Executive Excellence (June): 14–15.

Goman, C. K. 1992. *Adapting to Change: Making It Work for You.* Menlo Park, Calif.: Crisp.

Goodemote, E. 1995. "Managing in the Next Decade: A New Set of Skills for Nurse Managers." *Seminars for Nurse Managers* 3 (2): 84–88.

Gray, J. 1992. *Men Are from Mars, Women Are from Venus.* New York: HarperCollins.

Gummer, B. 1988. "Post-Industrial Management: Teams, Self-Management, and the New Interdependence." *Administration in Social Work* 12 (3): 117–132.

Hamilton, J. 1993. "Toppling the Power of the Pyramid." *Hospitals* (January 5): 33.

Hart, E. 1995. "Executive Leadership Teams: Exorcising Demons, Exercising Minds." *Planning Review* 23 (4): 14–19, 46.

Hawley, J. 1993. *Reawakening the Spirit in Work: The Power of Dharmic Management.* San Francisco: Berrett-Koehler.

Heifetz, R. A., and D. L. Laurie. 1997. "The Work of Leadership." *Harvard Business Review* (January/February): 124–134.

Helgesen, S. 1990. *The Female Advantage: Women's Ways of Leadership.* New York: Doubleday Currency.

Henry, B., and H. LeClair. 1987. "Language, Leadership, and Power." *Journal of Nursing Administration* 17 (1): 19–24.

Hersey, P. 1993. *Situational Leadership: A Summary.* Escondido, Calif.: Center for Leadership Studies, Inc.

Hersey, P., and H. K. Blanchard. 1993. *Management of Organizational Behavior: Utilizing Human Resources.* 6th ed. Englewood, N.J.: Prentice Hall.

Hesselbein, F., M. Goldsmith, and R. Beckhard, eds. 1996. *The Leader of the Future.* San Francisco: Jossey-Bass Publishers.

Holpp, L., and R. Phillips. 1995. "When Is a Team Its Own Worst Enemy?" *Training* 32 (9): 71–82.

Horak, B. J. 1991. "Building a Team on a Medical Floor." *Health Care Management Review* 16 (2): 65–71.

Hout, T. M., and J. C. Carter. 1995. "Getting It Done: New Roles for Senior Executives." *Harvard Business Review* (November/December): 133–145.

Huey, J. 1994. "The New Post-Heroic Leadership." *Fortune* (February 21).

Huret, J. 1991. "Paying for Team Results." *HR Magazine* (May): 39–41.

Jacobson, R. 1997. Correspondence with author. May 20.

Jacobsen-Webb, M. 1985. "Team Building: Key to Executive Success." *Journal of Nursing Administration* 15 (2): 16–20.

Jessup, H. R. 1990. "New Roles in Team Leadership." *Training & Development Journal:* 79–83.

Kanter, R. M. 1997. *On the Frontiers of Management.* Middlebury, Vt.: Soundview Executive Book Summaries.

Katzenbach, J. R., and D. K. Smith. 1993. *The Wisdom of Teams: Creating the High-Performance Organization.* Boston: Harvard Business School Press.

Kim, W. C., and R. A. Mauborgne. 1992. "Parables of Leadership." *Harvard Business Review* (July/August): 123–128.

Knowles, M. 1970. *The Modern Practice of Adult Education: Andragogy versus Pedagogy.* Chicago: Association Press.

Kohles, M. K., W. G. Baker, and B. A. Donaho. 1995. *Transformational Leadership: Renewing Fundamental Values and Achieving New Relationships in Health Care.* Chicago: American Hospital Publishing, Inc.

Kostner, J. 1994. *Knights of the TeleRound Table.* New York: Warner Books.

Kouzes, J. W., and B. Z. Posner. 1987. *The Leadership Challenge.* San Francisco: Jossey-Bass Publishers.

———. 1993. "The Credibility Factor." *Healthcare Forum Journal* (July/August): 16–24.

Larson, C. E., and F. LaFasto. 1989. *TeamWork: What Must Go Right/What Can Go Wrong.* Newbury Park, Calif.: Sage Publications.

Leander, W. 1994. "Layered Learning: Improved Learning through Phased Education." *Patient Focused Care Association Review* (summer): 2–7.

Leander, W., D. Shortridge, and P. Watson. 1996. *Patients First.* Chicago: Health Care Administration Press.

Linden, R. M. 1992a. "Flattening the Hierarchy through Self-Managing Teams: I." *Virginia Review* (October): 52–53.

———. 1992b. "Self-Managing Teams II: Dealing with the Issues." *Virginia Review* (November): 20–21.

Lorimer, W., and J. Manion. 1996. "Team-Based Organizations: Leading the Essential Transformation." *Patient Focused Care Association Review* (summer): 15–19.

Lumsdon, K. 1995. "Why Executive Teams Fail and What to Do." *Hospitals & Health Networks* (August 5): 24–31.

Manion, J. 1989. "Professional Collaboration: More Than a Committee Structure." *Nursing Options* 1 (4): 9–12.

———. 1990. *Change from Within: Nurse Intrapreneurs as Health Care Innovators.* Kansas City: American Nurses Association.

———. 1993. "Chaos or Transformation? Managing Innovation." *The Journal of Nursing Administration* 23 (5): 41–48.

———. 1994. "Managing Change: The Leadership Challenge of the 1990s." *Seminars for Nurse Managers* 2 (4): 203–208.

———. 1995. "Understanding the Seven Stages of Change." *American Journal of Nursing* 95 (4): 41–43.

———. 1997. "Teams 101: The Manager's Role." *Seminars for Nurse Managers* 5 (1): 31–38.

Manion, J., W. Lorimer, and W. Leander. 1996. *Team-Based Health Care Organizations: Blueprint for Success.* Gaithersburg, Md.: Aspen Publishers.

Manion, J., M. J. Sieg, and P. Watson. Forthcoming. "Managerial Partnerships: The Wave of the Future?" *The Journal of Nursing Administration* 28 (no. 4, April).

Manion, J., and P. Watson. 1995. "Developing Team-Based Patient Care through Reengineering." In *Reengineering Nursing and Health Care*, edited by S. S. Blanchett and D. L. Flarey. Gaithersburg, Md.: Aspen Publishers.

Manthey, M. 1989. "An Expert Answers Common Questions about Primary Nursing." *Nursing Management* 20 (3): 22–24.

Markels, A. 1997. "Memo 4/8/97, FYI: Messages Inundate Offices." *The Wall Street Journal* (April 8): B1.

McCarthy, D. 1997. *The Loyalty Link*. New York: John Wiley & Sons.

McDonald, T. 1997. "Send Clear Messages." *Team Management Briefings*. Sample, p. 4.

McGinnis, A. L. 1985. *Bringing Out the Best in People*. Minneapolis: Augsburg Publishing.

McNeese-Smith, D. 1992. "The Impact of Leadership on Productivity." *Nursing Economics* 10 (6): 393–396.

———. 1993. "Leadership Behavior and Employee Effectiveness." *Nursing Management* 24 (5): 38–39.

Melrose, K. 1996. "Leader as Servant." *Executive Excellence:* 20.

Miller, D., and M. Manthey. 1994. "Empowerment through Levels of Authority." *Journal of Nursing Administration* (no. 24, July/August): 23.

Minor, M. 1989. *Coaching and Counseling: A Practical Guide for Managers*. Menlo Park, Calif.: Crisp Publications.

Mintzberg, H. 1980. *The Nature of Managerial Work*. Englewood Cliffs, N.J.: Prentice Hall.

Moffitt, G., C. McCullough, and D. Sanders, 1993. "High-Performing Self-Directed Work Teams: What Are They and How Do They Work?" *Patient Focused Care Association Review* (fall): 8–12.

Morris, D. 1979. *Manwatching: A Field Guide to Human Behavior.* New York: Harry N. Abrams.

Moss-Kanter, R. 1989. *When Giants Learn to Dance: Mastering the Challenge of Strategy, Management and Career in the 1990's*. New York: Simon & Schuster.

Naisbett, J. 1982. *Megatrends: Ten New Directions Transforming Our Lives.* New York: Warner Books.

Naisbett, J., and P. Aburdene. 1990. *Megatrends 2000: Ten New Directions for the 1990s.* New York: William Morrow & Company.

Neuhauser, P. C. 1988. *Tribal Warfare in Organizations.* Cambridge, Mass.: Ballinger Publishing.

Nierenberg, J., and I. Ross 1985. *Women and the Art of Negotiating.* New York: Simon & Schuster.

O'Dell, C. 1989. "Team Play, Team Pay—New Ways of Keeping Score." *Across the Board* (November): 31–45.

O'Dooley, P. 1992. "Be Different—Stand Out in Others' Minds." *Flight Plan for Living: the Art of Self Encouragement.* New York: Master Media.

Oakley, E., and D. Krug. 1993. *Enlightened Leadership.* New York: Simon & Schuster.

Orsburn, J. D., L. Moran, E. Musselwhite, and J. Zenger. 1990. *Self-Directed Work Teams: The New American Challenge.* Homewood, Ill.: Business One Irwin.

Parker, G. 1997. "Teamwork and Team Players." *Team Management Briefings* 5 (5): 8.

Peck, M. S. 1978. *The Road Less Traveled.* New York: Simon & Schuster.

Perot, R. 1996. "Caring Leaders." *Executive Excellence* (April): 6–7.

Pesmen, S. 1990. *Orlando Sentinel* (May 27): E21.

Peters, T., and R. Waterman. 1982. *In Search of Excellence: Lessons from America's Best-Run Companies.* New York: Harper & Row.

Peters, T. 1987. *Thriving on Chaos.* New York: Harper & Row Publishers.

Peters, T., and N. Austin. 1985. *A Passion for Excellence.* New York: Random House.

Phillips, D. 1992. *Lincoln on Leadership: Executive Strategies for Tough Times.* New York: Warner Books.

Pinchot, G., and E. Pinchot. 1996. "Creating Space for Many Leaders." *Executive Excellence:* 17–18.

Pinchot, G., and E. Pinchot. 1996. *The Intelligent Organization: Engaging the Talent & Initiative of Everyone in the Workplace.* San Francisco: Berrett-Koehler.

Post, N. 1989a. *Working Balance: Energy Management for Personal and Professional Well-Being.* Philadelphia: Post Enterprises.

———. 1989b. "Managing Human Energy: An Ancient Tool of Change Experts." *OD Practitioner:* 14–16.

Ranney, J., and M. Deck. 1995. "Making Teams Work: Lessons from the Leaders in New Product Development." *Planning Review* 23 (4): 6–13.

Reddy, W. B. 1994. *Intervention Skills: Process Consultation for Small Groups and Teams.* San Diego: Pfeiffer & Company.

Rogers, R. 1994. "The Psychological Contract of Trust." *Executive Excellence* (July): 6.

Saarel, D. 1995. "Triads: Self-Organizing Structures That Create Value." *Planning Review* 23 (4): 20–25.

Schrubb, D. A. 1992. "The Implementation of Self-Managed Teams in Health Care." *Topics in Health Information Management* 13 (1): 45–50.

Scott, C. D., and D. T. Jaffe. 1989a. *Managing Organizational Change.* Menlo Park, Calif.: Crisp.

———. 1989b. *Managing Personal Change.* Menlo Park, Calif.: Crisp.

———. 1991. "From Crisis to Culture Change." *Healthcare Forum Journal* 34 (3): 31–39.

Scott, C. D., D. T. Jaffe, and M. Tobe. 1993. *Organizational Vision, Values and Mission.* Menlo Park, Calif.: Crisp.

Senge, P. M. 1990. *The Fifth Discipline: The Art & Practice of the Learning Organization.* New York: Doubleday.

———. 1996. "Leading Learning Organizations." *Executive Excellence* (April): 10–11.

Shelton, C. 1995. "Team Mania." *Executive Excellence* (June): 9–10.

Sherer, J. 1995. "Tapping into Teams." *Hospitals & Health Networks* (July 5): 32–36.

Shula, D., and K. Blanchard. 1995. *Everyone's a Coach*. Grand Rapids, Mich.: Zondervan Publishing House.

Siebert, A. 1993. *The Survivor Personality*. Portland, Ore.: Practical Psychology Press.

Spencer, S. A., and J. D. Adams. 1990. *Life Changes: Growing through Personal Transitions*. San Luis Obispo, Calif.: Impact Publishers.

Sprenger, G. 1996. Interviewed by author (November 22).

Tannen, D. 1994. *Talking from 9 to 5*. New York: Avon.

Tarkenton, F., with T. Tuleja. 1986. *How to Motivate People*. New York: Harper & Row Publishers.

Tjosvold, D., and M. Tjosvold. 1991. *Leading the Team Organization: How to Create an Enduring Competitive Advantage*. New York: Lexington Books.

Tuckman, B. W. 1965. "Developmental Sequence in Small Groups." *Psychological Bulletin* 63 (6): 334–99.

Vance, M. 1982. *Creative Thinking*. Audiotape series. Chicago: Nightingale-Conant Corporation.

Voluntary Hospitals of America. 1994. *Improving Patient Outcomes through System Change: A Focus on Changing Roles of Health Care Organization Executives*. Irving, Tex.: Voluntary Hospitals of America, Inc.

Warner, M. 1995. "Why Teams Fail, How Teams Succeed." *Executive Excellence* (June): 17.

Waterman, R. H. 1992. *Adhocracy: The Power to Change*. New York: W. W. Norton & Company.

———. 1987. *The Renewal Factor: How the Best Get and Keep the Competitive Edge*. New York: Bantam Books.

Watson, P., D. Shortridge, D. Jones, and R. Rees. 1991. "Operational Restructuring: A Patient-Focused Approach." *Nursing Administration Quarterly* 16: 45–52.

Wellins, R., W. Byham, and J. Wilson. 1991. *Empowered Teams: Creating Self-Directed Work Groups That Improve Quality, Productivity, & Participation.* San Francisco: Jossey-Bass Publishers.

Wellins, R., and J. George. 1991. "The Key to Self-Directed Work Teams." *Training* (April): 26–31.

Wheatley, M. J. 1992. *Leadership and the New Science.* San Francisco: Berrett-Koehler Publishers.

Wilson, J., and R. Wellins. 1995. "Leading Teams." *Executive Excellence* (June): 7–8.

Wilson, J., J. George, and R. Wellins. 1994. *Leadership Trapeze: Strategies for Leadership in Team-Based Organizations.* San Francisco: Jossey-Bass Publishers.

Wycoff, J. 1991. *Mindmapping: Your Personal Guide to Exploring Creativity and Problem-Solving.* New York: Berkley Publishing.

Yager, E. 1995. "Coaching Teams." *Executive Excellence* (June): 8.

Zemke, R. 1993. "Rethinking the Rush to Team Up." *Training* 30 (11): 55–61.

———. 1996. "The Corporate Coach." *Training* 33 (12): 24–33.

Zenger, J., E. Musselwhite, K. Hurson, and C. Perrin. 1994. *Leading Teams: Mastering the New Role.* Homewood, Ill.: Business One Irwin.

# Index